Tyndale Ol
Commi

CW00747096

VOLUME 23

───── TOTC ─────

DANIEL

Dedicated to
Kyle McClellan
Ben Mitchell
Richard Bailey
Jim Packer
Wendell Berry

Tyndale Old Testament Commentaries

Volume 23

Series Editor: David G. Firth
Consulting Editor: Tremper Longman III

Daniel

An Introduction and Commentary

Paul R. House

An imprint of InterVarsity Press
Downers Grove, Illinois

InterVarsity Press, USA　　　　　　　　*Inter-Varsity Press, England*
P.O. Box 1400　　　　　　　　　　　　*36 Causton Street*
Downers Grove, IL 60515-1426, USA　　*London SW1P 4ST, England*
ivpress.com　　　　　　　　　　　　　*ivpbooks.com*
email@ivpress.com　　　　　　　　　　*ivp@ivpbooks.com*

InterVarsity Press®, USA, is the book-publishing division of InterVarsity Christian Fellowship/USA® and a member movement of the International Fellowship of Evangelical Students. Website: intervarsity.org.

Inter-Varsity Press, England, is closely linked with the Universities and Colleges Christian Fellowship, a student movement connecting Christian Unions throughout Great Britain, and a member movement of the International Fellowship of Evangelical Students. Website: uccf.org.uk.

Unless otherwise indicated, Scripture quotations are the author's translation.

Scripture quotations marked ESV are from the Holy Bible, English Standard Version®, copyright © 2001 by Crossway Bibles, a publishing ministry of Good News Publishers. Used by permission. All rights reserved.

First published 2018

Image: © Erich Lessing/Art Resource, NY

USA ISBN 978-0-8308-4273-5 (print)
USA ISBN 978-0-8308-9100-9 (digital)
UK ISBN 978-1-78359-742-0 (print)
UK ISBN 978-1-78359-743-7 (digital)

Typeset in Great Britain by CRB Associates, Potterhanworth, Lincolnshire

Printed in the United States of America ⊚

InterVarsity Press is committed to ecological stewardship and to the conservation of natural resources in all our operations. This book was printed using sustainably sourced paper.

Library of Congress Cataloging-in-Publication Data
Names: House, Paul R., 1958- author.
Title: Daniel : an introduction and commentary / Paul R. House.
Description: Downers Grove : InterVarsity Press, 2018. | Series: Tyndale Old Testament commentaries ; Volume 23 | Includes bibliographical references and index.
Identifiers: LCCN 2018028460 (print) | LCCN 2018029824 (ebook) | ISBN 9780830891009 (eBook) | ISBN 9780830842735 (pbk. : alk. paper)
Subjects: LCSH: Bible. Daniel—Commentaries.
Classification: LCC BS1555.53 (ebook) | LCC BS1555.53 .H68 2018 (print) | DDC 224/.5077—dc23
LC record available at https://lccn.loc.gov/2018028460

P　21　20　19　18　17　16　15　14　13　12　11　10　9　8　7　6　5　4　3　2　1

Y　35　34　33　32　31　30　29　28　27　26　25　24　23　22　21　20　19　18

CONTENTS

GENERAL PREFACE

The decision completely to revise the Tyndale Old Testament Commentaries is an indication of the important role that the series has played since its opening volumes were released in the mid-1960s. They represented at that time, and have continued to represent, commentary writing that was committed both to the importance of the text of the Bible as Scripture and a desire to engage with as full a range of interpretative issues as possible without being lost in the minutiae of scholarly debate. The commentaries aimed to explain the biblical text to a generation of readers confronting models of critical scholarship and new discoveries from the Ancient Near East, while remembering that the Old Testament is not simply another text from the ancient world. Although no uniform process of exegesis was required, all the original contributors were united in their conviction that the Old Testament remains the Word of God for us today. That the original volumes fulfilled this role is evident from the way in which they continue to be used in so many parts of the world.

A crucial element of the original series was that it should offer an up-to-date reading of the text, and it is precisely for this reason that new volumes are required. The questions confronting readers in the first half of the twenty-first century are not necessarily those from the second half of the twentieth. Discoveries from the Ancient Near East continue to shed new light on the Old Testament, whilst emphases in exegesis have changed markedly. Whilst remaining true to the goals of the initial volumes, the need for contemporary study of the text requires that the series as a whole be updated. This updating is not simply a matter of commissioning new volumes to replace the old. We have also taken the opportunity to update the format of the series to reflect a key emphasis from linguistics, which is that texts communicate in larger blocks rather than in shorter segments such as individual verses. Because of this, the treatment of each section of the text includes three segments. First, a short note on *Context* is offered, placing the passage under consideration in its literary setting within the book as well as noting any historical issues crucial to interpretation. The *Comment* segment then follows the traditional structure of the commentary, offering exegesis of the various components of a passage. Finally, a brief comment is made on *Meaning*, by which is meant the message that the passage seeks to communicate within the book, highlighting its key theological themes. This section brings together the detail of the *Comment* to show how the passage under consideration seeks to communicate as a whole.

Our prayer is that these new volumes will continue the rich heritage of the Tyndale Old Testament Commentaries and that they will continue to witness to the God who is made known in the text.

David G. Firth, Series Editor
Tremper Longman III, Consulting Editor

AUTHOR'S PREFACE

The writers in the Tyndale Old Testament Commentary series have helped my teaching, preaching and writing for over thirty years. Thus, I was honoured when asked to join them. I was particularly honoured to take up Joyce Baldwin's work on Daniel, for I consider her a model expositor. Readers will note that I build on her work; I do not presume to replace it. I have tried to treat her and other scholars fairly. They are my teachers and colleagues, and I am grateful for them, even when we disagree.

Several people deserve thanks. I am grateful to series editor David Firth and to Philip Duce at Inter-Varsity Press for their invitation to write this volume, and for their editorial guidance. I thank Samford University Provost Michael Hardin, Beeson Divinity School Dean Timothy George and Associate Dean Grant Taylor for granting a fall 2017 sabbatical. This leave allowed me to write most of the commentary in the Pontifical Biblical Institute Library in Rome, where Dr Adam Wisniewski, Dr Alberto Bellavia and other hardworking librarians gave valuable assistance. Ralph W. Beeson's estate provided funds for books, travel and housing in Rome. Writing about Daniel in Italy was ideal, since churches and museums in Rome, Venice and Florence afforded several insightful visual images of Daniel's major characters.

My wife, Heather, encouraged me, made homes in Birmingham and Rome, and provided editorial expertise. Heather's parents, David and Dawn Oldfield, and my sister Suzanne Kingsley spent time in Italy with us and were very supportive. Suzanne deserves particular thanks for being planner, guide, art teacher and friend in Italy. I thank our Monday-night Bible study, family members Roy and Lee House, Martin, Molly, Caleb and Eleanor Spence, old friends Jim Dixon and Scott Hafemann and new friends Nic Seaborn and Josh Turner for praying for my writing.

Win Corduan and Hunter and Liz Twitty inspired me through their faith and courage amid great loss. We will not forget indefatigable June Corduan or tiny Charlotte Twitty, who now see God.

While writing, I imagined living models of the book's characters. Daniel's friends reminded me of Kyle McClellan, Ben Mitchell and Richard Bailey, long-time companions. Though they have not followed the diet in Daniel 1:8–16, defied a murderous king or faced flames of martyrdom, they could do all three, if necessary. Imagining Daniel required two individuals. Jim Packer, a skilful theological bookman who knew Joyce Baldwin, has shared seventy years of his story with me, and I have heard him pray like Daniel. Wendell Berry constantly reminded me of Daniel, though he will likely laugh at the comparison. Regardless, his poems, stories, essays and kindness show that he sees more than I do. Like Daniel, Packer and Berry have persevered, showing me and others how it is done. I dedicate this book to these five good men, in whom the spirit of Daniel, Shadrach, Meshach and Abednego abides.

For these and other kindnesses, I am grateful.

Paul R. House

CHIEF ABBREVIATIONS

AB	Anchor Bible
ABD	D. N. Freedman et al. (eds.), *The Anchor Bible Dictionary*, 6 vols. (New York: Doubleday, 1992)
AbOTC	Abingdon Old Testament Commentary
ANET	*Ancient Near Eastern Texts Relating to the Old Testament*, ed. James B. Pritchard, 3rd edn (Princeton: Princeton University Press, 1969)
AOTC	Apollos Old Testament Commentary
ARAB	*Ancient Records of Assyria and Babylonia*, Daniel David Luckenbill, 2 vols. (Chicago: University of Chicago Press, 1926–1927, repr., New York: Greenwood, 1968)
AUSS	*Andrews University Seminary Studies*
BDB	Brown, F., S. R. Driver and C. A. Briggs, *A Hebrew and English Lexicon of the Old Testament* (Oxford: Clarendon, 1906)
BLS	Bible and Literature Series
ConC	Concordia Commentary
EANEC	*Explorations in Ancient Near Eastern Civilizations*
EBC	*Expositor's Bible Commentary*
EvQ	*Evangelical Quarterly*
FOTL	The Forms of the Old Testament Literature
HDR	Harvard Dissertations in Religion
HSM	Harvard Semitic Monographs

IBC	Interpretation: A Bible Commentary for Teaching and Preaching
ICC	International Critical Commentary
Int	*Interpretation*
ITC	International Theological Commentary
JBL	*Journal of Biblical Literature*
JSOTSup	Journal for the Study of the Old Testament Supplement Series
LNTS	The Library of New Testament Studies
NAC	New American Commentary
NCBC	New Century Bible Commentary
NIDOTTE	*New International Dictionary of Old Testament Theology and Exegesis*, ed. Willem A. VanGemeren, 5 vols. (Grand Rapids: Zondervan; Carlisle: Paternoster, 1997)
NIVAC	NIV Application Commentary
OTL	Old Testament Library
TDOT	*Theological Dictionary of the Old Testament*, ed. G. Johannes Botterweck and Helmer Ringgren, trans. John T. Willis et al., 8 vols. (Grand Rapids: Eerdmans, 1974–2006)
Them	*Themelios*
TOTC	Tyndale Old Testament Commentaries
WBC	Word Biblical Commentary
WTJ	*Westminster Theological Journal*

Bible versions

| ESV | English Standard Version |
| LXX | Septuagint (pre-Christian Greek version of the Old Testament) |

SELECT BIBLIOGRAPHY

Albright, W. F. (1921), 'The Date and Personality of the Chronicler', *JBL* 40(3): 104–124.

Allison, D. C., Jr (2014), 'Apocalyptic Ethics and Behavior', in J. J. Collins (ed.), *The Oxford Handbook of Apocalyptic Literature* (Oxford: Oxford University Press), pp. 295–311.

Anderson, B. W. (1999), *Contours of Old Testament Theology* (Minneapolis: Fortress).

Anderson, R. A. (1984), *Signs and Wonders: A Commentary on the Book of Daniel*, ITC (Grand Rapids: Eerdmans).

Archer, G. L., Jr (1985), 'Daniel', in F. E. Gaebelein (ed.), *EBC* 7 (Grand Rapids: Zondervan), 7: 3–157.

Astin, A. E. et al. (1989), *The Cambridge Ancient History: Volume VIII, Rome and the Mediterranean to 133 B.C.*, 2nd edn (Cambridge: Cambridge University Press).

Averbeck, R. E. (1997), '*gʾl*', *NIDOTTE* 1: 794–795.

Baldwin, J. G. (1978), *Daniel: An Introduction and Commentary*, TOTC (Leicester: Inter-Varsity Press; Downers Grove: InterVarsity Press).

Bartholomew, C. G. and M. W. Goheen (2014), *The Drama of Scripture: Finding Our Place in the Biblical Story* (Grand Rapids: Baker).

Bengtson, H. (1988), *History of Greece: From the Beginnings to the Byzantine Era*, 4th edn, trans. and updated by Edmund F. Bloedow (Ottawa: University of Ottawa Press).

Berry, W. (1981), 'Discipline and Hope', in W. Berry, *Recollected Essays: 1965–1980* (San Francisco: North Point Press), pp. 151–220.

—— (2003), *Life Is a Miracle: An Essay against Modern Superstition* (Berkeley, CA: Counterpoint).

—— (2006), *The Way of Ignorance and Other Essays* (Berkeley, CA: Counterpoint).

—— (2013), 'Amish Economy', in *Sabbaths* (Berkeley, CA: Counterpoint), pp. 160–161.

—— (2014), *This New Day: Collected Sabbath Poems, 1979–2013* (Berkeley, CA: Counterpoint).

Bevan, A. A. (1892), *A Short Commentary on the Book of Daniel: For the Use of Students* (Cambridge: Cambridge University Press).

Booth, W. C. (1961), *The Rhetoric of Fiction* (Chicago: University of Chicago Press).

Breed, B. (April 2017), 'Daniel's Four Kingdoms Schema: A History of Re-writing World History', *Int* 71(2): 178–189.

Briant, P. (2002), *From Cyrus to Alexander: A History of the Persian Empire*, trans. P. T. Daniels (Winona Lake: Eisenbrauns).

Brueggemann, W. (2010), *Out of Babylon* (Nashville: Abingdon Press).

Casey, M. (1979), *Son of Man: The Interpretation and Influence of Daniel 7* (London: SPCK).

—— (2007), *The Solution to the 'Son of Man' Problem*, LNTS (London: T. & T. Clark).

Charles, R. H. (1929), *A Critical and Exegetical Commentary on the Book of Daniel* (Oxford: Clarendon Press).

Childs, B. S. (1980), *Introduction to the Old Testament as Scripture* (Philadelphia: Fortress Press).

—— (1985), *Old Testament Theology in a Canonical Context* (Philadelphia: Fortress Press).

Collins, J. J. (1984), *Daniel: With an Introduction to Apocalyptic Literature*, FOTL 20 (Grand Rapids: Eerdmans).

—— (1993), *Daniel*, Hermeneia (Minneapolis: Fortress).

—— (2016), *The Apocalyptic Imagination: An Introduction to the Jewish Apocalyptic Literature*, 3rd edn (Grand Rapids: Eerdmans).

de Miroschedji, P. (1992), 'Susa', *ABD* 6.

Dillard, R. B. and T. Longman III (1994), *An Introduction to the Old Testament* (Grand Rapids: Zondervan).

Dougherty, R. P. (1929), *Nabonidus and Belshazzar: A Study of the Closing Events of the Neo-Babylonian Empire*, Yale Oriental Series 15 (New Haven: Yale University Press).

Driver, S. R. (1900), *The Book of Daniel*, Cambridge Bible for Schools and Colleges (Cambridge: Cambridge University Press).

Drury, J. (2014), *Music at Midnight: The Life and Poetry of George Herbert* (Chicago: University of Chicago Press).

Ferguson, S. B. (1988), *The Communicator's Commentary: Daniel* (Waco: Word Books).

Fewell, D. N. (1988), *Circle of Sovereignty: A Story of Stories in Daniel 1–6*, JSOTSup 72/BLS 20 (Sheffield: Sheffield Academic Press).

Goldingay, J. (1989), *Daniel*, WBC 30 (Dallas: Word).

Goldsworthy, G. (2002), *According to Plan: The Unfolding Revelation of God in the Bible* (Leicester: Inter-Varsity Press; Downers Grove: InterVarsity Press).

Gowan, D. E. (2001), *Daniel*, AbOTC (Nashville: Abingdon).

Hafemann, S. J. and P. R. House (eds.) (2007), *Central Themes in Biblical Theology: Mapping Unity in Diversity* (Nottingham: Apollos; Grand Rapids: Baker).

Hanson, P. D. (1979), *The Dawn of Apocalyptic: The Historical and Sociological Roots of Jewish Apocalyptic Eschatology*, rev. edn (Philadelphia: Fortress).

Hartman, L. F. and A. A. Di Lella (1977), *The Book of Daniel*, AB 23 (Garden City: Doubleday).

—— (1978), *The Book of Daniel*, AB 23 (Garden City: Doubleday).

Hasel, G. F. (1977), 'The First and Third Years of Belshazzar (Daniel 7:1; 8:1)', *AUSS* 15(2): 153–168.

Havel, V. (1990), *Disturbing the Peace* (London: Faber & Faber).

Heaney, S. (1995), *The Redress of Poetry* (London: Faber & Faber).

Hölbl, G. (2001), *A History of the Ptolemaic Empire*, trans. Tina Saavedra (London: Routledge).

Holm, T. L. (2013), *Of Courtiers and Kings: The Biblical Daniel Narratives and Ancient Story-Collections*, *EANEC* 1 (Winona Lake: Eisenbrauns).

House, P. R. (1988), *Zephaniah – A Prophetic Drama*, JSOTSup 16 (Sheffield: Sheffield Academic).

—— (1990), *The Unity of the Twelve*, JSOTSup 27 (Sheffield: Sheffield Academic).

—— (1998), *Old Testament Theology* (Downers Grove: InterVarsity Press).

—— (Spring 2005), 'God's Character and the Wholeness of Scripture', *Scottish Bulletin of Evangelical Theology* 23(1): 4–17.

Humphreys, W. L. (1973), 'A Lifestyle for Diaspora: A Study of the Tales of Esther and Daniel', *JBL* 92: 211–223.

Jenson, P. P. (1997), '*swr*', *NIDOTTE*, 3: 790–791.

Jerome (1958), *Jerome's Commentary on Daniel*, trans. Gleason L. Archer, Jr (orig. 407; Grand Rapids: Baker).

Johnson, I. (2013), 'China Embarking on Vast Program of Urbanization', *The New York Times*, June 16, A1.

Johnston, P. S. (2002), *Shades of Sheol: Death and Afterlife in the Old Testament* (Leicester: Apollos; Downers Grove: InterVarsity Press).

Jones, G. H. (1984), *1 and 2 Kings, Volume II*, NCBC (Grand Rapids: Eerdmans).

Kaiser, W. C., Jr (1978), *Toward an Old Testament Theology* (Grand Rapids: Zondervan, 1978).

Keil, C. F. (1980), 'Daniel', in C. F. Keil and F. Delitzsch, *Commentary on the Old Testament*, trans. M. G. Easton (orig. 1869; Grand Rapids: Eerdmans), 9: 115.

Kitchen, K. A. (1965), 'The Aramaic of Daniel', in D. J. Wiseman et al., *Notes on Some Problems in the Book of Daniel* (London: Tyndale), pp. 31–79.

—— (2003), *On the Reliability of the Old Testament* (Grand Rapids: Eerdmans).

Koch, K. (1972), *The Rediscovery of Apocalyptic*, trans. M. Kohl (Nashville: Allenson).

LaCocque, A. (1979), *The Book of Daniel*, trans. D. Pellauer (Atlanta: John Knox Press).

Lederach, P. M. (1994), *Daniel*, Believers Church Bible Commentary (Sacramento: Herald Press).

Lewis, D. M. et al. (eds.) (1994), *The Cambridge Ancient History: Volume VI, The Fourth Century B.C.*, 2nd edn (Cambridge: Cambridge University Press).

Longman, T., III (1999), *Daniel*, NIVAC (Grand Rapids: Zondervan).

Lucas, E. C. (2002), *Daniel*, AOTC (Leicester: Apollos; Downers Grove: InterVarsity Press).

Lundbom, J. R. (April 2017), 'Builders of Ancient Babylon: Nabopolassar and Nebuchadnezzar II', *Int* 71(3): 154–166.

Maclean, N. (1976), *A River Runs through It and Other Stories* (Chicago: University of Chicago Press).

McComiskey, T. E. (1985), 'The Seventy "Weeks" of Daniel against the Background of Ancient Near Eastern Literature', *WTJ* 47: 18–45.

McCullough, C. T. (2008), 'Introduction to Daniel', in K. Stevenson and M. Glerup (eds.), *Ezekiel, Daniel*, Ancient Christian Commentary on Scripture 13, ed. Thomas Oden (Downers Grove: InterVarsity Press).

Martens, E. A. (1981), *God's Design: A Focus on Old Testament Theology* (Grand Rapids: Baker).

Millard, A. R. (1977), 'Daniel 1–6 and History', *EvQ* 49(2): 67–73.

Miller, S. R. (1994), *Daniel*, NAC 18 (Nashville: Broadman & Holman).

Montgomery, J. A. (1927), *A Critical and Exegetical Commentary on the Book of Daniel*, ICC (New York: Charles Scribner's Sons).

Murphy, F. J. (2012), *Apocalypticism in the Bible and Its World* (Grand Rapids: Baker).

Newsom, C. A. and B. W. Breed (2014), *Daniel*, OTL (Louisville: Westminster John Knox Press).

Olmstead, A. T. (1948), *History of the Persian Empire: Achaemenid Period* (Chicago: University of Chicago Press).

Owens, J. J. (1971), 'Daniel', in *The Broadman Bible Commentary, Volume 6: Jeremiah–Daniel*, ed. Clifton J. Allen (Nashville: Broadman Press).

Porteous, N. (1979), *Daniel*, rev. edn, OTL (London: SCM).

Redditt, P. L. (1999), *Daniel*, NCBC (Grand Rapids: Eerdmans).

Rendtorff, R. (1998), *The Covenant Formula: An Exegetical and Theological Investigation* (London: T. & T. Clark).

—— (2005), *The Canonical Hebrew Bible: A Theology of the Old Testament*, trans. D. E. Orton, Tools for Biblical Study (Leiden: Deo).

Rowley, H. H. (1950), *The Relevance of Apocalyptic*, 2nd edn (London: Lutterworth Press).

Russell, D. S. (1964), *The Method and Message of Jewish Apocalyptic, 200 BC – AD 100*, OTL (Philadelphia: Westminster John Knox Press).

Ryken, L. et al. (1998), 'Heavenly Armies/Hosts', *Dictionary of Biblical Imagery* (Downers Grove: InterVarsity Press), pp. 372–373.

Scheetz, J. M. (2009), *Reading Daniel as a Text in Theological Hermeneutics* (Cambridge: James Clarke).

Schürer, E. (2014), *A History of the Jewish People in the Time of Christ: Vol. I*, trans. John Macpherson et al. (orig. 1890; Peabody: Hendrickson).

Seow, C. L. (2003), *Daniel*, Westminster Bible Companion (Louisville: Westminster John Knox Press).

Steiner, G. (1989), *Real Presences* (Chicago: University of Chicago Press).

Steinmann, A. E. (2008), *Daniel*, ConC (Saint Louis: Concordia).

Sternberg, M. (1985), *The Poetics of Biblical Narrative: Ideological Literature and the Drama of Reading* (Bloomington: Indiana University Press).

Stevenson, K. and M. Glerup (eds.), *Ezekiel, Daniel*, Ancient Christian Commentary on Scripture 13, ed. Thomas Oden (Downers Grove: InterVarsity Press).

Thiel, W. (2003), '*sûr*', *TDOT*, 12: 306–311.

Towner, W. S. (1984), *Daniel*, IBC (Atlanta: John Knox Press).

Vallat, F. (1992), 'Elam', *ABD* 2.

Vanderhooft, D. S. (2000), *The Neo-Babylonian Empire and Babylon in the Latter Prophets*, HSM 59 (Atlanta: Scholars Press).

Vogel, W. (2010), *The Cultic Motif in the Book of Daniel* (New York: Peter Lang).

Vogt, E. (ed.) (2011), *A Lexicon of Biblical Aramaic: Clarified by Ancient Documents*, trans. and rev. J. A. Fitzmyer (Rome: Gregorian and Biblical Press).

von Rad, G. (1965), *Old Testament Theology, Volume Two: The Theology of Israel's Prophetic Traditions*, trans. D. M. G. Stalker (New York: Harper & Row).

Wills, L. M. (1990), *The Jew in the Court of the Foreign King*, HDR (Minneapolis: Fortress).

Wiseman, D. J. (1985), *Nebuchadrezzar and Babylon* (Oxford: Oxford University Press).

Wiseman, D. J. et al. (1965), *Notes on Some Problems in the Book of Daniel* (London: Tyndale Press).

Yamauchi, E. M. (1990), *Persia and the Bible* (Grand Rapids: Baker).

Yamauchi, E. M. and M. R. Wilson (2016), *Dictionary of Daily Life in Biblical and Post-Biblical Antiquity: Vol. III, I–N* (Peabody: Hendrickson).

Young, E. J. (1949), *The Prophecy of Daniel: A Commentary* (Grand Rapids: Eerdmans).

INTRODUCTION

Many commentaries introduce Daniel by examining a list – sometimes a long one – of the book's perceived difficulties. While Daniel has its share of complicated matters, this commentary seeks to emphasize its strengths and possibilities. As is true of any biblical book, Daniel rewards readers who embrace its historical, literary and theological features as key means of personal and community formation. Readers who welcome its insights will weather its seeming peculiarities. They will find comfort in the book's main theme, 'God's kingdom rising', to the extent that they believe it is true. They will experience the book's presentation of this message as imaginative and gripping if they embrace the challenge of reading vision reports and historical narratives that contain symbolic elements. They will find the book applicable if they are willing to follow Daniel's example of faithful living under oppressive conditions. This journey begins by examining basic aspects of Daniel's historical, literary, theological, canonical and formational elements.

1. Historical elements

a. Overview

This commentary focuses on the Hebrew and Aramaic text of
Daniel, which features several historical notations that position its
characters in specific times and places. Beginning in 1:1, these
markers direct readers from the beginning of the reign of Nebuchadnezzar II[1] of Babylon in 605 BC (1:1) to the third year of Cyrus
the Great[2] of Persia's rule in *c.* 537–536 BC (10:1). Along the way,
the book stops in Nebuchadnezzar's second year (*c.* 603–602 BC;
2:1), in unspecified years during his monarchy (3:1; 4:1), in
Belshazzar's first (*c.* 550–549 BC; 7:1), third (548–547 BC; 8:1) and
final (*c.* 539 BC; 5:1, 30–31) years of co-regency (see comments on
Dan. 5:1–31) with his father, Nabonidus (5:1), and the first year of
Darius the Mede (*c.* 539–538 BC; 6:1). To summarize, 1:1 and 1:21
introduce the book's basic historical-political scope, which spans
the Babylonian era to the Persian era. Chapters 2 – 6 then unfold in
chronological order from 603–602 BC to 539–538 BC. Finally,
chapters 7 – 12 occur in order from 550–549 BC to 537–536 BC.

Daniel also transcends these historical settings. The book
portrays times long after Daniel has died, including the end of
all time, in 2:31–45; 7:1–28; 8:1–26; 9:24–27; and 10:1 – 12:13.
Specifically, it envisions Greece supplanting Persia, which occurs by
331 BC, and a series of Greek rulers of Jerusalem that ends with
Antiochus IV in *c.* 175–164 BC. In fact, Daniel sees trouble for God's
people and Jerusalem beyond 164 BC, but also God's ultimate
triumph and giving of his kingdom to the Son of Man (7:9–27). He
sees death and destruction ahead, but also resurrection and peace
with God (12:1–4). Therefore, readers must hold Daniel's past,
present and future together, not separate them. They must read

---

1. Since I do not discuss Nebuchadnezzar I in the commentary, I will
simply refer to Nebuchadnezzar II as Nebuchadnezzar hereafter.

2. An unknown number of Persian rulers named Cyrus preceded Cyrus
the Great. Kenneth Kitchen (2003: 380) notes that one was an Assyrian
vassal in the seventh century BC. Since I will not discuss these
predecessors further, I will simply refer to Cyrus the Great as Cyrus.

Daniel the way they experience reality, combining memory, current experience and future hope.

b. Nabopolassar, Nebuchadnezzar and the Babylonian Empire (Daniel 1 – 4)

The whole book unfolds in or near Babylon, so it is necessary to grasp some specific parts of its history. Daniel opens with two major occurrences: Nebuchadnezzar's rise to power, and Judah's descent into exile (1:1–2). Nebuchadnezzar ascended Babylon's throne when his father, Nabopolassar, died. Nabopolassar (c. 626–605 BC) was an extraordinary leader (see Lundbom 2017: 154–162 on his achievements). When he was born, his people chafed under Assyrian rule. By the time he died, he and the Medes had driven the neo-Assyrian Empire (c. 745–612 BC) into the dust. Assyria had conquered Babylon many times (e.g. 729, 709, 700 and 689 BC). The most recent instance (652–648 BC) left the city and land devastated. Fortunately for Babylon, Assyria rebuilt Babylon before their last great king, Assurbanipal, died in c. 626 BC.

Upon Assurbanipal's death, Nabopolassar galvanized his people and his allies, defeated Assyria in a series of battles, conquered Assyria's capital, Nineveh, in 612 BC and effectively finished Assyria as a major power by 609 BC. He then turned to Egypt, Assyria's ally, the greatest remaining threat to his empire-building plans. He dispatched Nebuchadnezzar to fight Pharaoh's armies at Carchemish in 605 BC, and then died later that year. Having achieved his father's aim of driving Egypt southward, Nebuchadnezzar returned from Carchemish to take the throne. He inherited a strong kingdom, but one with much unfinished business. Throughout his reign Nebuchadnezzar laboured to keep Egypt as far south as possible, and regularly fought other enemies much closer to home.

Nebuchadnezzar's rise meant the diminishing of many other rulers and lands, including Judah and their king, Jehoiakim (c. 609–598 BC). Situated at the border between Babylon's and Egypt's nationalistic aims, Judah had little peace. Egypt placed Jehoiakim in power (see 2 Kgs 23:31–37), so Nebuchadnezzar had political reasons to harass, subdue, recruit or replace him. He made Jehoiakim pay tribute money at times, but never unseated him.

In fact, Daniel 1:1–4 states that Nebuchadnezzar extracted tribute payments consisting of precious temple treasures and talented individuals in his first year (see commentary on 1:1). The people included Daniel and his friends. Hezekiah (*c.* 715–687 BC) had paid Sennacherib (*c.* 705–681 BC), his Assyrian overlord, similarly in *c.* 701 BC (2 Kgs 18:13–17; *ARAB* 2: 119–121, entry 240). Jeremiah notes that Nebuchadnezzar threatened Jehoiakim in 604 and 601 BC (Jer. 25:1; 36:1). Nebuchadnezzar took control of Judah's political fortunes months after Jehoiakim had died. He subdued Jerusalem and replaced Jehoiakim's natural successor, Jehoiachin (598–597 BC), with Zedekiah (597–587 BC), who eventually rebelled against Nebuchadnezzar and faced his wrath (see 2 Kgs 24:10–20). Nebuchadnezzar sacked and burned Jerusalem in 587 BC (see 2 Kgs 25:1–21).

In all, Nebuchadnezzar took people from Judah in *c.* 605, 597, 587 and 582 BC (Jer. 52:1–30). Thus, there were many exiles, not just one. These exiles have profound theological significance in the Old Testament (see 2 Kgs 17; Ps. 89). Daniel pondered their significance and yearned for their end (9:1–9). Thus, the author almost certainly expected the book's first readers to know about them. After conquering and levelling Jerusalem, Nebuchadnezzar apparently did not place Babylonian officials there (see Jer. 40 – 41), as he did in most conquered lands. Rather, he left the area to the remaining people, and kept an eye on Egypt (Vanderhooft 2000: 9–59). Many survivors understandably looked to Egypt for help, a strategy Jeremiah decried (see Jer. 42 – 44).

Once taken to Babylon, Daniel lived there for the rest of his days (1:21; 10:1). Thus, the book portrays a captive's life, an existence filled with dangers, hopes and constraints. Indeed, Daniel and his friends had better opportunities than most exiles, but they still faced massive challenges. These challenges included surviving political intrigue and regime change. Daniel 2:1 mentions Nebuchadnezzar's second year, a time when the young king faced strong opposition on many fronts (Baldwin 1978: 86; Wiseman 1985: 24). It is not surprising that he had troubling dreams and a suspicious mind, and feared his kingdom might not last long. He also experienced internal opposition in his tenth year (Wiseman 1985: 34–35). Nonetheless, he met every challenge to his authority within and outside his kingdom.

c. Nebuchadnezzar's successors and Babylon's decline (Daniel 5:1–30)

Nebuchadnezzar died peacefully, and in power, in 562 BC. None of his successors did. Nebuchadnezzar's son Amel-Marduk succeeded him (see 2 Kgs 25:27–30), but ruled only two years (562–560 BC) before his brother-in-law Neriglissar (560–556 BC) replaced him. After four years, Nebuchadnezzar's son Labashi-Marduk ruled for a short while before Nabonidus (556–539 BC), who was perhaps another son-in-law of Nebuchadnezzar (Dougherty 1929: 60–63; Wiseman 1985: 11), reigned.

Nabonidus did not particularly like the city of Babylon, and he preferred another deity to Babylon's chief god, so he lived elsewhere and put his son Belshazzar in power there for ten years, before returning when Persia became a threat (see *ANET* 313 and the comments on Daniel 4:1 and 5:1). Scholars date this co-regency as beginning in *c.* 553–552 BC or *c.* 550–549 BC. The latter date seems the most likely (see comments on 5:1 and 7:1). Belshazzar was ruling the city of Babylon on his father's behalf when it fell in 539 BC.

d. Cyrus and Babylon's downfall (Daniel 5:31 – 6:28)

Cyrus began to rule Persia in 559 BC. His father came from the Persian royal household, but his mother was a Mede (Lucas 2002: 38–39). He conquered the Medes in 550 BC, thereby joining these two significant societies. Ancient peoples thereafter considered the Persians and the Medes as one entity, yet separable by ethnic origin. Beginning in 540 BC, the Medes and Persians fought a series of battles with Nabonidus's forces (see comments on 5:1, 30–31; 6:1). They took control of the land of Babylon, including the city of Babylon, in 539 BC. Babylon's officials apparently surrendered to avoid a siege, and perhaps due to their dislike for Nabonidus and Belshazzar. One of Cyrus's generals captured the city, and Cyrus came there some time later. He did not live in Babylon for long periods of time. His officials ruled in his name in his absence, which may explain the presence of Darius the Mede in 5:30–31; 6:1. As with the various Jewish exiles, Daniel does not discuss how these changes occurred. Rather, it focuses on God's rule over events that the author expects readers to know. Cyrus died in 530 BC.

e. Babylon, Persia-Media, Greece and beyond (Daniel 7 – 12)

Daniel always kept an eye on the future. In chapter 2 Nebuchadnezzar dreams about coming days, and Daniel describes three kingdoms that will follow Nebuchadnezzar's. His interpretation does not address all kingdoms that might ever arise. The metaphor of four kingdoms appears elsewhere in the book as a way of describing the periodic rise of normal evil monarchs (see comments on 2:21–45; 7:17; 8:22). From his years in Babylon, then, Daniel knew that the Babylonian Empire was not everlasting.

In Belshazzar's first (7:1; 550–549 BC) and third (8:1; 548–547 BC) years, Daniel had visions that supplemented Nebuchadnezzar's dream. As in 2:1–47, Daniel saw four kingdoms in 7:1–28, and, as before, God's kingdom capped history. When a new ruler arises, then, God reminds Daniel of who leads an eternal kingdom. Two years later Daniel envisioned the Medes and Persians fighting Greece (8:1–27). Though Cyrus's forces withstood Greece, Daniel saw a later powerful founding ruler rise out of Greece, followed, as in chapters 2 and 7, by four lesser kings (8:22). As before, God defeats the last of these rulers (8:25).

Thus, Daniel 7 and 8 push the book's vision of the future to the time of Alexander the Great of Greece and beyond. Alexander took Macedon's throne in 336 BC. Between 334 and 331 BC he conquered Persia and Egypt, thereby taking political control of Jerusalem (Lucas 2002: 39). He died in 323 BC in an interesting place: Nebuchadnezzar's palace in Babylon. His kingdom then split into two factions, the Seleucids in the north and the Ptolemies in the south. The Seleucids ruled Jerusalem. The last Greek ruler, Antiochus IV (175–164 BC), was especially harsh to the Jews and particularly determined to insult their religious beliefs (see the comments on 7:1–27 and 8:1–26). For example, he erected an altar to another deity in the temple in Jerusalem in 167 BC.

Daniel 9:1 and 10:1 push the vision beyond the Greek era. In 9:1–19 Daniel prays about the temple's renewal in the first year in which the Medes and Persians ruled Jerusalem (c. 539 BC), and he learns that the temple will face desolation for years. Indeed, the temple will face woes for 'seventy weeks of years' (lit. 'seventy sevens'), not 'merely' seventy years (9:24–27). Then, at the time when temple sacrifice begins afresh in Jerusalem (10:1), he receives a long vision that fleshes out this long era in 10:1 – 12:13. Trouble will accompany the temple and its people well beyond Daniel's death. Daniel must take comfort in God's promise of resurrection and vindication (12:1–13).

Jesus uses these visions to explain the eventual destruction of the second temple in AD 70 to his disciples (Matt. 24:15–28; Mark 13:1–22; Luke 21:20–24). He also declares that his people will suffer through the ages until God puts an end to human oppression (Matt. 24:29–51; Mark 13:24–37; Luke 21:25–36). In short, he confirms the visions Daniel conveys. Kingdoms will come and go. Persecution will continue, though not always at the same level of severity. God will eventually intervene. Until then, there will always be yet another fourth human kingdom, but God's kingdom is the ultimate kingdom. It will endure for ever.

f. Conclusion and implications
The book's vision of history spans from 605 BC to the end of time. Its narratives are anchored historically in Daniel's early and later years. It does not deal with all the historical and linguistic details historians and commentators might understandably like it to stress. Rather, it shines light on God's activities revealed through the life story and accurate future predictions of one of his exiled people. It highlights God's kingdom rising and human rulers falling. Therefore, it reverses the situation with which the book opens, and rejects the common human belief that world leaders dictate history. Those who preserved the book found it valuable because of its wide-ranging value for faith and life.

2. Literary elements

a. Overview
Historical analyses of various kinds have dominated Daniel studies for over a century. Though further historical discoveries and studies of Daniel will hopefully provide new information, this territory has been staked out fairly well. Though there has been progress on the study of Daniel's literary aspects, there remains room for growth. This commentary seeks to maintain contact with Daniel's historical details, but will highlight the book's literary and

theological contributions to biblical literature. Thus, it seeks to explain the text, not just interact with theories about the book's origins. As George Steiner (1989: 39–47) warns, it is easy for commentaries on commentaries to displace the text and its witness to God's powerful presence. Daniel's most important literary details are its text, characters, plot, imagery and genre.

b. Hebrew and Aramaic text of Daniel

Daniel features both Hebrew (1:1 – 2:4a; 8:1 – 12:13) and Aramaic (2:4b – 7:28) material (for discussions of Daniel's textual history, see Baldwin 1978: 73–74; Newsom and Breed 2014: 2–12; and Collins 1993: 2–24). Of all the Old Testament books, only Ezra and Jeremiah also have Aramaic passages (see Ezra 4:8 – 6:18; 7:12–26; and Jer. 10:11), and Daniel's is the longest. Daniel 2:4a introduces a speech in Aramaic, but the book gives no reason for continuing in Aramaic to 7:28, or for switching back to Hebrew in 8:1.

Aramaic was used in Persia from 700 BC to 200 BC, and became the Persian Empire's official language in 500 BC (Collins 1993: 14–15). The Assyrian and Babylonian Empires also used it in official documents. Thus, it is not unbelievable for a book set in the Babylonian and Persian eras to feature Aramaic. The Dead Sea Scrolls include eight manuscript fragments containing portions of Daniel, with the oldest dating from the second century BC (Lucas 2002: 19; Collins 1993: 2–3). These texts include the change from Hebrew to Aramaic in 2:4b and the transition back from Aramaic to Hebrew in 8:1 (Lucas 2002: 19). They also indicate that the Masoretic Text[3] stands on firm historic ground. Therefore, Daniel almost certainly included the Aramaic materials from the start, and the wide and long usage of Aramaic in ancient times precludes dating Daniel solely on linguistic grounds (see Kitchen 1965: 31–79).

Comparing the Old Testament's only two long Aramaic passages may be relevant. Ezra 4:8 – 6:18 is set in the Persian era, and intersperses official diplomatic letters and narratives. It is part of Ezra's summary of the fate of the temple and the community in

---

3. The Masoretic Text is the standard scholarly text of Daniel (*Biblia Hebraica Stuttgartensia*). It is based on the Leningrad Codex (*c.* AD 1005).

Jerusalem from Cyrus's first year in *c.* 539–538 BC to Ezra's journey there from Babylonia in the fifth century BC. It quotes official Persian documents, and includes third-person and first-person narration. Daniel includes these types of material, as well as some strikingly different subject matter. The books could date, then, from the same general era.

c. Greek and Latin texts of Daniel

Two significant Greek versions of Daniel have survived. The first, called the Old Greek (*c.* 150–100 BC; see Collins 1993: 8–9; Montgomery 1927: 38–39; Baldwin 1978: 70–71), appears in the Septuagint, the third-century BC translation of the Old Testament from Hebrew to Greek. Scarcity of early manuscripts makes the Old Greek version hard to date. The second is Theodotion's text, which dates from *c.* AD 200. These two texts differ in various respects, especially in chapters 4 – 6 (see Collins 1993: 6–7; Holm 2013: 302–303).

Jerome (347–420), who translated the Bible from the original languages into Latin, knew both Greek versions of Daniel. His version, known as the Vulgate, became the church's Bible for over a thousand years. He wrote that churches had set aside the Septuagint version of Daniel in favour of Theodotion's (1958: 17). New Testament writers usually cite a text like Theodotion's when they quote Daniel, so Theodotion likely depended on a similar, earlier Greek translation (Steinmann 2008: 65; Baldwin 1978: 70). Theodotion's translation conforms closely to a text form very much like the Masoretic Text (see Lucas 2002: 19–21), which affirms the integrity of the Masoretic text of Daniel.

The Greek manuscripts include three additions to Daniel's Hebrew and Aramaic text. Roman Catholic, Greek Orthodox and Russian Orthodox believers consider this material as Scripture. The first addition consists of prayers that Daniel's friends offer in the furnace (see Dan. 3), joined by a short prose statement. These prayers are known as the Prayer of Azariah (Abednego) and the Song of the Three Young Men. They appear between Daniel 3:23 and 24 in the Vulgate and both ancient Greek texts. The prayers lament sin, ask for deliverance and promise to praise God when deliverance comes. Therefore, they read like many psalms of lament, and like prayers in Daniel 9:1–19; Ezra 9:1–15; and Nehemiah 9:1–38. The second addition is Susanna, in which Daniel's wisdom delivers a virtuous young Jewish woman from sexually predatory elders. This material appears at the beginning of Daniel in Theodotion's version, and after Daniel 12 in the Old Greek and Vulgate. The third addition is Bel and the Dragon, in which Daniel exposes idol worship. Theodotion's text has Bel and the Dragon after Daniel 12. The Old Greek and Vulgate have it after Susanna. These narratives portray Daniel as devoted to God, wise, helpful and able to solve difficult problems. Scenes from all three additions appear on Christian sarcophagi (stone burial boxes) dating from the fourth century AD housed in the Vatican Museum. This demonstrates that these stories have encouraged suffering believers for centuries.

Jerome included the additions in his translation, mainly because the churches of his day read them as Scripture, though he duly noted that the additions did not exist in Hebrew (1958: 17). Christians used his Bible for centuries, so many believers considered these texts to be Scripture. During the sixteenth century, Protestants slowly came to count only the Hebrew and Aramaic-based Old Testament books as Scripture. At the Council of Trent in 1546, Catholics decided that Jerome's translation determined the approved books of the Old Testament. Thus, they included the Greek additions to Daniel in their Bible.

Early Protestants considered the additions helpful to Christian devotion. These texts do not contradict the author's portrayal of Daniel and his friends. They affirm prayer, holy living and worship of the one true and living God. They encourage persecuted believers. Therefore, they are worthy of respect, even if one does not consider them to be Scripture.

d. Characters

Literary scholars have debated whether characters or plot drive a story at least since Aristotle wrote his *Poetics* in the fourth century BC (see House 1988: 23–24; and House 1990: 111–219). This discussion will probably never end. Since Daniel's title and main character cannot be separated, I will begin with its characters, saving God's characterization for the section on theology. Though Daniel's characters are not as fully drawn as some in longer current fiction and historical studies (Dillard and Longman 1994: 346), they are hardly colourless. Daniel, Nebuchadnezzar, Shadrach, Meshach, Abednego, Belshazzar, Darius, Gabriel, Daniel's fellow courtiers and the last Greek king make a reasonably impressive cast of characters in a relatively short work.

Daniel is a reluctant main character, and a man of great wisdom. He does not seek exile, so he would rather *not* be at the centre of a story set in Babylon. His prayers in 6:10 and 9:1–19 show that his heart remains back home in Judah. Nonetheless, he steps forward in 1:8–16 as the leader of three other young men in the same predicament. About to die with all Babylon's wise men in 2:13, he asks prudently and discreetly (2:14) for time to fulfil Nebuchadnezzar's seemingly impossible demand. When he hears Nebuchadnezzar's dream in 4:8–18, he hesitates before interpreting the dream and offering advice (4:19–27). In 5:13–16 Belshazzar summons Daniel to explain the handwriting on the wall. As before, Daniel wisely does not seek reward for interpreting the writing, though his speech in 5:17–28 does not display the patience he had with Nebuchadnezzar. He does not seek the night visions that terrify him (7:28; 8:27; 10:10, 15). He seems by nature a studious, reticent man, and (thus) a wise man.

Daniel exhibits authentic devotion to God. He decides to refuse the king's food and wine in 1:8–16, for he believes it would 'defile' him in some unspecified way. He risks his life, the steward's, and his friends' by requesting another diet, so he has the courage needed for his convictions. His concern for Nebuchadnezzar (4:19) indicates not only that he loves his neighbour, but perhaps that he also loves his enemy (see Lev. 19:18; Matt. 5:43–48). Praying to God when to do so risks his life proves his sincerity (see 6:1–10). His willingness to receive visions that confuse and sicken him (see 8:27) shows his unselfishness, as do his fasting and prayer for his people and their future (9:1–3).

Daniel remains consistent throughout the book. Apparently, he goes about his business without fanfare, for decades pass between his service to Nebuchadnezzar and his words to Belshazzar.[4] Because

---

4. I owe this observation to David Oldfield, long-time lay Bible teacher.

of his faith, he never loses proper hope. Writing in a very different context, Vaclav Havel (1990: 181) describes this type of hope:

> It is an orientation of the spirit, an orientation of the heart; it transcends the world that is immediately experienced, and is anchored somewhere beyond its horizons. I don't think you can explain it as a mere derivative of something here, of some movement, or of some favorable signs in the world. I feel that its deepest roots are in the transcendental, just as the roots of responsibility are. . . . It is not the conviction that something will turn out well, but the certainty that something makes sense, regardless of how it turns out.

This is the type of hope that understands one cannot separate disciplined means from positive ends (Berry 1981: 151–220).

Nebuchadnezzar is the book's most volatile character. On the one hand, he acts like any ancient despot. He conquers foreign lands to line his nation's pockets (1:1–4). He worries about losing power (2:1–12), deifies himself (3:1–7), and builds a capital city as a monument to himself (4:28–30). Yet he grows, learning from Daniel (2:46), Daniel's friends (3:26–30) and circumstances (4:1–3, 34–37; 5:20–21). Nebuchadnezzar humbled himself before God (5:20–21). The author may present Nebuchadnezzar's last confession in 4:34–37 as true faith in God, but leaves just enough doubt to keep Nebuchadnezzar a bit of a mystery.

Daniel's three friends are steadfast. They follow Daniel's lead in 1:8–16 and pray for him in 2:17–18. In 3:1–18 they take centre stage, ready to die for their beliefs. Yet when they refuse to bow to the king's idol, they do not profess to know that God *will* spare them. They confess that he *can* do so, but refuse to bow regardless (3:16–18). They are completely faithful without possessing full knowledge of the future. This makes them realistic. They know that faithfulness does not guarantee self-preservation. Dozens of generations of believers have taken courage from their example.

Daniel and his friends' Babylonian colleagues are a mixed bag. On the one hand, the overseer in 1:8–16 and Arioch in 2:12–16 accommodate Daniel's requests. On the other, malicious men make sure Nebuchadnezzar knows that Shadrach, Meshach and Abednego have not bowed as ordered (3:8). Going one step further, colleagues of the elderly Daniel set a trap for him based on his religious beliefs (6:5). Though they end up dead in Daniel's place (6:24), the book never claims that the wicked never prosper. Like the overseer in 1:8–16, these men made their decisions and took their chances. They have been foolish, for Daniel has character and wisdom they cannot understand. Their increasing malevolence highlights his goodness.

Belshazzar is uncomplicated. The author presents him as a completely foolish co-regent, a playboy would-be king. He revels (5:1–4) when he should be preparing for invasion (5:30–31). He shows disrespect for God when he uses the vessels Nebuchadnezzar took from Jerusalem's temple to praise other gods (5:1–4). Perhaps he defies Nebuchadnezzar's belief that God gave Jerusalem into his hands (see 1:2; 4:34–37; 2 Kgs 24:13), or rejects a prophecy that Babylon will fall (e.g. Jer. 50 – 51). Regardless, he earns God's judgment and Daniel's denunciation (5:5–9, 17–28). Belshazzar represents the complete decline of earlier rulers' achievements, and foreshadows the terrible king that 8:22–26; 9:9–27; and 11:29–45 describe.

Darius has a small role in the book. As the commentary on 5:31 – 6:28 will discuss, scholars debate his identity. Officials dupe this new ruler into putting Daniel in the lions' den in order to gain power for themselves. He falls for their ploy. When Daniel survives, however, he shows that he has the vengeful nature normal for one in his position. Still, like Nebuchadnezzar, he praises Daniel's God as the living, enduring and rescuing God (6:25–27). He learns, and he respects God, at least to some degree.

The Bible first gives the name of an angel in Daniel 8:16 and 10:13, introducing Gabriel and Michael, respectively. The word translated 'angel' in English can also be rendered as 'messenger'. Gabriel is certainly God's messenger, for he interprets Daniel's dream about Greece fighting Persia (8:16–17). He also assures Daniel that God has heard his prayers in 9:20–23, and gives him the bad news that Jerusalem's suffering has just begun in 9:24–27. Interestingly, the angels that represent God fight angels representing Persia and Greece (10:1–21). Though more powerful than Daniel, angels are not as powerful as God is. Their work is not effortless. Gabriel appears again in the Bible. He informs Zechariah of John the Baptist's birth (Luke 1:6–25), and tells Mary she will bear the Christ (Luke 1:26–38).

Daniel 7 – 11 presents the book's most evil character, building his profile as surely as Daniel 1 – 6 builds Daniel's, yet without ever naming him. The author presents him as unnatural, twisted. He is a little horn growing out of a big horn (7:7–8; 8:9), a usurper (11:21). The author depicts him as the opposite of a wise man. He brags (7:11, 20), misuses his gift of understanding problems (8:23), and treasures deceit (8:25). Furthermore, the author characterizes him as the worst sort of king: brutal (7:19; 8:24; 9:26; 11:22), blasphemous (7:25; 8:9–14; 9:26–27a; 11:37–39), and committed to destroying God's people (7:23–25; 8:24–25; 9:26; 11:29–35). The only good thing about him is his mortality. God will overthrow him (7:11–12, 26; 8:25; 9:27a; 11:40–45) and give his kingdom to the Son of Man and the holy ones (7:13–14, 26–27).

e. Plot

One can read a literary work, note its characters and understand some of its imagery, yet fail to grasp its plot. A plot is not simply what happens in a story. It explains why what happens in a story takes place, and those events' causes and effects.

Daniel fits into the Bible's overall plot. This plot includes creation of all things by God, rebellion against God, redemption by God, instruction from God for living, resurrection of the dead by God, and eternal life with God in the new heavens and earth.[5] Abraham's family has a special role in this drama. They will bless all nations (Gen. 12:1–9) by serving as priests (Exod. 19:5–6) in a healthy community (Lev. 19:18) that declares that the Christ (2 Sam. 7; 1 Chr. 17) will redeem sinners (Isa. 52:13 – 53:12) and give eternal life with God (Isa. 66:18–23). When Abraham's family sins, God disciplines them, even removing them from their land if necessary (Lev. 26:13–39; Deut. 28:15–68; 2 Kgs 17). However, even then he will not discard them. He will bring them back to the land (Deut. 30:1–10), renew and repopulate the land, and reunite the people so they will be ready to receive the promised Saviour (Jer. 30 – 31) and take his message to the world (Isa. 66:18–23). Daniel knew this plot

---

5. On the Bible's unified plot, see Bartholomew and Goheen 2014;
   Hafemann and House 2007; and Goldsworthy 2002.

(see Dan. 9:1–19). He knew he was in the exile portion of it, and he desired to know when the plot would proceed to the renewal stage. Daniel realized his life was one small part of a much bigger story.

With these elements in mind, Daniel's plot revolves around what God *gives*. Daniel 1:2 asserts that God gave Jehoiakim into Nebuchadnezzar's hands. Daniel 1:9 claims that God gave Daniel favour with the overseer. Daniel 1:17 states that God gave the four young exiles the learning and skill needed to endure a lifelong exile. Daniel confesses that God gave him the wisdom to interpret Nebuchadnezzar's dream (2:21), and Nebuchadnezzar learns that God gives kingdoms to whomever he chooses (4:17). Belshazzar learns the same in 5:28. Most importantly, the book claims that God will give the world's kingdoms to one 'like a son of man' as a permanent gift (7:13–14). As this commentary will argue, this figure is the Davidic messiah that the Old Testament promises. Finally, God gives Daniel visions of the future (9:22), the promise of resurrection (12:1–4) and a fitting place in God's kingdom (12:13). Daniel learns exile is his place in the plot, but he also discovers that God will complete the plot.

Thus, the episodes in Daniel's life have purpose. When he goes into exile, he suffers with his people as they face God's righteous discipline. When he stays faithful, he shows his belief in God's universal rule and eventual redemption of his people. When he serves Nebuchadnezzar and Darius, he blesses other nations. When he endures and relates visions, he leaves a witness for later generations, as befits a member of a kingdom of priests. His devotion would please the psalmists, and his endurance would please Moses and Job. Taken together, these aspects demonstrate that Daniel's plot flows from imagery found in 2:31–45: God's kingdom is rising. It rises despite Judah's exile, despite Babylon's oppressive ways and despite Judah's weakness. It rises because of God the Creator's power in heaven and on earth, and because he gives the nations to his chosen 'son of man' (7:13–14).

f. Imagery
Daniel utilizes forceful, strange, vivid imagery. The author portrays kingdoms as parts of a statue (2:1–45), kings as mutant beasts (7:1–12) who fight one another (8:5–14), nations as stars that fall (8:10),

stupefying divine messengers as human beings (8:1–22), and time
as an entity that can be multiplied like a number (9:24–27; 12:11–
12). A disembodied hand emerges and writes on a wall (5:5). God
appears as the Ancient of Days, and his co-regent looks like a
man – but one who rides on clouds (7:13–14). Angels battle (10:13)
and support nations (11:1). Snow-white clothing and hair represent
purity one cannot fully fathom (7:13–14; 12:5–6).

Meanwhile, Nebuchadnezzar and Daniel have dreams in the
night (2:1–47; 4:1–37; 7:1). Daniel has visions (2:19; 8:1; 9:20–23;
10:1), yet also reads scrolls containing God's Word (9:1–2) and prays
three times a day. Extraordinary experiences do not replace normal
devotional habits. Daniel persevered through discipline and hope.
Visions and dreams and conversations with angels did not come
every day. Their timing was as mysterious to him as the imagery.

Numbers play a consistent symbolic role, especially the number
four. It seems to have the same type of meaning as in Proverbs
30:1–19, where the wisdom writer says there are three things too
wonderful for him to grasp – no, there are four. Amos 1 – 2 provides
a negative example, noting that God will judge various nations due
to three sins – no, four – that they have committed. In both cases,
adding the fourth item invites the reader to make a longer list, since
the original one does not exhaust the subject. In Daniel, as in world
history, there is always another kingdom coming along. One can
always divide history into four parts. Babylon follows Assyria; Persia
follows Babylon; Greece follows Persia; Rome follows Greece, and
on and on to this day. When Daniel 2:31–45 and 7:13–28 specify a
final kingdom beyond a fourth human kingdom, that final kingdom
will never end. It is God's kingdom. There are similar explanations
for the numbers seven and seventy in Daniel 9:24–27.

The commentary material will discuss the book's imagery as it
occurs, so I will only make some preliminary summative statements
here. First, it is impossible to know for certain all that the symbols
entail, but it is possible to know many things about what they
signify. For instance, humans portrayed as misshapen animals
symbolize people who do not perform their role in creation, who,
for example, exalt themselves above God, as Nebuchadnezzar does
in 4:1–37 and Belshazzar does in 5:1–4. Horns symbolize power
(see Ps. 75), but horns that sprout from mutant beasts represent

power that cannot last (7:19–28). Beast-like rulers will oppose God and his faithful ones. A character who looks 'like a son of man' has a human shape.

Second, revelatory dreams and visions occur often in the Bible. Jacob (Gen. 28:10–22; 46:1–4), Joseph (Gen. 37:5–11), Joseph's fellow prisoners and Pharaoh (Gen. 40 – 41), Moses (Num. 12:6), Gideon's opponents (Judg. 7:13–14), Solomon (1 Kgs 3:5), Joseph the husband of Mary (Matt. 1:20; 2:19) and Paul (Acts 18:9) all have revelatory dreams. God uses them to inform, instruct and encourage his people. They do not come on demand and they are not meant to entertain or satisfy morbid spiritual curiosity. Similarly, Peter has a vision (Acts 10:9–33), and so do Elisha (2 Kgs 6:15–17; 8:7–15), Isaiah (Isa. 6:1–13), Jeremiah (Jer. 1:4–19), Ezekiel (Ezek. 37:1–14, et al.), Amos (Amos 7:1–9; 8:1–3) and several other biblical characters. The initial verses in Isaiah, Nahum and Obadiah identify the books as 'visions', which indicates that the words these prophets write originate beyond them. As with dreams, visions come from God as he wills. The Bible does not promise visions to current readers simply because selected biblical characters had them.

Third, current readers may be more used to finding this sort of imagery in poetry than in prose. Hence, it may be helpful to consider how two selected contemporary poets and one seventeenth-century poet portray themselves and their art. Wendell Berry is a down-to-earth poet. Therefore, it is interesting that he states that he would not have been a writer except that he has been 'wakeful at night' and words 'have come' to him, words that needed 'to be remembered' (2014: 154). Berry does not claim to write Scripture. Yet what he describes as words that 'have come' to him sounds like what Daniel and other biblical writers call a 'vision'. The wakefulness at night he mentions sounds like how Daniel heard from God in 2:19.

Seamus Heaney (1995: 1) observes that poetry provides a bridge between helpful imagination and the flawed world we see every day. Poetry 'is the imagination pressing back against the pressure of reality'. One could easily say the same about Daniel's life and writing. Poetry seeks to probe what reality has been, is or could be. For this probing and bridge building, it utilizes heightened language suitable for grasping the nature and importance of what has been and what could be. Heaney (1995: 5–6) observes that many poets and their readers therefore wish for poetry to serve specific political change in a broken world, and concedes that poetry can provide such help. However, he believes that poetry must not just be utilitarian. It should also be free enough to call the human spirit 'beyond the course that the usual life plots for it' (1995: 16), so that it can serve diverse individuals, communities, situations and causes in many generations.

Both Berry and Heaney appreciate George Herbert's poetry. Herbert (1593–1633) was an Anglican minister whose religious poetry self-consciously relates his desire to link life on earth to God, without debasing either (on Herbert's life, see Drury 2014). Herbert used poetry to bridge the gap between time and eternity, a gap he believed is much smaller than most people imagine. Thus, he uses images that can apply to people and things (e.g. an altar, a pulley, etc.). Sometimes these images seem odd, so they jolt readers into thinking differently, which then helps him make his point.

Daniel's images, visions, dreams and angels serve the purposes Berry, Heaney and Herbert propose. Sometimes the words and images that come to him in the night bring comfort, as in 2:19. Sometimes they frighten, as in 7:28 and 8:17. Always they peel back the thin veil between time and eternity, demonstrating that God rules reality, and that reality includes things like angels fighting against Persia and other twisted beasts. God's warnings and encouragements may come to pass quickly, as in 4:1–37, or they may delay until the end of time, as in 12:1–13. Past and present readers must therefore follow Daniel's example and live in discipline, hope, imagination and steely resolve, paying due regard to intertwined life on earth and in heaven. Doing so removes some of the barriers between understanding Daniel's imagery in a world saturated with materialism.

g. Genre

Many works on Daniel begin with the book's genre and proceed to its contents. I have done so myself (House 1998: 498). This process has its place, since the contents of literature often follow the genre the author selects. In Daniel studies, however, following this method creates as many problems as it solves. For one thing, genres develop as many authors write in a similar way. Daniel is an early version of the apocalyptic genre regardless of when scholars date it. He did not seek to write an apocalypse in the way, for instance, that Shakespeare sat down to write a sonnet or play. For another, studies of apocalyptic literature have yielded a broad definition of the genre. So starting with Daniel's genre can feed the tendency to approach the book as a series of problems that must be solved before the book can speak. Thus, I have chosen to present Daniel's basic literary features before discussing its genre.

Virtually all scholars agree that Daniel is apocalyptic literature. Studies of apocalyptic literature are relatively new in biblical studies. John J. Collins (1993: 2–3) observes that the first major study of apocalyptic literature did not appear until 1832, when Friedrich Lücke published his seminal synthesis of then-known biblical and extra-biblical works. Several examples of apocalyptic literature were discovered later in the nineteenth century, thereby greatly changing the way interpreters approached Daniel and other similar works (Collins 1993: 3).

Though scholars offer differing lists of apocalyptic aspects, the following combination of characteristics is fairly common: highly symbolic language; division of future world history into specific periods; emphasis on God's sovereignty; angels and visions revealing the future; and God and his people's ultimate victory over the forces of evil (see Rowley 1950: 11–149; Russell 1964: 104–139; Koch 1972: 28–33; Hanson 1979: 1–31; Collins 1984: 67–71; and Murphy 2012: 1–26). Many commentators add pseudonymous authorship and prophecy after the fact to the list (e.g. Hartman and Di Lella 1977: 67–71), since many apocalyptic works have those traits. Though experts agree that its roots are much older, apocalyptic literature flourished from *c.* 250 BC to AD 250.

Genres develop over time. Citing Alastair Fowler, Collins observes that genres go through at least three stages. First, they begin with several authors writing parts of what become the genre's main features. Second, authors practise the form. Third, authors use some aspects of the genre for many purposes, until eventually the genre dissipates as a particular form of literature (Collins 1993: 4). Apocalyptic certainly underwent this sort of development. Virtually all experts agree that Daniel emerged during the early stages of this process.

Beginning in the 1970s, Collins and other scholars have sought a definition of 'apocalyptic' general enough to cover as many works as possible, yet specific enough to keep interpreters from assigning the term to any work they wish. They have suggested that apocalyptic literature is 'a genre of revelatory literature with a narrative framework, in which a revelation is mediated by an otherworldly being to a human recipient, disclosing a transcendent reality which is both temporal, insofar as it envisages eschatological salvation [salvation at the end of time], and spatial insofar as it involves another, supernatural world' (Collins 2016: 5). He provides a further helpful distinction between apocalyptic works 'with an interest in the development of history' and works 'marked by otherworldly journeys with a strong interest in cosmological speculation' (Collins 2016: 6).

The above survey of Daniel's literary aspects indicates that these definitions are helpful. All genres have variations, as any reader of narrative fiction, biography, lyric poetry and drama will quickly know. Daniel uses symbolic imagery freely, divides history or portions of history into four periods several times, highlights God's sovereignty, includes angels and visions, and asserts that God and his people will triumph over evil. The book also combines historical narrative like that found in the Old Testament historical books, poetic prayers like those found in the psalms, visions such as many biblical characters experienced, statements about future salvation given by an angelic being, and summaries of divine deliverance like those found throughout the Bible. However, Daniel also has great interest in what happens during his lifetime (see 9:1–19). He understands that salvation from oppression does not only occur at the end of time. Furthermore, he was not as famous as many of the other figures apocalyptic writers often chose (e.g. Moses, Abraham, etc.) when writing pseudonymous works. Daniel does not just have a narrative framework; it includes several separate stories and visions that follow a chronological sequence. Thus, there are clear differences.

Given these similarities and differences, and their general interest in how the genre evolved, scholars have sought to determine the sources that influenced apocalyptic authors. At least four are pertinent to Daniel. First, the prophetic literature influenced Daniel and subsequent writers (Hanson 1979: 1–31). As I noted above, several prophets report revelatory visions. These accounts include disturbing or unusual sights: locust swarms forming (Amos 7:1–6), God measuring Israel for judgment (Amos 7:7–9), and Israel rotting like fruit in a summer basket (Amos 8:1–3). They also include positive images: God putting death to death (Isa. 25:1–9), Judah's future budding like an almond tree (Jer. 1:4–12), and God's glory flying in a series of wheels caught in a storm (Ezek. 1:4–22). The book therefore contributes to a very long tradition of compelling imagery. Daniel's prayer in 9:1–19 also links him to the prophets' view of Israel and Judah's history. However, he does not speak and write to effect repentance, purity and witness in the way the prophets do.

Second, Daniel participates in an extensive Ancient Near Eastern literary tradition. Daniel reflects ideas and storytelling techniques that occurred in Babylon, Persia, Greece and Egypt before and after Daniel's setting (Collins 2016: 26–46). Predictive prophecy, dreams and visions, life after death, royal court intrigue, foreigners flourishing against long odds, dividing history into periods of time, and royal decrees all precede Daniel (Lucas 2002: 22–27). Daniel 1:1–21 presents Daniel as one trained in the history and practice of various sorts of Babylonian literature, and the book's contents support that characterization.

Over the past forty years, several scholars have particularly noted that Daniel parallels ancient court stories and story collections. Writing in 1973, Lee Humphreys concluded that Daniel 2 – 6 resembles court tales of *conflict* between a hero and opponents (e.g. Dan. 3, 6), and tales of court *contest* (e.g. Dan. 2, 5). He argued that the stories intend to instruct exiles how to flourish in their situations (Humphreys 1973: 211–223). Tawny Holm (2013: 2) writes that from this starting point a series of excellent works (e.g. Wills 1990) devoted to ancient court tales and Daniel have been published. For her part, Holm has argued that Daniel has many similarities not just to single accounts, but to ancient story collections that existed as early as 1500 BC.

Citing Helen Cooper, Holm defines a 'story collection' as having three major traits: (1) a collection of stories that are separable from one another and still make sense; (2) a collection of stories compiled, written or rewritten by a single author; and (3) shaped into a collection of stories that circulates in a coherent form (Holm 2013: 12). Holm notes that the fact that Daniel has both stories and visions makes it unusual, and that this combination transforms the book into a diverse whole shaped as a life of Daniel (2013: 205–208, 219). The book's goal is to instruct, not entertain (2013: 208–210), and, more specifically, to help people choose the side of wisdom instead of foolishness (2013: 219). Holm's work makes a significant contribution to literary studies of Daniel by suggesting ways in which Daniel and other Old Testament books that blend narrative and vision operate. Many of her observations about story collection apply to historical works. In ancient, no less than in modern, times, there is significant overlap between the style and structure of writing in historical and fictional texts.

Third, Old Testament narrative books influence Daniel. Scholars rarely mention this point. Readers might not notice tremendous differences between Daniel 1 – 6 and any number of texts in Joshua – 2 Kings, Ezra – 2 Chronicles, Isaiah 6 – 7 and 36 – 39 or Jeremiah 36 – 45. The prayer in Daniel 9:1–19 reads very much like Ezra 9 and Nehemiah 9. Daniel and Esther both occur in a royal setting that still leaves the main character's survival very much in doubt. These narrative books relate historical settings, use previous written source material and display a shared view of history. They present their material in a variety of ways, as befits careful literary work. But there is a strong family resemblance.

Fourth, Gerhard von Rad (1965: 306–308) asserted that Daniel and other apocalyptic literature grew out of wisdom teaching. Though I disagree with his conclusion that apocalyptic and prophecy have little in common (1965: 301–306), I think he is right to note the connections between wisdom literature and apocalyptic. Daniel received training in Babylonian wisdom literature (Dan. 1:1–7). Thus, he grappled with the sort of daily issues one finds in the book of Proverbs. Yet he also examined the future for Nebuchadnezzar's sake (Dan. 2:1–47) and for Jerusalem's (Dan. 9:1–19). Doing so in the Babylonian wisdom tradition included using accumulated wisdom to discern the future. His ability to discern the best course of action in the present (1:8–16; 4:27) mirrors Proverbs. His knowledge of the future also fuels his positive actions in the present (Dan. 9:1–19; 12:1–13). He is a great sage.

Taken together, this data indicates that it is correct to consider Daniel a work of apocalyptic literature. However, it is important to note how the book combines traditional biblical genres with Ancient Near Eastern works. It fuses narrative, poetry, wisdom, rich symbolism and two languages to present a deportee from Judah encouraging subsequent readers with the news that God's kingdom inevitably rises in history and beyond it. One should let Daniel's contents define the type of apocalyptic writing it is.

h. Narrator

Narrators are the implied voices that present a literary work of history or fiction (see Booth 1961; and Scheetz 2009: 30–51). To simplify matters greatly, narrators are typically recognizable by the presence of first-person or third-person voices. They are usually omniscient (all-knowing) or limited in their knowledge of events, and reliable or unreliable. Meir Sternberg has argued persuasively that biblical narrators almost always present themselves as omniscient and reliable (1985: 180–186). Daniel 1 – 6 features accounts about Daniel and the other characters that include what they did, said and thought. Therefore, those chapters reflect a third-person omniscient narrator who stands behind the whole section. Daniel 7 – 12 begins with a third-person statement that Daniel received a vision and committed it to writing (7:1), and then proceeds to convey Daniel's first-person account of what he experienced. Daniel 8:1 simply proceeds to recount Daniel's first-person account of another vision, and 9:1 does the same. Then, 10:1 provides a third-person introduction to Daniel's first-person account of his long final vision.

Daniel's narrator therefore presents stories about Daniel that occur and have been written down over many decades (see 1:1, 21; 2:1; 5:31; 6:1). This narrator uses a third-person narrative voice within a first-person account by Nebuchadnezzar (4:1–37; see 4:19), and presents a third-person narrative framework for Daniel's first-person accounts, two that begin in the first person (8:1; 9:1–2), and two that begin in the third person (7:1; 10:1). The book's narrator presents all the material as received, not witnessed. Nonetheless, the narrator purports to be reliable, just as the narrators in 1 and 2 Kings and 1 and 2 Chronicles do. He does not claim to have received Daniel 7 – 12 through a personal vision. Rather, 7:1 and 10:1 indicate that the narrator has one or more documents containing Daniel's visions to use in composing the book. The presence of Hebrew and Aramaic sections implies this narrator had access to materials in both languages. In short, the narrator presents himself as an accurate, careful guide.

i. Authorship, date and setting

The authorship and dating of Old Testament books have provided fuel for fiery scholarly debates over the past two centuries. This is probably as it should be, since important theological and historical matters have been at stake. Nonetheless, besides offering cautions against attacking and misrepresenting others, the history of these debates provides some necessary standards. Among other things, it is important to stick to what the Bible actually claims. It is also important to avoid making grandiose statements for one's view-point. It is important to examine historical data carefully, and it is important to avoid simply repeating earlier publications rather than weighing evidence and making balanced judgments. It is important to proceed with humility, caution and conviction.

Most experts hold some variation of the following pattern for Daniel's authorship (see Collins 1993: 24–34; Lucas 2002: 313–315; Holm 2013: 184–330; and Newsom and Breed 2014: 6–12), so I will summarize rather than deal with every individual opinion separately. They think Daniel is an example of apocalyptic literature. Daniel 1 – 6 probably conveys legendary stories about a literary character, not about a historical person. Several factual errors mark the material as written by an author living long after the settings the book gives. These stories had a good purpose, which was to inspire Jewish people living under foreign control. Since Daniel 7 – 12 states that Greece will succeed Persia, and includes accurate information about Greece's rule from 323 BC to c. 164 BC, the book originated during the reign of Antiochus IV (175–164 BC), who tormented his Jewish subjects living in Palestine. These visions fuel Jewish efforts against Antiochus. Because Daniel 11:40–45 incorrectly predicts that Antiochus will die in Palestine, however, the book as it exists now emerged before that event. There may have been earlier versions of parts of the book, especially chapters 2 – 6, but the whole dates to just before Antiochus died in *c.* 164 BC. The differences between the Greek and Hebrew/Aramaic versions show that the book had not settled into its final form before the second century BC. The book exhibits unity in its final form, but likely developed through several stages of composition.

A few writers have held to the traditional view that Daniel wrote the book in the late sixth century BC in Babylon to encourage fellow exiles. Again, I will summarize (see Baldwin 1978: 13–72; Miller 1994: 22–43; Archer 1985: 4–6). They note that there are good reasons why Jewish and Christians writers have held this position for centuries. They offer solutions to the historical and linguistic questions that other scholars have raised, and argue for the reality of predictive prophecy. They contend that the date of the relevant Dead Sea Scrolls of Daniel, the date of the Septuagint, the wide geographical use of the material, the book's acceptance as Scripture in all major sources and the book's roots in biblical sources make a date as late as *c.* 165 BC unlikely. The book's unity comes from its author, not careful subsequent editorial activity.

In response to these well-conceived positions, I think it is important to note that the book does not claim that Daniel wrote everything in it (Lucas 2002: 313–315). There is no superscription as prophetic books have (e.g. Isa. 1:1; Jer. 1:1, etc.). However, Daniel 1 – 6, 7:1 and 10:1 present a third-person narrative framework for the whole. Daniel's autobiographical sections do not reveal who wrote its third-person narrative material. That said, the book claims to reflect accurately what happened to Daniel and the book's other characters. It claims to provide accurate reports of Daniel's autobiographical first-person reports of his visions. The inclusion of both Hebrew and Aramaic documents within the book testifies to a desire to present Daniel's life and times accurately through relevant sources.

Thus, the book's third-person narration and historical framework indicate that in the matter of its authorship, Daniel is like 1 and 2 Kings and Ezra. Daniel could be the author of the third-person narrative material. If so, he decided to distance himself in much of the material. Though point of view in autobiographical writing can vary a great deal, even in modern works, this does not appear likely to me. It is important to note that Daniel does not have to write the third-person sections for the book to be accurate, theologically sound and helpful. Still, an excellent historian and writer is necessary. Those who consider the author of 1 and 2 Kings an accurate interpreter and historian of Elijah and Elisha's lives will find Daniel's author similarly skilled.

Furthermore, the book is historically accurate. As I noted above, and as the commentary below will discuss, many scholars flatly deny this assertion. Yet scholars holding various theological views have argued that the claims about historical inaccuracies in Daniel 1:1; 5:31; 6:1, 28; and 10:1 – 11:45 have been exaggerated, or have plausible historical answers. The book's author did careful work. Again, this author should be compared to the writers of historical books, not just to those who penned apocalyptic literature.

The book's contents make it possible to conclude that it is an example of early apocalyptic literature and as part of ancient story collections written by a single author. Yet the book provides no specific statement that the author set out to write an apocalyptic work of the sort that appeared later. The book's contents should therefore not be judged negatively by someone starting with a definition of the whole apocalyptic genre which they then impose on Daniel's contents. For example, it is an inadequate approach to note that many, even most, apocalyptic works are pseudonymous, and then to state that since Daniel is an apocalyptic work it is pseudonymous. It is probably as circular to argue that Daniel is a prophet (see Matt. 24:15), so the book is a prophecy and therefore immune from the frailties of apocalyptic literature.

Also, predictive prophecy is a real phenomenon. Peoples ancient and modern have believed this is the case, and have provided examples as proof. This evidence ought to be weighed, but predictive prophecy should not be discounted as automatically arising after the fact. Also, many, if not most, biblical prophecies have general and specific aspects. The commentary below will contend that Daniel 10 – 11 is not so specific that current interpreters can prove the author composed these chapters during the second century BC before Antiochus IV died. While predictive prophecy will always require faith open to reason, this does not mean that a naturalistic worldview that denies it is possible deserves full acceptance.

In conclusion, the author of the book of Daniel most likely lived in Babylon, since that is the place the author emphasizes. Some scholars have started to suggest that this is true of at least a large portion of the book. For example, though Carol Newsom holds a post-167 BC date for Daniel 8 – 12 (Newsom and Breed 2014: 11; see also LaCocque 1979: 35–36), she writes that 'the focus on the Babylonian court suggests that the origin of the narratives in Dan 2 – 6 is to be sought among the Jewish exiles in Babylonia and their descendants' (Newsom and Breed 2014: 9). She also considers it possible that 'a first edition of ch. 7' emerged soon after Greece conquered Persia in 331 BC (Newsom and Breed 2014: 10).

The date of the Septuagint and the Dead Sea Scrolls place the writing as no later than *c.* 250–150 BC. The accuracy of Daniel 1 – 6 indicates the sources, and thus the time of composition, could be as early as the late sixth century BC, soon after Daniel's death in the Persian era. Daniel 8:26 and 12:4 mention sealing the scroll for some time, so the narratives and visions may not have been identified until later. It is hard to be more specific than that. To utilize 1 and 2 Kings and Ezra as examples again, their authors relate accurately events that occurred centuries earlier. Thus, the issue is not solely whether or not Daniel wrote the whole book.

Based on the book's contents, Daniel's author had access to court documents, written prophetic statements such as existed in the Assyrian, Babylonian, Persian and Greek Empires, and written records preserved by Jewish exiles. These records included Daniel's personal remembrances. The books of Jeremiah, Ezra and Nehemiah indicate that there was more communication between Babylon and Jerusalem than many readers may realize. Therefore, it is not the case that the book of Daniel aimed at only one or the other audience, or that only readers inside or outside of Palestine would take heart from its contents.

Like Daniel and Ezra, this person was probably a scribe and teacher with strong faith in God's plans for the Jewish people. Like them, this individual suffered in exile, and desired release, renewal and repopulation. This author worked hard to link the materials in Daniel. He succeeded well enough that most scholars now consider Daniel a unified work, well enough that some historians conclude that he presents viable historical information, and well enough that Jewish and Christian communities of faith have counted the book as Scripture since before the second century BC.

3. Canonical elements

a. Overview

As was noted above, Daniel has its own plot that fits the whole Bible's wider plot. Daniel reflects various genres found in the Old Testament and the ancient world, yet configures them in a fresh and an imagery-laden manner. Daniel demonstrates knowledge of Jeremiah's prophecies (cf. 9:1–2 and Jer. 25:1–14), and the New Testament cites Daniel. Thus, Daniel is 'canonical' in that it is part of the Old Testament 'canon', or list of books considered Scripture. It is also canonical in the sense that it has a place in the order of biblical books that falls between books it cites and books that cite it. Finally, it is canonical in the sense that it had, and has, continuing significance for previous and subsequent biblical writers and readers. Scholars debate the ways, means and timing of how the books currently in the Old Testament came to achieve the status of Scripture. I will not rehearse those healthy and necessary discussions here. Rather, I will focus on relatively secure information related to Daniel.

b. The Old Testament canon

As I noted above, the Dead Sea Scrolls prove that the book of Daniel, in the form that it appears in today's standard Hebrew editions, is an ancient and reliable text form. Daniel was part of the Septuagint, the Greek translation of the Hebrew and Aramaic scriptures. Though estimates vary, it is safe to conclude that this translation began by c. 250 BC. Furthermore, Daniel appears either explicitly or implicitly in all the ancient lists of Old Testament Scripture. There is no reason to doubt its canonicity (Gowan 2001: 23).

As was also noted above, there are three Greek additions to the Hebrew and Aramaic text of Daniel that Catholics accept as Scripture. The Septuagint translation predates the oldest Dead Sea Scroll fragment of Daniel. However, as Joyce Baldwin (1978: 68) observes, none of the fragments includes any portion of the additions, and a fragment that includes 3:23–24 does not have the Prayer of Azariah between the verses. She concludes that the additions 'originated outside Palestine, possibly in Egypt. This would easily explain their acceptance in LXX, which was translated in Alexandria' (1978: 70). The oldest manuscript evidence certainly points to the Hebrew and Aramaic text as Scripture. The oldest Christian usage outside Palestine points to the three additions as Scripture. While I affirm the former tradition, the latter tradition does not contain false doctrine.

c. Daniel's placement in the Old Testament canon

Of the many options that existed in the ancient world, two major traditions of the Old Testament books' order prevail in contemporary editions. The first is the threefold order from Palestine: Law, Prophets and Writings. The New Testament reflects this order in Matthew 23:35, when Jesus mentions the first and last murders in the Hebrew canon, and in Luke 24:44, when Jesus teaches two disciples 'all the things concerning himself'. Jewish Bibles still use this format. In this list, Daniel appears in the Writings after Lamentations, which introduces the Babylonian exiles. Then Esther and Ezra–Nehemiah follow. Thus, together Daniel–Nehemiah provides books about a man who becomes a royal servant in Babylon (Daniel), a woman who becomes queen in Persia (Esther), a priest who leaves Babylon to aid the people of Jerusalem spiritually (Ezra), and a Persian official who travels to and from Jerusalem, seeking to build its physical and spiritual infrastructure (Nehemiah).

The second is the Latin order, which reflects the Septuagint. It places Daniel as the fourth major prophet after Isaiah, Jeremiah and Ezekiel, and before the Book of the Twelve (Minor Prophets). This order appears in virtually all Protestant editions. This tradition likely highlights Daniel's prophecies about the Son of Man (7:13–14) and other future events. It also takes Jesus' calling Daniel a prophet very seriously (Matt. 24:15). It provides a historical end to the Major Prophets, just as Malachi does for the Minor Prophets.

However, prophecy is its own genre (see House 1990: 37–52), and not every book that includes predictive statements belongs in the Prophets. For example, Psalms includes several promises about the messiah, but no-one would place it in the Prophets. Prophetic books emphasize proclamation of sin, punishment and restoration to turn people to God. Their view of history is that God rules events through his Word, which he reveals through his servants the prophets (see Amos 3:7–8). Prophets intercede for the people, preach the covenant and sometimes predict the future.

Daniel agrees with the prophets' views. The book teaches faithfulness and hope through its narratives, dreams and visions, and it speaks about the future. Daniel does not, however, exhort people to repent, with the exception of 4:27. Even then, he does so after God has already warned Nebuchadnezzar through a dream. Instead, the book stresses that God is ruler of creation, protector of his followers and giver of wisdom, themes particularly evident in the Writings.

Daniel's combining of narrative and visionary materials makes it an appropriate book to appear near the end of the Old Testament canon. The narrative's emphasis on miraculous deliverance of the faithful reminds readers of similar accounts in the Law and Former Prophets (Joshua – 2 Kings). The lives of Elijah and Elisha easily come to mind as examples. Likewise, Daniel 7 – 12 reminds interpreters that Isaiah, Jeremiah, Ezekiel and the Book of the Twelve highlight God's universal rule and knowledge of the past, present and future. Daniel makes a significant individual contribution to the Old Testament canon, but it does so in part by synthesizing previously revealed truth while confronting a new and harsh reality. The book's blending of older ideas into newer literary forms provides an interesting context for arresting theological ideas. While both canonical orders make their own kind of sense, the Palestine order respects Daniel's predictive prophecy while maintaining its other qualities, which often get neglected by users of the Latin order.

d. Daniel's canonical significance

A book's position in the biblical canon does not exhaust its canonical significance. Its placement helps highlight the way it accesses previous traditions and texts, and how subsequent books access it (see Childs 1980; Rendtorff 2005; and House 1998). Together, the books develop themes that enrich Christian liturgical and ethical practices.

The preceding paragraphs have introduced many of the ways in which the author of Daniel incorporates previous biblical materials into the book's own fabric. Thus, I will merely summarize a few points here. First, Daniel 1:1–2 indicates the author's agreement with the historical perspective in 1 and 2 Kings and 1 and 2 Chronicles. Indeed, those verses could easily fit into 2 Kings 24. This indicates that Daniel's author has a similar opinion of why exile occurred. Second, Daniel's narratives include details that fit well with the Joseph accounts in Genesis 37 – 50, and the Elijah and Elisha materials in 1 Kings 17 – 2 Kings 13. These stories are not embarrassed to recount divine intervention, predictive prophecy or extraordinary personal encounters with God. Third, Daniel 7 – 12 includes episodes and imagery that correspond to Amos 7:1 – 8:3; Isaiah 6; 24 – 27; and 65 – 66, practically all of Ezekiel, and Zechariah 9 – 14. Fourth, Daniel presents the life and times of a wise man who is also a deportee. His behaviour matches the description of 'the wise' in Proverbs and other wisdom texts. His portrayal in Susanna and Bel and the Dragon underscores his wisdom. Fifth, Daniel continues Lamentations' emphasis on exile. Daniel, Esther, Ezra and Nehemiah present concrete examples of the abstract concept of 'exile'. Daniel introduces exile's origins and challenges. It stresses the necessity for real-life devotion amid hard times, and the importance of desiring to participate in the rebuilding of God's people.

Bernhard Anderson (1999: 327–329) has observed that the New Testament authors used Daniel as a bridge between the Old Testament and their works. He notes that the New Testament continues the Old Testament's respect for wisdom teaching (e.g. John 1:1–18) and highlights preaching the kingdom of God. Citing Howard Kee, he then lists three ways in which Daniel influences the New Testament's apocalyptic perspective: (1) revelation of God's secret plans; (2) martyrdom due to the opposition of evil powers; and (3) the coming new age (1999: 329–330). He adds that Paul's emphasis on the resurrection of believers in 1 Corinthians 15 also depends on apocalyptic texts (1999: 330). He concludes by differentiating between the views of apocalyptic writing before and after Christianity. While Christianity shares the view that there is a current age and an age to come, he believes that the New Testament transforms this distinction by adding the fact that there is overlap between the present and future age (1999: 331–336).

Anderson is right about the consistencies between the testaments, and his analysis is extremely helpful. However, Daniel 9:24–27 and 12:1–13 prepare readers to accept the New Testament's 'now-and-not-yet' emphasis. Daniel must persevere, knowing that God already pursues his kingdom goals on earth (see 10:10–21), and that a long time will pass before woes end (9:24–27). Until then, like Paul and the Corinthians, he looks to the resurrection for strength to live in the present. That said, the New Testament writers know that Jesus of Nazareth is the Son of Man described in Daniel 7:13–14 (see Mark 14:61–62). That knowledge provides a canonical highway beyond the bridge Daniel builds.

4. Theological elements

a. Overview
Theology focuses on God's character and how he shapes reality. Because of Daniel's interpretational issues, it is easy to lose sight of the book's marvellous vision of God. Through narratives, visions and prayers, the book portrays God as revealer of life-shaping truth, creator and ruler of history whose kingdom will rise in due time, protector of his people, and the one to whom all humanity must answer.

b. God, the revealer of life-shaping truth
Daniel features both direct divine revelation and revelation through God's written words. Direct revelation saturates Daniel 2 – 12. God speaks to Daniel and Nebuchadnezzar through dreams and visions. These are not just for their personal growth, however, since both share what they have received verbally or through writing. The author has made it possible for these dreams and visions to influence readers for over 2,000 years.

Written revelation is implied in Daniel 1:8–16 and 6:10, and used explicitly in 9:1–19. In the first text, Daniel believes accepting the king's set diet will defile him in some way. This belief may come from rules governing purity in Genesis–Deuteronomy, or from wisdom passages about how to behave in front of the king (e.g. Prov. 23:1–9). In the second text Daniel prays three times a day towards Jerusalem, as has been his habit, apparently, throughout his life. Psalm 55:16–19 mentions prayer offered morning, noon and night, and 1 Kings 8:41–43 and 2 Chronicles 6:34 expect people outside the land to pray towards the temple (Baldwin 1978: 129). It is impossible to know if Daniel had such passages in mind, but it is certainly possible.

Daniel 9:1–19 cites Jeremiah, and demonstrates knowledge of several texts. Three points are particularly important. First, 9:1–19 indicates Daniel's reverence for the Law of Moses. His confessional prayer discloses that Daniel knows Israel's disobedience to Moses was disobedience to God. Moses' voice was God's voice (9:10), and Moses' law was God's law (9:11). Second, Daniel shares the Former Prophets' (Josh. – 2 Kgs) view of history, and he reveres the Prophets' (Isa. – Mal.) words. He mirrors 2 Kings 17 when describing how and why Israel and Judah went into exile. He conceived of Jerusalem as God's chosen city, the mountain of the Lord (9:16–17). Thus, he mirrors major themes in Isaiah (see 4:2–6; 25:1–12; 56:1–8; 65:17–25; 66:18–24) and Zechariah (see 14:10–21). Daniel believed Jeremiah's prophecies were God's words (9:1–2). Third, he intercedes and laments like many of the exilic prayers in Psalms 90 – 106.

Daniel was wise enough to understand that his role as an exile was that of a penitent, consistent, faithful, hopeful and prayerful servant of God and God's people. Like the other deportees, he must wait on God for the end of their suffering. God's written Word helps him do that no less than God's immediate, direct revelation. Both demonstrate God is the true ruler of all creation.

c. God, history's everlasting ruler

Daniel opens by asserting that God gave Judah into Nebuchadnezzar's hands (1:1–2). It closes with a promise about the end of all days (12:13). In between, the author relentlessly places God in the foreground of every episode. The prayers and proclamations Daniel, Nebuchadnezzar and Darius make provide good syntheses of the book's theology. Having received the content and interpretation of Nebuchadnezzar's dream, Daniel confesses that 'the God of heaven' (2:19) owns wisdom and might, changes seasons and rulers as he wills, reveals hidden things and deserves praise (2:20–23).

After seeing God protect the three Hebrews from the furnace's flames, Nebuchadnezzar proclaims that no other god can rescue like their God (3:29). Having finally learned his human frailty after experiencing madness brought on by pride, Nebuchadnezzar praises God's power and wonders (4:3), claims that God's kingdom never ends, and bows to God's supreme authority (4:34–35). He adds that God's ways are right, including the ways in which he humbles the proud (4:37). After God protects Daniel from the lions, Darius declares God able to rescue through signs and wonders, and the living God whose kingdom never ends (6:26–27).

d. God, the ruler whose kingdom rises

Though God rules all nations and peoples, his kingdom will be fully revealed later. Daniel 2:31–45 envisions a kingdom that will not be destroyed and that will not be left to another people. Daniel 7:9–14 adds to this previous vision. God appears as 'the Ancient of Days' (7:9), a person of complete purity (7:9), who judges all the world's kingdoms (7:10). He gives all the kingdoms of the world to one who has the form of a son of man, a human being, and all peoples will serve him for ever (7:13–14). The 'holy ones' who follow God will also receive this kingdom (7:18, 27). When God's kingdom fully rises, it will never fall. God's chosen ruler and chosen followers share that kingdom. Similarly, 9:24–27 indicates that God and his people will prevail, but only after suffering at the hands of God's enemies (9:25–26).

The commentary on 7:13–14 will argue that the Son of Man is the messiah. He receives what earlier texts attribute to the heir of David, the chosen one. God promises David an eternal kingdom in 2 Samuel 7:16. Isaiah 9:6–7 and 11:1–10 claim the Davidic king will rule endlessly over a kingdom free from strife. Isaiah 52:15 – 53:12 presents one who dies to redeem the people. Ezekiel 37 foresees the Davidic ruler governing the people after God's Spirit raises them from the dead. Psalms 2 and 110 foresee God giving a universal kingdom to the chosen one, despite the nations' opposition. No other Old Testament figure is cut off and still able to redeem his people. No-one else is said to transform, judge and inspire all at the same time. Only a messianic figure receives God's kingdom in the Old Testament (von Rad 1965: 312).

e. God, his suffering people's protector

God's people suffer in Daniel. The author depicts Daniel, his three friends and others losing their homes and loved ones in the first two verses. Daniel and his friends have done nothing as individuals to merit this punishment. They are simply part of the covenant people, who as a whole have refused to follow their God's ways (see Lev. 26:13–39; Deut. 28:15–68; and 2 Kgs 17). Therefore, the author indicates that suffering and joy are both community experiences. Members do not simply get what is coming to *them*, but what is coming to everyone involved. Daniel 9:1–19 certainly makes this point. Daniel does not ask, 'Why *me?*' He asks when the whole *community* can expect forgiveness and renewal (see Lev. 26:40–45; Deut. 30:1–10; and Jer. 25:1–14).

God's people endure threats in Daniel. Though rescued in the end (see below), Daniel and his friends endure hostility related to their faith, having escaped hostility to their professional guild in 2:1–47. The three friends will not bow to an idol (3:1–18), and Daniel will not pray to a man (6:10). Malicious foes (3:8; 6:4–5) make sure that they face death for daring to have authority and daring to have secure convictions. Daniel 7:13–28 promises that such threats will arise as long as God's 'holy ones', his 'different ones', walk the earth.

God rescues his people. The fires do not consume the three friends, and the lions do not devour Daniel. No god delivers like the everlasting living God (3:28–30; 6:25–28). Early Christian sarcophagi (stone burial boxes) include depictions of Daniel in the lions' den, the three friends praying in the furnace, Daniel condemning the elders who accused Susanna, and Daniel exposing Bel and the dragon. On one, the lions lick Daniel, so transformed are they by God's power as creator. Their message is clear: God is able to save from any catastrophe (see 3:17). But not everyone lives through such trials, as early Christians knew all too well. Thus, it is fair to ask in what way God really rescues.

God preserves his people's most-cherished treasures. Above all, God's people value God, their relationship with him and their love for neighbour and enemy. Nothing can take these from them, as their willingness to accept loss of home, property and life before surrendering them shows (see 3:18; 6:10). They will always have

God, one another and the chance to show love to friend and foe (e.g. Nebuchadnezzar) alike.

God preserves his people for ever. Exiles like Daniel, Jeremiah, Baruch, Ezekiel, Esther, Ezra and Nehemiah still exist. At the time of writing, millions of Christians and people of other faiths have refugee status. This comes after a century of two global wars and countless smaller ones. Daniel 7:13–28; 9:24–27; and 12:1–13 warn that woes will follow many of God's own. Daniel 12:1–4 and 12:13 offer the greatest vindication of such persons' faith in him. He will resurrect them (body, mind and soul) after their years of useful, living belief have ended. One piece of early Christian art in the Vatican Museum shows believers rising from their sarcophagi to be with God. Images of resurrection vary, but they all count on God's promise.

f. God, the one to whom all must answer

As the section above on Daniel's genre indicates, apocalyptic literature takes special interest in the future. In this sense it emphasizes eschatology, the study of the end of time. It also emphasizes how people, especially suffering people, live now, and how God dispenses justice in his world prior to the day of final justice. Therefore, people always struggle to balance ethics now and judgment then. Again, it is important to begin with Daniel's contents, not with a definition of 'apocalyptic literature' and then look for particular elements in Daniel. The book features several points about days beyond Daniel's lifetime, some of which deal with final days, and all of which point to God as the one to whom all people will eventually answer.

Daniel asserts that God will end human injustice once and for all. It does not state a specific date for that reckoning. As D. S. Russell (1964: 263) observes, for most writers of apocalyptic literature, and 'in particular to the writer of the Book of Daniel, the fact of the End and its imminence were of greater importance than their ability to predict the day of its arrival'. Daniel 7:13–28 envisions God destroying all twisted human rulers, portrayed as deformed beasts, and giving the everlasting kingdom to the Son of Man and the saints. Daniel 12:1–4 and 12:7 promise that faithful ones like Daniel will rise from the dust, and wicked ones will face punishment.

Daniel learns that he must rest before that time comes. Those who long for that day must be prepared to serve like Daniel and wait like Daniel.

Daniel indicates that a long time will pass between Daniel's lifetime and the end. In fact, I disagree with Russell's assessment that the book of Daniel teaches an imminent end. If one takes 7:1; 8:1; 9:1–2; and 10:1 as real historical markers, and the details that follow as God-revealed messages about the future, then one must agree that Daniel learned that a lot of time will pass before the end. He has known since 2:1–47 that more than one kingdom will succeed Nebuchadnezzar's. Daniel 8:19–26 reveals that Persia and Greece are to come. If one takes these notations as fiction written in the second century BC to declare that wicked Greek rule will end soon (see e.g. Murphy 2012: 79–88), then perhaps one could argue that Daniel claims the end could come at any time. Even then, one would have to deal with the fact that Daniel 12:1–13 tells the main character to rest and wait through a mysterious number of days before resurrection. Death will overtake him first. Every believer in Christian history to this day has had to accept the same verdict, not adjust the timetable, as Murphy (2012: 88) suggests an editor did in 12:1–13.

Daniel encourages steadfast discipline and hope as the way to please God in the present and stand with God in the future. Daniel does not support passive waiting for the end of time. Nor does it recommend frantic activity or austere living.[6] Daniel 9:1–19 proves that Daniel possesses enduring hope. He desires to know if the end of seventy years of exile will begin the renewal process that Leviticus 26:40–45, Deuteronomy 30:1–10 and several of the prophets proclaim. He knows that such renewal will take time. He has proven faithful. Thus, Gabriel answers Daniel's pleas for mercy, calling him 'greatly loved' (9:23). Likewise, the messenger in 10:12 praises Daniel for setting his heart to understand and humbling himself before God.

To borrow from Wendell Berry's poem 'Amish Economy' (2013: 160), Daniel knows he lives by mercy, so he has worked well, thanked

---

6. For a survey of these types of ethical behaviour in apocalyptic communities, consult Allison 2014: 295–311.

often, loved God, loved neighbour and thus kept the world's community. He has done so while working for the Babylonian and Persian Empires, and receiving visions hard to understand and accept – all jobs God gave him to do. There is no apocalyptic escapism in Daniel, just hope anchored in good work by one 'greatly loved' by God.

5. Formational elements

a. Overview
Historical, literary, canonical and theological reflection feeds application in concrete situations, or can do so. It is important to remember that a commentary writer does not have access to a reader's heart, congregation or study group. Most of the hard work of application must occur at the local level. Daniel and his friends certainly knew that. Nonetheless, a few observations may help stimulate thought about those local communities.

b. The New Testament
The New Testament affirms the necessity of endurance and hope. Though it has been a common scholarly belief in the last century (see e.g. Allison 2014: 300–301), the early Christians did not necessarily expect Jesus to come soon. In Acts 1:6–11 Jesus tells the disciples not to wonder about times and dates and the return of Israel's kingdom. Rather, they must take the gospel to the ends of the earth, beginning with their home regions. This handful of people surely did not think this would take only a few days. Thus, their sharing of food and necessities (see Acts 2:42–47) probably stemmed from their practices with Jesus rather than from thoughts that they would not need any worldly goods for very long. Since Jesus told them the temple would be destroyed, their ministry in its environs surely reminded them of work to be done. Paul tells the Thessalonians to keep working, for the end is not yet (2 Thess. 2:1 – 3:15). They must look forward to Christ's coming, but they must not quit their jobs. Revelation ends with a prayer for Jesus to come soon *and* a prayer for continued grace to serve (Rev. 22:21). Daniel's endurance surely fuels such teaching.

c. Contemporary times

Currently, millions of Christians are displaced by wars, economic privation, government decrees such as the Chinese government's forced relocation of 250 million rural people (*The New York Times*, 17 March 2014), and the impersonal industrial-technological culture in which the modern West lives. In a lesser vein, many people live away from their families because of education or work. Some will go home, most will not, and many no longer have a home to which they *can* go.

For all these variations of exiles, Daniel offers instruction, not entertainment; hope, not despair; endurance, not surrender. It offers people dreams bigger than themselves, and ministry that reaches down the ages. It also reminds them that there is a home here on earth well worth caring about, and a home with God beyond the dust of death. While Daniel has much more to contribute, in offering these, the book provides what no-one can take away.

ANALYSIS

As stated above, Daniel is a story of kingdoms: human kingdoms that rise and fall, and God's kingdom, which rises and remains. Within this story Daniel and his friends persevere in their witness through his power, often mediated through angels. The author presents this plot in Hebrew and Aramaic passages structured by ten distinct, yet interlocking, settings. The dates of these sections span from *c.* 605 to 536 BC, and they feature the four foreign kings Daniel serves: Nebuchadnezzar, Belshazzar, Darius and Cyrus. They address the future beyond Cyrus's time, incorporating apocalyptic interests and imagery within both narrative and visionary texts. This careful linking of the book's various parts highlights its unity within exceptional diversity. The ten sections take readers slowly and systematically from Judah's loss of kingdom, to the promise of God's everlasting kingdom, to the necessity of long-standing perseverance, to the promise of resurrection, the means by which faithful ones inherit God's everlasting kingdom. God's kingdom rises continually, and will reach its goal in God's time.

1. GOD GIVES EXILE AND GRACE (1:1–21)
  A. God gives his people into Nebuchadnezzar's hands (1:1–7)
  B. God gives his servants grace (1:8–21)

2. GOD GIVES WISDOM, MIGHT AND HIDDEN KNOWLEDGE (2:1–49)
  A. Nebuchadnezzar's troubling dream and hasty decree (2:1–13)
  B. God reveals hidden knowledge (2:14–23)
  C. Daniel reveals Nebuchadnezzar's dream and its interpretation (2:24–45)
  D. Nebuchadnezzar praises God and promotes Daniel and his friends (2:46–49)

3. GOD DELIVERS HIS SERVANTS FROM THE FLAMES (3:1–30)
  A. Nebuchadnezzar's golden statue (3:1–7)
  B. Conflict in the court (3:8–12)
  C. Confrontation, confession and condemnation (3:13–23)
  D. Deliverance, confession and decree (3:24–30)

4. GOD HUMBLES THE PROUD (4:1–37)
  A. Nebuchadnezzar's letter to his people (4:1–3)
  B. Another helpful troubling dream (4:4–18)
  C. A reluctant interpreter and some wise counsel (4:19–27)
  D. God humbles Nebuchadnezzar (4:28–33)
  E. God heals and restores Nebuchadnezzar (4:34–37)

5. THE HANDWRITING ON THE WALL: THE END OF BABYLON (5:1–31)
  A. The handwriting on the wall (5:1–12)
  B. Daniel interprets the writing (5:13–28)
  C. Honours at the eleventh hour (5:29–31)

6. GOD SAVES DANIEL FROM THE LIONS (6:1–28)
  A. New regime, new dangers (6:1–9)
  B. Daniel's faithfulness and the king's anguish (6:10–18)
  C. God delivers Daniel (6:19–24)
  D. Darius's decree and Daniel's security (6:25–28)

COMMENTARY

1. GOD GIVES EXILE AND GRACE (1:1–21)

Context

This chapter provides an excellent introduction to the whole book. The author sets its historical context as beginning with the third year of Jehoiakim (*c.* 606–605 BC; 1:1) and ending with the first year of Cyrus (*c.* 539 BC; 1:21). This story takes nearly seven decades to unfold. These verses mention most of the book's most important characters: God, Nebuchadnezzar, Daniel, Hananiah, Mishael and Azariah (1:1–7). They stress the moral fibre that Daniel and his friends display when forced to serve their nation's conqueror (1:8–21). They also convey the important theological points – that God gave his people to Babylon because of covenant breaking (1:1–7), but protects his faithful ones through his grace (1:8–21). In short, this chapter introduces a long exile in Babylon faithfully navigated by God's servants through his gifts. It thereby states the book's value for all subsequent readers.

Comment
A. God gives his people into Nebuchadnezzar's hands
(1:1–7)

By Jehoiakim's reign (*c.* 609–598 BC), the majority of Judah's people had long ignored the covenant consequences that Moses detailed in Leviticus 26:14–39 and Deuteronomy 28:15–68. They had likewise rejected the prophets' warnings to repent (see 2 Kgs 17:13; 21:1–18; and 24:20). Daniel and his colleagues were too young to have participated much in this long national disobedience. Yet they suffered as community members when God disciplined his covenant people. When God gave Judah to Nebuchadnezzar, he gave young, innocent ones to him along with old, wicked folks. This corporate discipline simultaneously magnifies the wicked people's sin and the righteous ones' patient suffering.

   1. This verse has long sparked debate (see Montgomery 1927: 115–116) because of its historical statements. The narrator describes events in the straightforward manner one finds in 1 and 2 Kings, 1 and 2 Chronicles, Esther and Ezra. Certain things are clear. *Jehoiakim king of Judah* was by all biblical accounts a shrewd political operator with little interest in God's Word (2 Kgs 23:31 – 24:7; Jer. 36:1–26). Egypt placed him in power (2 Kgs 23:31–35), and he was a loyal subordinate to Egypt when circumstances allowed. *Nebuchadnezzar king of Babylon* (*c.* 605–562 BC) had recently taken over his father's realm (see Introduction: Historical elements, p. 2). He worked to eliminate Egypt as a threat to his empire-building plans. As 2 Kings 24:1 recounts, Nebuchadnezzar 'rose up, and Jehoiakim became his servant for three years. Then he [Jehoiakim] turned and rebelled against him.'[1] The second book of Chronicles (36:6) states that at some point Nebuchadnezzar moved towards Jerusalem to place Jehoiakim in chains, but this statement is not specific enough to tie it to Daniel 1:1.

   The debates begin with the fact that no other Old Testament or Babylonian text states explicitly that Nebuchadnezzar took successful military action against Judah in Jehoiakim's *third year*. In

---

1. Unless otherwise noted, all translations of biblical texts are the author's.

contrast, the Bible documents Nebuchadnezzar's conquests of *Jerusalem* in *c.* 597 and 587 BC (2 Kgs 24:1 − 25:26; Jer. 37 − 39, 52). Also, Jeremiah 25:1 links the first year of Nebuchadnezzar's reign with Jehoiakim's fourth year. Jeremiah 46:2 states that in Jehoiakim's fourth year, 'Nebuchadnezzar king of Babylon' defeated Carchemish, a strategic trading city located on the western side of the Euphrates River in today's southern Turkey (Wiseman 1985: 16). By Hebrew reckoning, Jehoiakim's third year was 606 BC, not 605 BC. Therefore, there are at least three basic problems: (1) how the chronology of Nebuchadnezzar's first year fits Jehoiakim's fourth year (Jer. 25:1; 46:2); (2) when and in what way Jehoiakim served Nebuchadnezzar before rebelling (2 Kgs 24:1); and (3) what sort of military action, if any, Nebuchadnezzar took against Jerusalem in his first year (Dan. 1:1).

On the first matter, Babylon used a dating system for the beginning of a king's reign that was different from that of Hebrew writers. Baldwin explains that the system in 'the history books of the Old Testament counts the months between the king's accession and the new year as a complete year, whereas the method most usual in Babylon called those months the accession year and began to count the years of a king's reign from the first new year' (Baldwin 1978: 20–21; see also Wiseman et al. 1965: 17; Millard 1977: 69; and Lucas 2002: 51). Similarly, today some cultures count a baby as one year old when born, while others do not count babies as one year old until their first birthday. By Babylonian reckoning, then, the events took place in Jehoiakim's third year, not his fourth. By Hebrew reckoning, the events occurred in Jehoiakim's fourth year. Babylon is the book's setting, so it is natural for the author to employ that dating system.

On the second issue, Babylonian records contain key dating information. The Babylonian Chronicles indicate that in spring and summer 605 BC, Nebuchadnezzar, Nabopolassar's co-regent, led Babylon's armies at Carchemish. He routed the Egyptians, took at least northern Syria, and forced many kings to pay tribute (Wiseman 1985: 17). Since Egypt put Jehoiakim in power (see 2 Kgs 23:31–35), he was probably one of the kings forced to pay tribute (Wiseman 1985: 23–24). When Nabopolassar died in August, Nebuchadnezzar returned to Babylon, and took the throne in September (Wiseman

1985: 17–21). He rejoined his forces shortly, and came home to
Babylon in 604 BC (Wiseman 1985: 21–23). In *c.* 601 BC Egypt
defeated Babylon in a key contest, so Jehoiakim may have withheld
tribute then (Jones 1984: 634).

On the third matter, the typical English translation of Daniel 1:1
may be too specific, and thus unintentionally misleading. Most have
something like 'Nebuchadnezzar king of Babylon came to Jerusalem and besieged it' (ESV; Collins 1993: 127; Lucas 2002: 45).
There are two basic problems with this translation tradition. First,
both 1:1 and 2 Kings 25:1, which describe Babylon's action against
Jerusalem in 587 BC, contain the Hebrew word translated 'came/
went'. However, there is no Hebrew preposition corresponding to
'to' in 1:1, as there is in 2 Kings 25:1. Thus, Daniel 1:1 states that
Nebuchadnezzar went towards Jerusalem, but does not indicate
that he marched all the way there, as a similar phrase in 2 Kings
24:10 makes certain to do. He may have achieved his objectives
without going all the way to Jerusalem. Second, 'besieged' implies a
city surrounded by enemy armies building siege ramps and machines
of war. For example, 2 Kings 25:1–2a reports that during the 587 BC
invasion Nebuchadnezzar 'came with all his army against Jerusalem
and encamped, and they built siege works all around it, and the city
came under siege until the eleventh year of King Zedekiah'. None
of this gathering of large forces, encamping or building siege works
occurs in 1:1. The word translated 'besieged' in the ESV can mean
that, or it can mean 'confined', 'opposed' (see Esth. 8:11), 'initiated
conflict' or 'treated as an enemy' (see BDB 848; *NIDOTTE* 3: 790–
791; *TDOT* 12: 306–311; and Wiseman 1985: 23). Context must
decide. Nebuchadnezzar may have achieved his aim without having
to lay siege to the place.

Given the lack of other textual evidence, it seems logical to take
the latter set of definitions as reasonable explanations of the post-
Carchemish tribute gathering that the Babylonian Chronicles
mention. That is, as part of chasing Egyptian forces south, Nebuchadnezzar's army 'initiated conflict' with Jehoiakim's army on
account of his alliance with Egypt, or 'confined' him to his capital
city. The king's submission was Nebuchadnezzar's ultimate goal.
When Jehoiakim saw Nebuchadnezzar's power and Egypt's weakness, he agreed to pay tribute rather than risk further consequences.

This scenario could account for Jehoiakim deciding to serve Nebuchadnezzar three years, before turning to Egypt again in *c.* 601 BC. It could also alleviate the necessity of explaining a full-blown siege that the Old Testament never mentions.

2. This verse agrees with 2 Kings 24:1–2 that God punished Jehoiakim for his disobedience. It also agrees with Jeremiah 25:1–14 that God specifically used Nebuchadnezzar to punish other nations. Nebuchadnezzar did not just happen to defeat Egypt and put pressure on Judah. God sent him, as a king sends a messenger (Jer. 25:9), and God *gave Jehoiakim king of Judah into his hands.* This theme of what God gives continues in verses 9 and 17 and in the rest of the book (see discussion of Daniel's plot above). The fact that God alone gives and takes power from rulers becomes a vital emphasis in chapters 2, 4, 5, 7, 8 and 10–12. Realizing this crucial element of reality humbles Nebuchadnezzar in chapter 4, but has no effect on Belshazzar in chapter 5. Despite Jeremiah's warnings in 25:1–14 and 36:1–26, Jehoiakim never learned this lesson.

When God gave Jehoiakim into Nebuchadnezzar's hands, he also gave *part of the vessels of the house of God* into Nebuchadnezzar's hands as tribute payment. Jehoiakim was the human instrument of this payment, but God was behind it. Montgomery (1927: 116) wrongly states that this verse assumes Jerusalem has been captured. Instead, the situation is like the one described in 2 Kings 18:13–16, where Hezekiah gives Sennacherib king of Assyria some of the temple's treasures to get him to leave Judah. Later, when Nebuchadnezzar captured Jerusalem and took King Jehoiachin (*c.* 598–597 BC) captive, he removed 'all the treasures' in the 'house of the Lord' and 'the house of the king', and cut the temple's gold vessels into pieces for other use (2 Kgs 24:13). Judah then made more vessels (though likely not of gold), since the temple continued to operate. These vessels are significant in 5:1–4.

Nebuchadnezzar took these vessels to *Shinar*, an ancient name for Babylon (see Gen. 11:2), and put them *in the treasury of his god.* Transferring treasure from a defeated deity's temple to the home of the triumphant one was standard practice in ancient times. By 2:46–49 Nebuchadnezzar learns that Israel's God is not a typical deity. By 4:34–37 he will confess that Israel's God rules him.

3–5. Empires do not run on money alone. They require enormous human resources. Thus, like tyrants before and after him, Nebuchadnezzar takes captives into his service. He tells *his chief official, to bring from the sons of Israel*, that is, males from the conquered people (1:3). More specifically, they are *from the family of the king and from the nobility*. Assyrian records indicate that Hezekiah sent such persons to Sennacherib as tribute to avoid losing his throne (*ARAB* 2: 119–121, entry 240). Nebuchadnezzar took large groups of such people when he captured Jerusalem in 597 BC (2 Kgs 24:10–17). The word translated *official* can be rendered as 'eunuch', though it is a general term that does not necessarily indicate castration (Collins 1993: 134–136).

Goldingay suggests that bringing 'young nobles to Babylon might have various objectives: to bring home Judah's vassal status in relation to Babylon (not to Egypt now), to add to the manpower of temple and palace' (1989: 15). Gowan suggests that the 'verses display him as one who intends to do well by selected members of the Israelite royal family' (2001: 44). Of course, these possibilities are not mutually exclusive. Nonetheless, his actions rob the captives of their homes and independence.

Besides a notable lineage, these captives had to be young and good looking (1:4a). This requirement no doubt shrank the number of candidates. Furthermore, they had to have certain mental qualities: they were to be *skilled in all wisdom, knowledgeable* and possessing *discernment* (1:4b). They needed good physical attributes so they could *stand in the king's palace* when he met his subjects and foreign dignitaries. They needed the intellectual attainments so they could advise the king publicly and privately, and oversee the king's affairs.

The word translated *wisdom* summarizes the teaching found in Proverbs, Job and Ecclesiastes. It stresses balanced and careful living, in both normal and extreme situations. The term *knowledgeable* indicates the ability to learn, to retain information internally and apply it externally (Miller 1994: 61). One with *discernment* has the ability to examine situations and make sound decisions. These requirements would have limited the pool of candidates even more. With these characteristics proven, they were to receive training *in the scroll and the tongue of the Chaldeans*. They would learn to read, write and speak like Babylonian wise men. Their native texts and tongue would now take second place. The *Chaldeans* were the nation's old ruling class, and here it refers to its wise men (Collins 1993: 137). These captives would have lots of old literature to learn.

They joined an elite class of individuals. Goldingay writes that Babylonian wise men 'were the guardians of the sacred traditional lore developed and preserved in Mesopotamia over centuries, covering natural history, astronomy, mathematics, medicine, myth and chronicle. Much of this learning had a practical purpose, being designed to be applied to life by means of astrology', and by the study of internal organs and the practice of 'rites of purification, sacrifice, incantation, exorcism and other forms of divination and magic' (1989: 16). They also interpreted dreams and made predictions (Collins 1993: 137). There was precious little that they were *not* expected to do for the king, but this demanding profession gave them social prestige (Newsom and Breed 2014: 42–45).

Such valuable people received the king's support. He provided *a daily portion of food* and *wine* (1:5; see 10:3). Candidates had *three years* of thorough preparation, a period that, like the dating of the king's accession, might not include three full calendar years. Afterwards, they were to stand *in the presence of the king*, which means they would do whatever he required whenever he required it (Baldwin 1978: 81).

6–7. Now the author introduces the main character and his friends: *Daniel, Hananiah, Mishael and Azariah of the tribe of Judah* (1:6). The *chief of the officials* gives them Babylonian names: *Belteshazzar, Shadrach, Meshach and Abednego* (1:7). The power to give them new names shows the Babylonians' authority. The book does not always recognize that authority. It refers to Daniel (e.g. 4:19; 5:12) and his friends (e.g. 2:17; 3:12, 14, 19, 20, etc.) by their Hebrew and Babylonian names. Royal renaming was supposedly 'an honor conferred by the king to mark the recipient's new status and a sign of the expectation of loyalty to the king who bestows the name' (Newsom and Breed 2014: 47). This 'expectation of loyalty' gets the friends into trouble in chapter 3.

B. God gives his servants grace (1:8–21)

So far, Nebuchadnezzar has benefited from God's gifts. Jehoiakim is his vassal, and some of Jehoiakim's best young subjects are training for service in his court. The author has highlighted four young men from Judah, but has not revealed their relationship with God. This section portrays them as his faithful followers. From the first days of their training, their commitment to God dictates their actions. Therefore, they seek alternatives to eating the king's food and drinking his wine, and God gives them grace with the authorities (1:8–16) and great learning and skill (1:16–20). As for their length of service, God gave Daniel, though apparently not his three friends, a very long life, but in exile (1:21).

The Bible presents a long and honourable tradition of persons showing themselves faithful to God under enormously difficult circumstances. These characters span the Bible's various genres and sections. Many live outside their homelands. Abraham (Gen. 11:10 – 25:18), Joseph (Gen. 39 – 50), Moses (Exod. 3 – 4), David (1 Sam. 27), Ruth and Naomi (Ruth 1), Jeremiah and Baruch (Jer. 42 – 44), Ezekiel (Ezek. 1:1), Daniel, Esther, Ezra, Nehemiah and the apostles (see Acts and Rev.) all serve God in foreign places. Even in Israel, God's good servants can become a minority. However, as God told Elijah (1 Kgs 19:18) in such a time, he still has followers when a hurting individual feels all alone. This passage places the four exiles in this class of stalwart people. They prove they are part of 'the remnant' (see Isa. 6:11–13; 7:3), the minority that serves God despite the high cost of doing so.

8. Daniel demonstrates his allegiance to God from the outset. Nebuchadnezzar had ordered that the candidates receive the food and drink he enjoyed (1:5), *but Daniel had set his heart that he would not defile himself with the king's food, or with the wine he drank*. God's ways took precedence over all other considerations.

The word translated 'defiled' occurs nine other times in the Old Testament (*NIDOTTE* 1: 794–795), and always has religious connotations. It basically means: (1) someone or something does not qualify for a specific purpose; (2) someone or something has been used for bad purposes; (3) someone or something has come in contact with blood. The term describes men excluded from the priesthood in Ezra 2:62 and Nehemiah 7:64; people who misused God's name and table in Malachi 1:7, 12; rulers who misuse their hands to oppress and kill in Isaiah 59:3 and Zephaniah 3:1; priests who misused their office for personal gain in Nehemiah 13:29; and blood that stains skin or garment in Numbers 31:19; Isaiah 63:3; and Lamentations 4:14. Only the Malachi passages and Daniel 1:8 deal with food, though that does not necessarily determine the context.

The text does not state exactly what Daniel has in mind. Experts have suggested that the king's food was offered to idols, was not 'clean' (acceptable) according to Moses' teachings, or that it came from the oppressive king – but then note that no food in Babylon avoided these issues.[2] Longman (1999: 53) suggests a solution close to the heart of the story. He writes,

> Daniel and his friends are in a process of education and preparation for service. Their minds as well as their bodies are being fed by the Babylonian court. If they prosper, then to whom should they attribute their development and success? The Babylonians. However, by refusing to eat the food of the king, they know it is not the king who is responsible.

Also, Daniel did not want to use his position for personal gain, in contrast to the priests who 'defile the priesthood' in Nehemiah 13:29. As the book proceeds, he seeks nothing for himself in return for his service (2:21–49; 5:17), and he always credits God with his successes (e.g. 2:17–23, 27–28; 5:17–23; 6:21–22). Thus, he unites the source and motives of his service.

As the book continues, it becomes very clear that Daniel does not just seek to survive. Rather, he desires to make God known to his captors. His asking *the chief of the officials* for permission *not to defile himself* makes this point clear, since it shows that he stated his conviction. As a discerning man (1:4), he knows that motives and witness must link.

9. This verse summarizes God's relationship with Daniel: *God gave Daniel covenant kindness and compassion in the sight of the chief of the officials*. Both *covenant kindness* and *compassion* appear in Exodus 34:6–7, the Old Testament's best summary of God's character.

---

2. See the excellent summary of these issues in Newsom and Breed 2014: 47–48; Longman 1999: 52–53; and Goldingay 1989: 18–19.

Here, God gives them as gifts in a way that benefits Daniel. The first term includes loyalty, kindness, enduring love or mercy given to a person in covenant with the giver, or even to a person who is not. The second includes the sort of tenderness a good mother (see 1 Kgs 3:26) or father (Hos. 11:8) has for their child.

10. The proof of God's covenant kindness and compassion develops in stages over the next few verses. The first stage includes a conversation with the man in charge of their care. While sympathetic to Daniel's concern to avoid defilement, the *chief of the officials* knows the king will hold him responsible if the four Israelites look worse than the other candidates. Indeed, he says that granting the request could cost him his life (*endanger my head*). Nonetheless, he does not deny the request.

11–13. The second stage requires a way to avoid the consequences that the chief official rightly fears. Daniel shows his wisdom by suggesting a plan to the steward who serves the chief official (1:11). This plan does not insult the king, endanger the chief official or steward, or compromise his and his friends' convictions. Daniel makes certain to protect everyone concerned (Newsom and Breed 2014: 49). This plan will also show the chief official and steward that God watches over his servants. All four exiles will participate in Daniel's proposal (1:11). There will be a time limit of ten days, so this is a test, not a permanent decision (1:12). After ten days, the steward can decide if this has been a wise course of action (1:13).

The word for the food Daniel chooses comes from the Hebrew word translated 'seed', so it is something that comes from, and contains, seeds. In the Old Testament the word describes the seasons of planting and harvesting (Gen. 8:22; 26:12; Isa. 17:11; *TDOT* 4: 144). Basically, then, the word describes common food made from grain (Montgomery 1927: 132), the most fundamental part of a diet. Likewise, they will drink water, the most fundamental of all fluids. The point is not to figure out what sort of 'health food' they ate. Rather, the point is that they will eat and drink what God alone can provide. By stating that this is how they will avoid defilement, the four invite their supervisor to see that the God they serve can provide what they need through the most basic sustenance. They also invite God to protect his name by protecting them. This whole scheme offers the book's first glimpse into the sort of wisdom Daniel possesses.

14–16. The third and final stage of the proof of God's covenant kindness and compassion is that Daniel's plan succeeds. The steward agrees (1:14). After *ten days . . . they were better in appearance and fatter* [i.e. 'healthier'] *in flesh*, one of the chief qualifications for their job (1:4), than the other candidates (1:15). Therefore, the steward let the four continue eating and drinking what they requested (1:16). This result can be considered miraculous (Gowan 2001: 47), though the text does not provide all the details involved (Goldingay 1989: 26–27).

17. Now the author begins a summation that closes the chapter. At this point, the four Judeans are still *young men*. Once again, the author states that *God gave* something (see 1:2, 9). This time he gives them success in the training 1:4 describes: *learning and skill in all literature and wisdom*. Then, very deftly, the author slips something new into the narrative. God specifically gives Daniel *understanding in all dreams and visions*. The next chapter demonstrates this gift, and his skill makes his puzzlement over the meaning of the visions in chapters 7 – 12 even more dramatic.

18–20. When their period of preparation ends (1:18), *the chief of the officials* presents them to Nebuchadnezzar, apparently without knowing or mentioning their unusual diet. Perhaps the steward kept this potentially explosive information from his chief and his king. The exiles from Judah are the elite of the elite in their class (1:19). Their conversation with the king sets them apart from the other *magicians and enchanters* (1:20).[3] This superiority prevails throughout the book. God has given Nebuchadnezzar excellent advisors for the time he acts as God's instrument of punishment (see Jer. 25:1–14). God has given the four friends the capacities needed to show that 'it is possible to be faithful in a foreign court' (Goldingay 1989: 27). God has given centuries of readers instruction in the wisdom of demonstrating God's supreme power.

21. Daniel will outlive the Babylonian Empire, which ends in 539 BC. Wiseman (1985: 98) writes that of the 2,997 scribes that the

---

3. For definitions of these types of wise men, see the commentary on 2:2 and 2:10.

Babylonian records mention, several have lifespans comparable to Daniel's. Though God gives Daniel long life, the absence of Hananiah, Mishael and Azariah in this summary is notable. Daniel most likely outlived his friends. Though he never outlived his love for Jerusalem (see 9:1–19), he never went home.

Meaning

In 1:1–7 God gives Jehoiakim, Judah and these four intelligent, attractive men into Nebuchadnezzar's hands. Nebuchadnezzar's hands have taken their homes, livelihoods and names. They have also provided food, drink, education and opportunity. As the book unfolds, it becomes apparent that these men are God's gift to this foreign king. The men accept this role, but their losses cannot be minimized.

Daniel 1:8–20 reveals several things about suffering and faithfulness. First, Daniel and his friends proved loyal to God when sent away to Babylon. Second, their self discipline prepared them for future harder tests (Baldwin 1978: 84). Third, they maintained their dignity, identity and witness while accepting their place in Nebuchadnezzar's service. There were lines of assimilation they would not cross (Collins 1993: 146). Fourth, the Judeans and the Babylonians alike learned that physical beauty, good appearance and health come from Israel's God, not from the king of Babylon (Longman 1999: 53; Newsom and Breed 2014: 50). Fifth, God's name was kept pure before a watching world, the reverse of what Malachi 1:7–12 describes. This witness will continue as more episodes unfold. Sixth, God chose to give them gifts of wisdom that carried them through difficult times.

Sadly, 1:21 indicates that Daniel never gets back home. However, he lives long enough to know that some of his people will go home (see comments on 10:1). As is true of Moses, part of Daniel's greatness is his willingness to serve God without getting what he probably desires most. God gives him what he needs, and more, but this verse reveals that the book's plot includes Daniel spending a lifetime in exile. Therefore, his witness of God bestowing gifts in exile will remain one of the book's chief interests, and among its most enduring legacies.

2. GOD GIVES WISDOM, MIGHT AND HIDDEN KNOWLEDGE (2:1–49)

Set in Nebuchadnezzar's accession year of 605–604 BC, chapter 1 introduced the major themes of God giving exile (1:2), covenant kindness and compassion (1:9) and wisdom (1:17). God bestows these gifts on whom he will, whether on a king like Nebuchadnezzar, or on exiles like Daniel, Mishael, Hananiah and Azariah. This authority to give gifts includes who conquers others, and who will survive in such times. Dated in Nebuchadnezzar's second year (2:1),[1] this chapter continues those themes, but also introduces concepts that will span the rest of the book. In particular, it stresses how divine disclosure of hidden knowledge saves the exiles and their associates from certain death.

---

1. The Old Greek text has 'twelfth year' rather than 'second', which seems an attempt to remove difficulties associated with collating 1:1–2; 1:8–20; and 2:1. See the discussion of 2:1 below.

Context

The chapter has four sections. First, in 2:1–13 Nebuchadnezzar has a troubling dream that he does not understand (or fears he does understand), so he calls on his wise men to help him (2:1–3). They are eager to do their job, and as they begin to wrestle with the hidden matters of dreams, the text changes from Hebrew to Aramaic (2:4). When Nebuchadnezzar assigns them the seemingly impossible task of telling the dream and its interpretation, they protest (2:5–11). In frustration, he orders them all to be killed, an edict that includes Daniel and his friends (2:12–13). Second, in 2:14–23 Daniel requests and receives time to do what the king demands. God reveals to him what he must know (2:19), and Daniel praises God for his power and willingness to reveal hidden matters (2:20–23). Third, in 2:24–45 Daniel tells the king what he wants to know. This segment introduces the concept of four kingdoms that will figure largely in chapters 7, 8, 9 and 11. Fourth, in 2:46–49 Nebuchadnezzar praises God, and promotes Daniel and his friends.

Humphreys (1973: 211–223) and others (e.g. Newsom and Breed 2014: 64) have identified this chapter as a 'court tale of contest' between the hero and other wise men based on its similarity to other ancient stories, especially the Egyptian text *Ahiqar* (see *ANET* 427–430; Hartman and Di Lella 1978: 55–56; also see Introduction: Literary elements, p. 7). Holm defines this type of story as one in which 'a wise hero of undistinguished status solves a problem that the native courtiers have not been able to solve and thereby wins elevation to a higher position (Daniel 2, 4, 5 and Genesis 40 – 41)' (2013: 195). She argues that, when included in story collections, such accounts mean to instruct, not entertain (2013: 208–210). This is especially true here, since life and death are at stake.

Interpreters have long observed the similarities between Daniel and Joseph. In particular, Joseph interprets the dreams of his prison colleagues in Genesis 40, and Pharaoh's dreams in Genesis 41. Both aid a foreign king by interpreting dreams, both credit God with the interpretation and both receive promotions. Lucas points out several differences between the two, however, such as Nebuchadnezzar's demand to hear the dream first, the helplessness of the sages in Daniel, and the status of Daniel as opposed to Joseph's position (Lucas 2002: 65). Thus, as Collins rightly claims (1993: 155), Daniel 2 does not simply retell the Joseph narratives in a different text. Rather, the author of Daniel 2 combines these familiar literary elements with Daniel-specific ones[2] to tell how God proves his universal authority, covenant loyalty and gracious willingness to reveal his plans in yet another unprecedented situation.

Comment

A. Nebuchadnezzar's troubling dream and hasty decree (2:1–13)

Disturbing dreams and visions span the book, linking characters and events. The initial dream occurs here, and it sets the stage for the others. Since the king receives this troubling dream and makes a disturbing decree, it involves everyone in the account. The author does not divulge the contents of the dream until Daniel reveals all to the king. Thus, readers are kept as much in the dark as the king, though they know Daniel will survive, having read 1:21.

1. The setting of *the second year[3] of the reign of Nebuchadnezzar* has led to discussions about the book's historical accuracy. The main issues are as follows: (1) Daniel 2:1 seems to contradict 1:5, which says that Daniel's training lasted three years; (2) 2:1 seems to contradict 1:18–20, since Nebuchadnezzar does not appear to know Daniel in 2:25–26; and (3) 2:14 seems to contradict 1:18–20, since Daniel seems to be a wise man already, not as one still needing to 'graduate' (see Longman 1999: 75–76; Collins 1993: 154–155; Montgomery 1927: 140–141; and Newsom and Breed 2014: 66), since he lives among the wise men.

On the first issue, R. H. Charles (1929: 26), S. R. Driver (1900: 17) and E. J. Young (1949: 56) suggest the three years in 1:5 and the

---

2. Thus, I do not think the inclusion of aspects of court drama, visions and repetition indicates that 'Daniel 2 readily reveals several redactional levels', as Wills (1990: 82) argues.

3. The Old Greek reads 'twelfth year', but few scholars accept this as the original reading.

second year of 2:1 can be reconciled if the author is using the Babylonian accession-year method of dating (see p. 47). Others think the book's editor did not notice the discrepancy (e.g. Collins 1993: 155), or did not attempt to iron out all the discrepancies between the accounts (e.g. Newsom and Breed 2014: 66).

On the second matter raised, Daniel 2:25–26 says nothing about Nebuchadnezzar's knowledge of Daniel. If he had not completed his course of study, then lack of knowledge about young Daniel on Nebuchadnezzar's part is completely understandable. Daniel 1:18–20 only summarizes the completion of the four Judeans' training. It says nothing about any previous acquaintance with the king. The fact that Daniel was not apprised of the king's problem makes sense if he was too new to consult. Therefore, since reasonable chronological solutions have been suggested, the book places this account either right after the training ended, or during Daniel's training. The second option seems more likely to me, given the introduction of Daniel's ability to interpret dreams in 1:17 and the fact that he was not among the wise men called to interpret Nebuchadnezzar's dream in 2:1–2.

On the third concern, it is hardly inconceivable that Daniel was living among the wise men while he was in training. He received rations from the king (1:3–16), and had to learn the curriculum assigned (1:3–7) from people who already possessed that knowledge. It seems more likely that he would live among the wise men than not. Also, why would the king spare the trainees when he had decided to eliminate the wise men? After all, they had come under the malignant influence of their teachers.

The king's second year (*c.* 603–602 BC in Babylonian reckoning) was a reasonable time for Nebuchadnezzar to have *dreams* that *troubled* his *spirit*. He was under considerable pressure. The kingdom his father left him was barely a decade old (see Introduction: Historical elements, p. 2). He had defeated the Egyptians at Carchemish and chased them and their allies south just before his father died. He had taken the throne and resumed battle into 604 BC. After a brief respite, he had to subdue Ashkelon later that year (Baldwin 1978: 86). Now he faced a western enemy that required him 'to organize a more powerful force' (Wiseman 1985: 24–25), and kept him from pressing further south towards Egypt.

2. Something about these dreams particularly worried Nebuchadnezzar. The author creates anticipation by not divulging exactly what that was. Since Nebuchadnezzar keeps a bevy of wise men with different skill sets on retainer, and is in the process of training more (1:3–20), he calls them together and seeks their help. Four categories of them are listed here: diviners, enchanters, sorcerers and Chaldeans. The first term signifies Egyptian wise men able to interpret dreams (Lucas 2002: 69); the second refers to individuals able to discern illness and to suggest a cure or perform an exorcism (Lucas 2002: 69); the third may indicate persons able to cast spells against an enemy (Yamauchi and Wilson 2016: 206–207); and the fourth represents the ancient leadership group of wise men in Babylon. They come *to tell the king his dreams*, but they have no idea that the king takes this phrase very literally.

3–4. Nebuchadnezzar tells them what the narrator revealed in 2:1. His troubling dream needs explaining, so perhaps the diviners can help. He needs healing for his troubled spirit, so maybe the enchanters will have a solution for him. If an enemy has attacked him through sorcery, then he may need to find and punish that enemy through sorcery. If there has been a similar case in Babylonian history, then the Chaldeans can tell him about it.

As if to increase their mysterious powers, when the wise men speak the text switches from Hebrew to Aramaic, and stays with Aramaic through to 7:28. Perhaps 2:4 – 7:28 was an Aramaic text to which the book's author added the introductory material in 1:1 – 2:3 and the visionary materials in chapters 8 – 12. It is impossible to know for certain, but if this scenario is accurate, the work was done with extreme care (see Introduction: Authorship, setting and date, p. 24). Assyria, Babylon and Persia used Aramaic as a court language (see Introduction: Hebrew and Aramaic text, p. 8), so the language fits the situation. Indeed, similar lists of wise men occur in both the Hebrew and Aramaic sections.

These servants have no doubt that they can do what they have been trained to do. They eagerly tell the king in reassuring tones: *O king, live for ever! Tell the dream to your servants, and your servants will expound its interpretation.* They believe they can interpret and dispel any ill effects the dream has caused (Collins 1993: 156).

5–6. Calm for the moment, the king clarifies their task. He has made a *firm* decision. They must *make known* both *the dream and its interpretation*, or they will be *dismembered* (cut in pieces; see 3:29) and their *households made into a dung heap* (see Ezra 6:11). They will die, and their families and property will be taken. In short, he will treat them as traitors or disobedient ones, which he may already suspect them to be. At any rate, he intends to discover if they are as good as they claim in 2:4. Since he requires such a difficult task, he quite reasonably promises *rewards and great honour* for solving his problem. This is a high risk and high reward situation. As Robert Anderson writes, Nebuchadnezzar has decided 'to ascertain beyond all doubt whether his retainers had the required capacity to render an interpretation other than one concocted simply in order to placate an unstable master' (1984: 12–13).

7–9. As if they have not heard correctly, *they answered a second time*. This time they are a bit more cautious. In 2:4 they use an imperative ('Tell us'). Here they use the more polite, permissive form: *Let the king tell us the dream, and we will expound its interpretation*. They have tried to ease any tension and eliminate any misunderstanding.

Undeterred, Nebuchadnezzar speaks even more plainly than before. He claims he *knows with certainty* that they are *buying time* the way one negotiates when buying a field or a house (see Vogt 2011: 121–122). In other words, they are bargaining for a better price. He believes they know his *word is firm*, that is, fixed, and that they consider it harsh. They know what he wants and what is at stake, yet are determined to give him something less.

Nebuchadnezzar is not in a bargaining mood. In fact, he thinks their refusal to give both dream and interpretation shows that they are traitors, frauds or both. He can only conclude that they *have agreed to speak lying and corrupt words* to him *until the times change*. Only by their giving him the dream can he trust them to give the appropriate interpretation. As the chapter unfolds, it becomes clearer why the king is wise to take this position.

The author gives a hint about the king's nervousness. The phrase *until the times change* does not simply mean 'until more time has passed'. As Newsom notes, in 2:21 it means 'the time to change kings', and thus 'may be a euphemistic way of referring to the king's demise and replacement by another monarch' (Newsom and Breed

2014: 69). He may accuse them of not wanting him to be their king, or of conspiring against him. At the very least, he believes that if they know the dream is negative towards him, and they wish him off the throne, they might not give him their best advice (Newsom and Breed 2014: 69). No, he can only trust someone who can perform both tasks.

10–11. Speaking with authority, these students of the scrolls of Babylon, Egypt, Assyria and other lands (see comments on 1:3–7) tell the king that his demand is unprecedented and impossible to fulfil by any *diviner or enchanter or Chaldean* (see comments on 2:2). They claim no *great and mighty king* has asked such a thing, and they are almost surely right about that. Assyrian and Babylonian monarchs used this phrase to describe themselves, so the wise men try to get the king to act like his predecessors (Charles 1929: 33). As he is the son of the first king to throw off the yoke of Assyrian rule, and one trying very hard to live up to his father's example, however, their comment can only anger him further. They are doing a poor job of bargaining with him. They conclude by adding a remark that foreshadows 2:14–47: *no-one can show it to the king except the gods, whose dwelling is not with flesh.* They make their living trying to navigate the distance between divinity and humanity, but realize that deities reserve some knowledge for themselves. The advisors have nothing in their arsenal of arts that can penetrate that veil.

12–13. Frustrated by his servants and his own fears, Nebuchadnezzar *became angry and furious.* He gives the order *to destroy all the wise men of Babylon.* As Collins (1993: 157) observes, this sort of anger and harsh decision also occurs in Daniel 3:13 and 19 (see also Esth. 1:12; 7:7). By now, readers may have let Daniel and his friends slip their minds. So far, this story has seemingly had nothing to do with them. Not surprisingly, *the decree went out,* but now the author reminds readers that Daniel and his friends are part of *the wise men of Babylon.* Their exalted social status proves a hindrance that not even their ethnic heritage had posed. The executioners *sought Daniel and his friends, to kill them.* They have now been part of two communities (see 1:1–7) Nebuchadnezzar has put at risk.

The text does not say why Daniel and his friends were not part of the group standing before the king. If they were still in training (see comments on 2:1), then they would not have been qualified or had sufficient seniority. What is clear is that in Nebuchadnezzar's second year, whether he was still in training or had recently finished, Daniel was a very young and untested wise man. One could hardly expect the veteran Chaldeans to choose him to stand before the king at such a crucial time.

B. God reveals hidden knowledge (2:14–23)

As in 1:8–16, this situation brings out Daniel's discerning wisdom. Under great pressure, he poses the right questions and at least tries to do as the king asks, rather than joining the chorus of wise men declaring it cannot be done (2:14–16). Nebuchadnezzar therefore grants him time. Like any good and humble wise person, he knows that he needs help from friends and from God in order to succeed. Prayer plays a big role in Daniel, and this section depicts the first instance of its importance. Having accepted the responsibility of trying to save himself, his friends and the other wise men, Daniel has his friends pray for him (2:17–18). After God reveals the dream and its interpretation, Daniel prays with thanksgiving (2:19–23).

14–15. One obedient servant meets another. Daniel encounters *Arioch, the king's executioner, who had gone out to kill the wise men of Babylon* (2:14). Arioch is an old Babylonian name (Gen. 14:1), so its usage may signal first-person testimony. The text does not reveal if Daniel heard about the decree and went to see Arioch, thus putting himself in danger, but taking the situation in hand, or if Arioch had sought and found Daniel to kill him. Either way, Daniel remains very cool under pressure, a trait that serves him well throughout his career.

Instead of words that enrage the king, Daniel offers words of *prudence and discretion* (2:14). Wisdom takes over from foolishness (see Prov. 26:16; Charles 1929: 34). Unlike the wise men in 2:4–11, he does not call the decree hasty or brutal. Instead, he wonders why it is so *urgent* (2:15).[4] Arioch buys time to *make the matter known* to the respectful wise man. Daniel's discretion will help him succeed where his colleagues have failed.

---

4. The word can also convey both urgency and severity (see 3:22). See Vogt 2011: 140.

16. Lucas (2002: 71) notes that several scholars have argued that this verse contradicts 2:24–25, since Daniel seems already to have access to the king here, but in 2:24–25 must go through an intermediary because the king does not know him. As with the objections to 2:1, this one seems overstated. Daniel *went and sought from the king that a time be given to him that he might expound the interpretation to the king.* He could have sought this time through an intermediary (Lucas 2002: 72), for an intermediary was necessary in 2:24–25. Arioch, an intermediary, is part of the account from 2:14 through to 2:25. Furthermore, the wording differs in 2:16 and 2:24–25. The latter text states explicitly that Daniel was 'brought before the king'.

Regardless, neither text specifies that the king did not know Daniel. The issue in the text remains the speed of the king's command and the speed with which Daniel must respond. Neither Nebuchadnezzar nor Arioch wants to carry out the order. Arioch is clearly not bloodthirsty, and the king wants someone to tell and interpret his dream.

17–18. A reprieve granted, *Daniel went to his house, then to Hananiah, Mishael and Azariah, his friends, to make the matter known.* The word translated *friends* refers to a person who is both a companion and an ally (Vogt 2011: 126). They have regard for one another and are loyal to one another. Their lives were also at risk. Because of his prowess in dream interpretation (see 1:17), they agree that Daniel must bear the weight of meeting Nebuchadnezzar's demands.

Their job is to pray for him (2:18), *to seek compassion from the God of heaven.* God gave them fatherly 'compassion' in the eyes of the chief official in 1:9 (see comments), and they need the same now. They are his children, and they seek their Father's help (see Hos. 11:8). Otherwise, they will be *destroyed with the rest of the wise men of Babylon.* Bevan (1892: 72) observes that 'God of heaven' occurs in Genesis 24:7 and 'was a favorite expression among the post-exilic Jews (Ezra 5:11; 6:9–10; 7:12, 21, 23; Neh. 1:4–5; 2:4, 20)'. Unlike their colleagues, these men believe their God does indeed reveal normally hidden knowledge to his servants. They intend to find out if the particular knowledge they seek belongs to God alone, or if he will entrust them with it (see Deut. 29:29). Chapters 3, 6 and 9 will demonstrate that prayer is a way of life with these friends. It is not a last resort.

19. God answers their prayers: *in the vision of the night the mystery was revealed* [lit. 'uncovered'] *to Daniel.* Steadfast to his narrative purpose, the author does not yet reveal to the reader what Daniel saw. The phrase *vision of the night* is a technical term found in Job 4:13; 33:15; and Zechariah 1:8. Baldwin (1978: 90) writes that based on the two Job passages, 'It seems that the recipient of the vision was in a deep sleep, but he was not said to be dreaming, perhaps because the imagery was arising not out of his own mind, but by God's direct intervention.' Through this vision, the *mystery*, the matter beyond human comprehension (Longman 1999: 78), became known. Praise for answered prayer comes as naturally as the prayer for help. Daniel *blessed the God of heaven*, which means he spoke of God's good acts on his behalf (see Ps. 103).

20–23. Daniel answers God's answer with a prayer of thanksgiving similar to those in the book of Psalms (see Pss 72:18; 103:1–22). This poem/prayer has at least three parts. First, Daniel focuses on God's name, his attributes (2:20). God's *name* means 'his character' revealed (see Exod. 6:3) to human beings. Daniel speaks highly (*Blessed be*) of two complementary aspects of God's nature: his *wisdom and might*, both of which he owns (*to whom belong*) and distributes (2:20). Having the power (might) to implement his carefully balanced plans for the world (wisdom) makes him a perfect ruler. Though this portion of the prayer speaks generally about God, its elements also address the current situation.

Second, he recounts God's deeds (2:21–22). As the all-powerful 'God of heaven' (2:19), he *changes times and seasons* (2:21; see Gen. 8:22). Nature's rhythms move at his command (see Job 38:1 – 42:6). Just as he removes one season and replaces it with another, so he *removes kings and raises up kings.* Daniel 1:1–2 has made this point. God also provides *wisdom for the wise, and knowledge for the ones knowing discernment.* Daniel 1:3–20 made this point about wisdom's true source, and 2:1–13 has emphasized the king's need to *know* something important to him.

Third, he praises God for what he has done in this particular instance (2:23). God's answer proves that he *reveals the dark and secret things*, the things that lie beyond human comprehension, such as the meaning of troubling dreams in the night (2:22). Nothing is too dark for him to see, for his light *dwells with him* always. He reveals his plans to whom he will according to his purposes, to people as different as Nebuchadnezzar and Daniel.

Therefore, Daniel directs his praise at the covenant God of Israel (*my fathers*). The one who chose Israel for deliverance and service has not changed, even though, or precisely because, he has given Judah's king into Nebuchadnezzar's hands (1:1–2). He merits praise *for ever and for ever* (2:20) for good reason (2:23). God has given him wisdom, might and knowledge, which means God shares his character with his servants (see Exod. 34:6–7; Pss 111 – 112). That he does so and why he does so may constitute the greatest mysteries of all. Daniel has not merited these gifts. They result from God's grace (see 1:9). This whole prayer confesses that God shows compassion (see 2:18; see Exod. 34:6–7; Ps. 103:8) to those who call on him.

C. Daniel reveals Nebuchadnezzar's dream and its interpretation (2:24–45)

Daniel wastes no time. Without delay, he seeks out Arioch, who in turn presents Daniel to Nebuchadnezzar (2:24–25). Continuing to demonstrate humble wisdom and deep devotion to God, Daniel credits God alone with revealing the future things in the king's dream. Daniel recounts the dream (2:31–35), and then retells it while giving the interpretation (2:36–45).

Everyone is happy. The wise men of Babylon survive, including Daniel and his friends. Arioch does not have to slaughter dozens of people. Nebuchadnezzar can relax, for he will not be overthrown. However, the dream and its interpretation continue to trouble many readers. Its fourfold division of history starting with Nebuchadnezzar has caused lots of discussion. Thus, it is important to gain some basic understanding of what sort of literature this is. Doing so will aid interpretation of the rest of the book, since schemes of four occur in chapters 7, 8, 9 and 11.

24–25. Armed with unprecedented (see 2:10) knowledge from the 'God of heaven' (see 2:11, 19), Daniel goes *to Arioch* (2:24).[5] To

---

5. Note that this verse uses a preposition and a name to specify whom Daniel encounters. These elements are lacking in 2:16.

return the reader's attention to the pressing matter at hand, the text repeats the fact that Nebuchadnezzar *had appointed* Arioch to *destroy the wise men of Babylon*. No-one is safe yet, but Daniel claims he can *expound the interpretation*. He does not mention the dream, perhaps because they are in a hurry (2:25a).

Arioch has access to the king due to his mission. He rushes in and hurriedly announces Daniel (2:25). In fact, he may try to take credit for the expected good result, since he declares, *I have found a man* (Baldwin 1978: 91). Indeed, this man was not present for the meeting in 2:1–13. Arioch implies that he was obscure, hard to find, since he is *a man from the sons of the exile, from Judah*. Arioch leaves out that Daniel was seeking to help. No matter. Daniel feels no slight, as 2:26–30 will demonstrate. Nor does he resent Arioch highlighting his parental roots, since he has not been ashamed of his fathers' God (2:23) or their religion since he came to Babylon (1:8–16). Regardless, Arioch's hurried speech is not an auspicious introduction.

26. Indeed, the king sounds dubious. In effect, he asks, *Are you really able to make known to me the dream that I have seen and its interpretation?* Nonetheless, he has little to lose in hearing what Daniel has to say, for no-one else has stepped this far forward. This Judean, newly trained and hustled in at the last second, will get a chance.

27–28. Daniel does not fail in wisdom or accuracy. As in 1:8–16, Daniel tries to avoid having losers in this situation. He exonerates his fellow wise men, telling the king that no human *can expound the mystery to the king* (2:27). As in 2:2, four experts appear in Daniel's list. He adds a new one, *astrologers*, who study the history of planetary movements and human activities to determine the importance of what is happening currently (Wiseman 1985: 88–89). At first, his answer sounds like the other wise men's, but he is building his speech towards a strong conclusion.

As in 2:20–23, Daniel gives God all possible credit. He does not say one thing to God and another to Nebuchadnezzar. He asserts that no man can discern the mystery Nebuchadnezzar poses, *but there is a God in heaven who reveals mysteries* (2:28). Daniel leaves himself out of the story, in contrast to Arioch (2:25). He emphasizes God's kindness for making *known to King Nebuchadnezzar* [not to Daniel] *what will be in later days* through *dreams* and *visions*. Nebuchadnezzar was probably most concerned about his own time, not the times long after his death. God has revealed to him more than he expected, so he should begin to feel God's comforting hand at work.

The phrase translated *later days* is more literally 'after days', as in 'after current days', or after Nebuchadnezzar's reign (see 2:39). Often translated 'the latter days', this phrase has come to be synonymous with 'the end of time' in many people's minds. However, Collins (1993: 161) writes that its usage here and in the Old Testament emphasizes turning points in Israelite history (see Deut. 4:30; 31:29), or 'a definite transformation of Israel in the distant future' (see Isa. 2:2; Ezek. 38:16; Hos. 3:5; Mic. 4:1). It can also indicate a 'closing period' of a future era (Newsom and Breed 2014: 74). Interpreting this dream as depicting specific world events at the end of time can therefore cause unnecessary misunderstandings.

29–30. Once more Daniel stresses what God has done for Nebuchadnezzar (2:29). Bearing witness to God's greatness remains Daniel's highest priority. As for Daniel himself, God has given him wisdom (2:30a; see 1:17), in this case to help the king (see 1:3–7), through whom God has revealed such marvellous things (2:30b). Normal wisdom alone would not have sufficed. In chapters 2 – 4 God reaches out to Nebuchadnezzar through Daniel and his friends. They give unselfish and even loving counsel to someone they could easily despise. Wisdom from God does not allow them to love God and hate their neighbour. It does not allow Daniel to take credit for being a great dream interpreter (see 1:17), or to give credit to his friends' prowess in prayer. He keeps God's concerns primary.

31. At last, readers learn what until now only God, Nebuchadnezzar and Daniel have known. Daniel says the king had an intense vision (*seeing, you saw*), which anyone could have gathered from the king's agitation. Daniel describes what the king saw and what it felt like to encounter it, which no-one could have known. Nebuchadnezzar saw *a big statue, and this statue was very large and very bright*, and even to a king *its appearance was frightening*.

32–33. Specific details follow. Descending from head to toe, the statue consists of five substances in descending order of monetary value. The head was made of gold, the chest and arms of silver, the waist and thighs of bronze, the legs of iron and the feet of a mixture of iron and clay. A looter of artefacts would likely cut the statue in pieces and sell the precious metals to the highest bidder. Even an amateur viewer of statues would know that the strongest metal visible here is the iron, and that having clay feet will eventually destabilize the whole. It is bad workmanship to make a big statue that has a weak base.

34–35. While the king watched, he saw *a stone cut* (in two; see Steinmann 2008: 130) seemingly on its own, but at least *by no human hand, and it struck the image on its feet.* The word translated *struck* can indicate an object coming from above or below (Vogt 2011: 200). As will become clearer in 2:44, a rock has split because part of it rises (2:34). The rising rock destabilizes the statue's feet, much as normal shifting over time would do. A rock has not fallen from the sky. Shelf rock rising above the soil takes time to emerge. Once the feet of mixed iron and clay begin to give way, the whole slowly cracks, reels, breaks and falls (2:35a). Once on the ground, wind blows its metal away, *like chaff from a summer threshing floor,* as if it had never been there (*not a trace of them could be found*).

In contrast, *the stone* that undermined and toppled the statue *became a large mountain, and filled the earth.* It grew until it was the highest of all mountains, an image Isaiah 2:2 and Micah 4:1 employ to describe cleansed and holy Zion, God's chosen mountain, the home of Jerusalem and the temple. This stone will possess all Nebuchadnezzar has ruled, and more. No wonder the king wanted to know the interpretation. He worried that the statue represented him and his imminent fall. No wonder he wanted someone to tell him the dream. Otherwise, how could he trust the honesty and loyalty of the dream interpreter?

36–38. So much for the dream, it is time for the interpretation (2:36). Daniel's sequential interpretation in verses 37–38 lengthens Nebuchadnezzar's anxiety. He once again makes certain to place God and his purposes before the young king. Nebuchadnezzar is indeed, as many Assyrian and Babylonian texts call their monarch, *king of kings.*

But there is a reason that this is so: *the king of heaven has given you the kingdom, the power, and the might, and the glory* (2:37). Just as Daniel has received the wisdom necessary for his work from 'the God of heaven' (2:19), so Nebuchadnezzar has received from 'the God of heaven' the power and glory he oversees. The God to whom belong people, animals and land (2:38a) has given these to Nebuchadnezzar to rule. This order of God giving stewardship to human beings derives from creation itself (see Gen. 1:26–31). Nebuchadnezzar is *the head of gold* (2:38b), but the God of heaven made him so. It will take Nebuchadnezzar until 4:34–37 to understand and confess this fact.

39–45. He next depicts three kingdoms that succeed Nebuchadnezzar's (2:39–43), and then portrays a final kingdom that lasts for ever (2:44–45). Thus, he notes four kingdoms and a fifth one that surpasses them. Many schemes of fours occur in Daniel. The book features four young men (1:17), four groups of wise men (2:2, 27) and four men in the fiery furnace (3:25). Four winds of heaven and four parts of bodies figure in 7:2, 7; 8:8; and 11:4. Four kingdoms and/or kings appear in 2:40; 7:3, 17, 19, 23; 8:22; and 11:2.

This part of Daniel's interpretation has long stimulated scholarly and popular discourse. Since this literature is vast, perhaps the following summary and references will suffice for this commentary's purposes. First, dividing history into three, four or five eras is an ancient literary device. No-one can ascertain its first usage with certainty, but Persian, Greek and Roman writers all utilized some variety of it. Wiseman (1985: 94) notes, 'The representation of four metallic ages goes back at least to Hesiod's *Work and Days* of the seventh century BC.' Writing in the fifth century BC, Herodotus used a three-nation (Assyria, Media and Persia) scheme, and credited Persian sources for his viewpoint (Newsom and Breed 2014: 80). Collins (1993: 167–168) writes that the *Fourth Sibylline Oracle*, which dates from the first century AD, but includes material that dates to Alexander the Great's era in the fourth century BC, features a four-nation (Assyria, Media, Persia and Greece) scheme that ends with Rome as the fifth and greatest land. Thus, Daniel participates in a long and valued tradition. God communicates with Nebuchadnezzar, Daniel and the original readers through a known format. Current readers may not know this format, but are used to historians dividing history into significant periods of time.

Second, the beginning and end of the four-part list matter a great deal. Though most schemes began with Assyria, Daniel begins with Babylon, thus highlighting its prominence. Most writers end with the most recent nation, probably to signify that nation's importance. For instance, as noted above, the *Sibylline Oracle* highlights Rome by making it the fifth, and finest, kingdom. This strategy corresponds to Daniel 2:44–45, and is a natural deduction for someone attempting to include the longest-surviving great empires. Interestingly, Babylon routinely gets left out of these ancient lists, which may underscore its short tenure compared to the others.

Third, experts are divided over whether Greece or Rome constitutes the fourth kingdom in Daniel, with most recent scholars choosing the former and most ancient writers the latter (Lucas 2002: 76–77). Daniel mentions Babylon, Media, Persia and Greece (see 2:38; 5:31; 6:28; and 8:21), so those nations are certainly in the author's mind. Nonetheless, this disagreement highlights the fact that the literary scheme can change as history does. The fourth nation basically stands for 'the most recent empire', so later writers could with integrity change the first or fourth nation as needed.

Fourth, everyone agrees that the kingdom 2:44–45 describes is God's kingdom. Thus, all conclude that it is the most important kingdom, the one that incorporates and ends all others. All Christian commentators stress that this is the most important element of eschatology.

Verse 39 quickly summarizes two kingdoms that will follow Nebuchadnezzar, the head of gold. The second does not seem to have the extensive rule of the first and third ones. If so, then the two can fit Nebuchadnezzar's Babylonian descendants during 562–539 BC, or the Medes, who rule Babylon briefly in Daniel (see 5:31; 6:28). Persia likely ruled the world that the original readers inhabited.

Verses 40–43 deal with the fourth kingdom, the most controversial one. This kingdom will be like iron, *because iron breaks and shatters . . . all these* (i.e. gold, silver and bronze; 2:40). Prior kingdoms will fall to this one. Like all human kingdoms, however, this one has a flaw. Its feet are *partly iron*, and *partly clay* (2:41). With this unstable base, it can stand *partly strong and partly brittle* (2:42) for some time.

But it cannot stand indefinitely. As Baldwin comments, 'Unity is impossible and the kingdom is vulnerable because it is seeking to unite elements which will not coalesce' (1978: 93). Leaders will try to stabilize the kingdom by *mixing the seed of man*, which may refer to intermarriage of royal families (see comments on 11:6) or relocating people in new lands.

Most scholars prefer the intermarriage possibility, and many (e.g. Charles 1929: 49; Montgomery 1927: 177; and Newsom and Breed 2014: 82–83) particularly point to the intermarriage between the Seleucids and Ptolemies, the inheritors of Alexander the Great's empire (see Dan. 11:6, 17). The relocation possibility derives from the fact that similar language occurs in Jeremiah 31:27, where God promises to sow the land of Israel and Judah with 'the seed of man and the seed of beast'. The language in this verse is not so specific as to refer to particular intermarriages. Steinmann writes that 'the expression here is unusual, and its meaning is far from certain' (2008: 131). The text does not specify here what sort of mingling takes place. Nonetheless, it is clear that whatever they try will fail.

While these kingdoms exist, God will be raising *a kingdom that will not be destroyed*, that will not be *handed over* [see Vogt 2011: 319] *to another people* (2:44). As I stated above, it takes some time for a rock to push through the ground and compromise a statue's base. Still, it makes slow, steady, unrelenting progress. This rock will break all other kingdoms, *and bring them to an end*. In sharp contrast to them all, even the ones with the greatest longevity, this kingdom *will stand for ever*. This is the kingdom kings and exiles alike must seek. Daniel 7:9–14 explains who will inhabit and who will rule this kingdom, but for now it is enough to look forward to the kingdom itself.

Daniel closes his speech with a flourish. Just as this mountain will rise by the power *of no human hand*, so this interpretation has come to Nebuchadnezzar by divine power, not by human hands. How can he be so sure? Because *a large God has made known to the king what will happen after this*, the day in which they live. Daniel knows the king has seen 'a large statue' (2:31), and he wishes him to see this *large God*, the 'God of heaven' (2:19, 28), who kindly reveals hidden knowledge to a fretful young king (2:29–30).

D. Nebuchadnezzar praises God and promotes Daniel and his friends (2:46–49)

Nebuchadnezzar partly recognizes God. He bows before Daniel, God's messenger (2:46). He praises God as the revealer of great mysteries, though he remains fixated on Daniel (2:47). As promised (2:6), he lavishes honours on Daniel (2:48). For his part, Daniel continues to look out for others, not just himself. He accepts Nebuchadnezzar's reverence for God (2:46–47), and asks that his friends receive promotions (2:49).

46–47. Upon receiving the revelation of his dream and its positive interpretation, *King Nebuchadnezzar fell on his face* (2:46a), a normal ancient way of showing respect to God and human beings (see Gen. 17:3; 2 Sam. 9:6; 14:4; Charles 1929: 51). The next part, *and paid homage, and commanded that an offering and incense be offered to him* (2:46b), has troubled some readers at least since the late third-century philosopher Porphyry doubted its truthfulness and reverence, a challenge Jerome still felt compelled to answer in his commentary on Daniel written *c.* AD 407 (McCullough 2008: 151; see Jerome 1958: 16).[6] Why would a king bow to his servant? Why would Daniel allow the king to do so?

In response, Nebuchadnezzar's bowing demonstrates his understanding that what he has heard comes from God. He seems overwhelmed by the stupendous revelation. His commanding of those around him proves, however, that he has not released his sovereignty over Babylon, or over Daniel. Furthermore, Nebuchadnezzar and Daniel probably understood that the gifts were given to the deity's representative in honour of the deity (Baldwin 1978: 94; Newsom and Breed 2014: 84; Montgomery 1927: 181). The next verse supports this conclusion.

Like Daniel in 2:20–23, Nebuchadnezzar praises God. Speaking to Daniel as God's messenger, he focuses on three issues. First, he asserts that *truly, your god is indeed a god of gods* (2:47). I do not capitalize the word 'god' because of the Aramaic grammar (Charles 1929: 51) and because the very next chapter shows Nebuchadnezzar has not

---

6. For surveys of this discussion, see Montgomery 1927: 180; Charles 1929: 50–51; and Collins 1993: 171–172.

become a monotheist (Collins 1993: 172; Baldwin 1978: 95). Still, he respects God for what he knows of him, which is that no other deity helped him in this situation. Second, he recognizes God as *lord of kings*. He sees that God aided him by telling him the future. He also sees that in doing so this God has power over present and future kings. As he will continue to discover in the next two episodes, this power is absolute. Third, Nebuchadnezzar states that God is *a revealer of mysteries*, of the things beyond human reach and understanding. Now he knows he will survive as king, and he knows that the God of heaven has committed nations, people and animals into his hand. He has learned more than kings can logically expect to know. This trio of truths instructs him and all readers in what to expect from God in the rest of the book, and the rest of history.

48–49. Nebuchadnezzar recognizes quality servants when he sees them. He gives Daniel *honours and gifts*, for *he made him a ruler over the whole province of Babylon, and a head over all the wise men of Babylon* (2:48). The passage does not indicate that Daniel was necessarily head of all matters in Babylon or of every wise man.[7] However, Daniel rises well above his former rank. He is now one of the leaders of an elite class. He has responsibility within the province of Babylon, one of many areas in the kingdom, and responsibility among the wise men of Babylon, whose lives he has saved.

As a newly appointed advisor, Daniel recommends that Nebuchadnezzar promote his three friends (2:49). The king obliges, giving them responsibility within the province of Babylon, thereby keeping them close to the palace. Their proximity helps set the stage for chapter 3. Nebuchadnezzar kept Daniel closer still, *in the gate of the king*, so the king could summon him to help make decisions.

Meaning

What did this chapter convey to its first readers, Jews in exile, and what does it contribute to all subsequent readers? Ernest Lucas

---

7. There are no definite articles ('the') on his titles, as there is on 'the king' in 2:48. Also, in 4:6 he may be 'merely' head of the dream interpreters, which fits with him serving as one head (among many) of a group of wise men.

(2002: 79) warns that it is easy to get caught up in the details of the vision and forget the vision's main point, which 'is not the details of the course of events in history, but the fact that history is under the control of God and that it has a purpose, which will be achieved'. Breed agrees, and demonstrates that for the early readers the four-kingdom scheme 'transforms a chaotic mass of events involving subjugation and brutal oppression into a logical, divinely ordained sequence that would result in the redemptive transformation of the world. As a schema, it helped persuade Jews that God had not abandoned them, and that history was not an inexorable series of meaningless brutalities' (Breed 2017: 180–181). It can do the same for modern readers who understand its purpose.

Elmer Martens observes that this chapter also intended to foster hope, for it shows that God will triumph, bringing salvation and deliverance to all who believe in his kingdom (1981: 202). Daniel kept God and his kingdom in mind at all times. This focus guided his speech, for he presents God as the source of all revealed knowledge (2:27–30). Many of today's exiles, refugees and stable believers share these priorities.

Finally, the account conveyed then, and imparts now, the need for strength borne by wisdom. God's gift of wisdom guided Daniel's speech, decisions and treatment of others. In short, God's gifts made him a good worker in a hard place, one who never forgot that giving witness to God's character undergirds all responsibilities. Discipline and hope are inseparable. Those who neglect the former will not likely find the latter. Only those who integrate discipline and hope have the patience to persevere while God's kingdom slowly rises to shatter the toes of the last oppressive kingdom, bringing the whole human-made image crashing down.

3. GOD DELIVERS HIS SERVANTS FROM THE FLAMES (3:1–30)

Daniel 3 has long stimulated faithfulness and comforted believers under trial. Hebrews 11:34 alludes to the chapter. Christian sarcophagi from the fourth century AD in the Vatican Museum feature Shadrach, Meshach and Abednego with hands raised in prayer, surviving the flames. The presence of the fourth person in the flames has long intrigued interpreters. All this is fitting, since this chapter provides one of the Bible's most vivid examples of God's power to save his faithful ones from seemingly certain death. At the same time, it does not promise that God will eliminate martyrdom. Rather, it encourages trust in God no matter what the outcome.

Context

As I noted above, Lee Humphreys pioneered the idea that Daniel 1 – 6 stems from ancient court tales. He argues that Daniel 2 represents the category of 'court contest' (see comments on Dan. 2), and Daniel 3 the category of 'court conflict' (1973: 211–223). Tawny Holm (2013: 195–196) defines the 'court conflict' as a story in which 'native courtiers seek the ruin of a wise hero of prominent status, who first suffers a setback but is later vindicated before the foreign king'. While this designation helps to explain the chapter's basic elements, Newsom and Breed are correct to argue that the story combines aspects of several genres. After all, scholars have also identified its genre as 'martyr legend, or wisdom didactic tale' (Newsom and Breed 2014: 100). As is the case with the book as a whole, the passage's contents determine what genre they represent. This episode is masterfully crafted to integrate a variety of narrative techniques and genres. It may be the book's best-told story.

This account has seven clear segments (3:1–7, 8–12, 13–18, 19–23, 24–25, 26–27 and 28–30; Collins 1993: 179–180), though one can combine them. For example, Newsom and Breed (2014: 102) helpfully divide the material into four parts that move from command (3:1–7), to conflict (3:8–12), to confrontation (3:13–23) and finally to resolution (3:24–30). Repetitions link the whole, as do familiar characters and themes. The chapter revolves around the exiles' confession in 3:16–18, and Nebuchadnezzar's declaration of God's greatness in 3:28–30.

Interestingly, this is the book's only segment that does not include Daniel. Readers know he lives on for years (see 1:21). They do not have that certainty for his three friends. Similarly, readers know God's kingdom is rising (2:44–45), but the flames of martyrdom seem to rise faster, and Nebuchadnezzar, the man to whom God gave Judah (1:1–2), is stoking the fire. Having been saved from defilement in chapter 1, and death in chapter 2, will these men fall victim to scheming colleagues and a furious king?

Comment
A. Nebuchadnezzar's golden statue (3:1–7)

This section introduces the problem that drives the rest of the chapter. Nebuchadnezzar orders an image to be made that represents his lordship, and probably also the gods he believes gave him power (3:1). Having assembled all types of officials (3:2–3), he orders them to bow down and give homage to this image (3:4–5).

Failure to do so carries a terrible penalty: death by burning (3:6–7). Common words from 2:24–45 help readers compare and contrast the king's previous and current behaviour.

Repetitions provide this and subsequent sections with rhythms more akin to songs or poems than a 'normal' narrative (whatever that is). Rhythms create beauty and power (Maclean 1976: 2), so readers must embrace them to appreciate the passage fully. In these verses the author mentions five times the monument Nebuchadnezzar 'raised' (3:1, 2, 3, 5, 7). Twice the author repeats a list of officials (3:2, 3), twice a list of musical instruments (3:5, 7), and twice the fact that the officials come from various peoples, places and languages (3:4, 7). Perhaps most importantly, three times the author repeats the requirement to 'bow down and pay homage' (3:5, 6, 7) to the image Nebuchadnezzar 'raised up'. These verses thereby read like a song sung well, perhaps sung as a round. All goes as the king plans in this section.

1. The Aramaic text does not date these events, but the Greek versions place them in Nebuchadnezzar's eighteenth year, when he conquered Jerusalem and burned the temple (see Jer. 52:29). Montgomery (1927: 199) notes that this would provide a dramatic setting by 'identifying the date of Nebuchadnezzar's impious creation with that of the destruction of the holy city', but considers it an addition to the text. C. F. Keil agrees, and suggests that the fall of lowly Jerusalem 'can hardly be regarded as having furnished a sufficient occasion for this' dedication ceremony (1980: 115). Thus, it seems best to accept the Aramaic version, leave the episode without a particular date and allow the textual connections to provide links between chapters 2 and 3. This approach lets the story begin with sheer action (Fewell 1988: 65).

The account starts by stating that Nebuchadnezzar *made an image* [lit. 'a thing cut out'; see BDB 853–854] *of gold*. The words translated as *image* and *gold* are the same as in 2:31–32, 38. By *made* the author means 'had made', for Nebuchadnezzar would have needed skilled workers to construct it, and by *of gold* he means 'overlaid with gold', as was the custom then. This is not a solid-gold monument. Wood or stone would be under the overlaid gold. The text does not state what was engraved on this monument's face, only its measurements. It is rather tall and thin, about 90 ft by 9 ft (27.4 m by 2.7 m). The height is not unprecedented in ancient times, but the slender width would have required solid anchoring.

Nebuchadnezzar *raised it*, which reminds readers of the kingdom God raises up in 2:44. He puts it *on the plain of Dura, in the province of Babylon*. This location is unknown, 'but *Dura*, which means "walled place", is an abbreviation of a longer name compounded with Dur-, such as Duru sha-karrabi, a suburb of Babylon' (Baldwin 1978: 101). Wiseman suggests the setting may have been outside the walls near a place by that name (1985: 111). Its setting in *the province of Babylon*, where 2:49 states that Shadrach, Meshach and Abednego work, is the most important point about the location.

The text does not divulge the reason for the monument's measurements. Fewell (1988: 65) suggests, 'The identical word (*slm*), the comparable size, and the matching component of gold prompt the understanding that Nebuchadnezzar is duplicating, with some variation, the image he had in his dream.' She adds that Nebuchadnezzar may have drawn some incorrect conclusions from his dream and its interpretation: 'Taken by Daniel's interpretation that he is the head of gold, Nebuchadnezzar builds a corresponding image of gold. His created image remedies the weaknesses inherent in his dream-image: His is made of a unified substance; his has no feet of clay' (1988: 65). If so, Nebuchadnezzar may have taken Daniel's interpretation as a warning of events he could avoid by assertive action. He certainly did not take it as evidence that he ought to give sole allegiance to the deity who made and rules the universe.

2–3. Nebuchadnezzar summons seven types of officials *to the dedication of the stele that* he *had raised*. Such ceremonies were common in Assyria, Babylon and Persia (Goldingay 1989: 69; Montgomery 1927: 197–198), and they remain so in many countries. The word translated *dedication* occurs in Ezra 6:16–17 to describe the temple's reopening (Vogt 2011: 138), so the author edges closer to the monument's religious purpose. The persons mustered include those in charge of various portions of provinces, those who advise them and those who keep track of expenditures. In short, major and minor officials alike are required to attend a state event celebrating the empire's power (Newsom and Breed 2014: 104). The list does not include the palace advisors, which explains Daniel's absence (see 2:49; Longman 1999: 99). The provincial servants all come as commanded, and stand *before the stele that King Nebuchadnezzar had raised* (3:3). Their unanimity, shown by the repetition of their titles, is impressive.

4–5. Now the assembled servants learn the gathering's purpose. Like the exiles from Judah, these officials hail from many lands. They represent the defeated *peoples, nations and languages* placed in the Babylonian Empire's service (3:4). To show Babylon's power and their loyalty, when they hear the music made by players of horns, reed instruments, stringed instruments and wind instruments,[1] a large and melodious band indeed, they must *fall down and pay homage to the stele of gold King Nebuchadnezzar has raised.* The words for *fall down* and *pay homage* are the same as in 2:46, where Nebuchadnezzar bows before Daniel.

6–7. Failure to obey will result in dire consequences – death by burning – a well-attested means of execution in the ancient world (Lev. 20:14; 21:9; Jer. 29:22; see Collins 1993: 185; Lucas 2002: 89). Montgomery (1927: 202) suggests that the *furnace* 'must have been similar to our common lime-kiln, with a perpendicular shaft from the top and an opening at the bottom for extracting the fused lime', and notes that 'similar ovens' existed 'in Persia for the execution of criminals'. With this penalty in mind, when the assembly heard the music of the instruments, the representatives of the conquered *peoples, nations and languages fell down and paid homage to the stele King Nebuchadnezzar had raised*, as uniformly as they had assembled.

B. Conflict in the court (3:8–12)

Prior to this section, the other royal servants Daniel and his friends encounter are not unfriendly. In fact, the ones in charge were willing to take Daniel's suggested change in diet as far as possible (1:8–20), and Arioch seemed happy to find an alternative to the king's decree against the wise men (2:12–16, 24–25). Now colleagues who wish Shadrach, Meshach and Abednego ill, or who wish to ingratiate themselves in the eyes of the king, or are simply obnoxious

---

1. For a discussion of these instruments, consult Collins (1993: 183–184); and Wiseman (1985: 111).

busybodies, enter the story. People like them will figure in chapter 6. Here they drive a wedge between the king and the exiles that only faith and miracle can resolve.

8. Nebuchadnezzar may have thought his dedication event had gone smoothly. If so, he soon gets disappointed (Longman 1999: 99). Some Chaldeans (see comments on 1:4; 2:2, 5, 10) come forward with disturbing news they are happy to relate. The text literally says that 'they ate pieces of the Jews', an old Akkadian phrase for bringing an accusation (Goldingay 1989: 66). This is an interesting expression, since Daniel and his friends did not eat the king's food in 1:8–16.

9–11. The Chaldeans greet Nebuchadnezzar with proper deference (3:9), and repeat the decree given in 3:4–6 (3:10–11). While they leave out the part that the king 'raised up' the stele, they highlight the order to *fall down and pay homage* and the dreaded death sentence (3:10–11). Thus, they guide the king towards the conclusion they desire (Fewell 1988: 69–70). A similar situation unfolds in Esther 3:1–15.

12. They get to the points they came to make. First, they highlight the fact that the men they report are *Jews*. Collins rightly observes, 'The Jewish identity of the three youths is recognized as the key to their disobedience' (1993: 186). This opening declaration throws suspicion on all Jews, not just the men in question. Second, they mention that Nebuchadnezzar had set *them over* [certain] *matters of the province of Babylon*, referring to the decision reported in 2:49. Perhaps they have been jealous all along, or simply see such reporting as how one advances in their profession. They barely avoid telling the king that he has made a big mistake, and eventually lay all blame on *Shadrach, Meshach and Abednego*. They have mastered underhanded arts. Third, and most damning, they claim that the accused *do not obey you, O King; they do not give reverence to your gods, and they do not pay homage to the gold stele you have raised.*

C. Confrontation, confession and condemnation (3:13–23)

This segment presents the chapter's moment of truth. Nebuchadnezzar confronts Shadrach, Meshach and Abednego, and offers them a second chance (3:13–15). To highlight their importance, from 3:13 to the end of the chapter the author repeats the three men's names twelve times (3:13, 14, 16, 19, 20, 22, 23, 26 [2×], 28, 29 and 30). Their ringing confession of loyalty to God includes their willingness to die rather than serve another deity (3:16–18). Extremely angry, Nebuchadnezzar decides to give them the chance to do just that (3:19–23). Everything hangs on their confession, not on their deliverance, though they believe God can rescue them (3:17).

13–15. The Chaldeans' words do their job. Nebuchadnezzar has *fury and rage* (3:13), emotions similar to those he exhibited in 2:12. Still, he does not simply take the Chaldeans' word for fact. He is not out of control with rage. Nebuchadnezzar sends for the men (3:13). He asks them three questions: (1) is it true that you have not bowed? (2) will you bow if given a second chance? (3) what god can save you from the fires? This last question amounts to a challenge. He implies that their religious commitments are about to get them killed. This scene's repetitions and key questions build suspense. How will these men respond?

16. Unequivocally, as it turns out. In answer to this first question, they say *we have no need to answer you.* Montgomery rightly thinks this phrase means they have no legal defence to make to the charge; this is not a sarcastic answer (Montgomery 1927: 205–206). They admit they have not bowed. Their respectful addressing of the king indicates they do not reject his authority. They just cannot obey it in this instance.

17. Now they deal with the third question: *If it be so, our God, whom we are serving, is able to deliver us from the furnace of burning fire, and he will deliver us from your hand, O King.* The *it* in this case is death by burning. The word for *serving* is the same as in 3:12 and 14. They admit that they put their God's will above Nebuchadnezzar's commands, and their God does not allow them to bow before images. They add that their deity can deliver them. Several commentators believe their expression leaves some doubt as to their God's ability to save (see the summaries of opinions in Collins 1993: 187–188; Baldwin 1978: 104–105; and Miller 1994: 119). Context determines meaning, of course. In this context, they give a balanced, faithful answer to a rash question, the sort of answer trained wise men give. They do not express doubts about God.

18. Finally, they answer the second question. They will not bow if given a second chance. God may deliver them from fire, or not. Nebuchadnezzar may give them a second chance, or not. Regardless, they tell the king, *we will not serve your gods or pay homage to the gold stele you have raised.* They will die rather than bow. Nebuchadnezzar need not waste a reprieve on them, hoping they will change. They admit they have not bowed, they have not served Nebuchadnezzar's deities, they have a deity able to save and they are ready to burn. Their reply does not mean they will not serve the king, as the charges in 3:12 imply. It does indicate that they will keep the first two of the Ten Commandments, come what may (Childs 1985: 67).

19. The author maintains a steady narrative course after this great statement. Now the text describes Nebuchadnezzar as *full of rage,* not just having 'rage' (see 3:13). Using the same word as the one translated 'image' in all the verses that describe the stele, the verse states that *the image* [or *expression*] *of his face changed concerning Shadrach, Meshach and Abednego.* That is, he has no more mercy for them. He will delay the execution order no longer. As his fury burned, he commanded *the furnace to be heated seven times more than was customary.* He wants to leave no doubt about their God delivering them, perhaps through an ebbing fire.

20–23. He also wants to make sure they reach the flames, and that the flames have plenty of fuel. Therefore, he has some of his soldiers (*mighty men*) take them to the flames, making certain their garments stayed on them (3:20–21). Apparently, previous victims had struggled, and had sought to take off their clothing, perhaps doing anything to avoid the inevitable. Sadly, the orders were given with such urgency (3:22; see 2:15, where the same word occurs) that they conflicted. The fire gets stoked while the captors take Shadrach, Meshach and Abednego to the oven. The soldiers do their job (3:23), but die in the process (3:22). The author leaves no room for doubt that the furnace is as dangerous as Nebuchadnezzar intends.

D. Deliverance, confession and decree (3:24–30)

The author has not revealed whether the faithful men will survive. There has been no prediction or promise that they will, and no notice of their longevity like the one about Daniel in 1:21. This creates tension in the plot. Nebuchadnezzar learns the outcome quickly. He seeks counsel as to how many they have put in the fire, for he sees four persons, and one does not look like a human being (3:24–25). God preserves the three friends, causing Nebuchadnezzar to call them from the flames (3:26) and find them unharmed (3:27). The king praises the 'Most High' God and his servants (3:26, 28), and then makes it illegal to speak against this God (3:29). Finally, Nebuchadnezzar promotes Shadrach, Meshach and Abednego (3:30). Their opponents fail in their attempt to discredit and do away with them.

24–25. Newsom notes that 3:19–23 is a very visual text, much concerned with garments, stoking fires and men falling into flames. Thus, it is not surprising that Nebuchadnezzar believes he is seeing things in 3:24–25 (Newsom and Breed 2014: 111). Staring into the dancing flames, *Nebuchadnezzar the king was astonished, and rose quickly* to seek *his counsellors*. These may be the ones in 3:8–12, though the text uses a different term to describe them. He confirms that they put three men in the furnace, for he sees *four men unbound, walking unhurt in the midst of the fire* (3:25). The fire seems to have dissolved what the guards used to bind them, but has not hurt them. What is more, *the appearance of the fourth is like a son of gods*.

Who, or what, is this fourth figure? Nebuchadnezzar calls the being God's 'angel', or 'messenger', in 3:28. It is important to remember who is speaking and under what circumstances (Longman 1999: 111–112). Nebuchadnezzar is still learning about the living God. He still believes in many gods (see 3:13–15; 4:8). Thus, it is most likely that he describes a being whom he believes resembles deity (Archer 1985: 57), one who fits the category of a divine being (Collins 1993: 190). He does not confess seeing a messianic figure, nor is this a pre-incarnate visitation by God the Son, as Miller argues (1994: 123–124).

Furthermore, it is not helpful to treat the being as a type or pattern of Jesus Christ, which Christians have done for centuries (see Stevenson and Glerup 2008: 181–182). Doing so shows disregard for the messenger God actually sent. Angels appear throughout the Bible as God's messengers sent on a variety of missions, including ministering to Jesus (Matt. 4:11). They deliver the apostles from prison in Acts 5:17–25, and Peter from a potential death sentence in Acts 12:1–19. This is the first appearance of an angel in Daniel, but not the last. God has not left his faithful ones alone. Nebuchadnezzar's messengers take the three to the furnace, and God's messenger protects them there.

26. Seeing his plan thwarted by this miracle, Nebuchadnezzar calls the men out of the furnace. They obey his word, as they have always done when his commands have not conflicted with their higher commitments to God. He gives them a new title: *servants of the 'Most High' God.* It no longer matters that they will not serve his gods (see 3:8–15). Charles (1929: 76) writes that Nebuchadnezzar's name for God appears often later in Daniel (see 4:17, 24, 25, 26, 32, 34; 7:25), and also in other works (see Isa. 14:14; Tobit 1:13; 1 Esdras 2:3; 6:31; Mark 5:7; Acts 16:17). Paul Redditt (1999: 72) writes that this name reminds readers of 'the name El Elyon, used of God in the Old Testament. It is also reminiscent of the title of the highest god in polytheistic religions. That god in some cultures was thought to be so far above mortals as to be uninterested in them.' Nebuchadnezzar has begun to understand something of God's power, but Daniel 4 indicates that he still has much to learn.

27. This miracle has certainly saved Shadrach, Meshach and Abednego. God has done a great thing for them. Beyond that, he has done a great thing for those who witnessed this deliverance: the king, *the satraps, the prefects, and the governors, and the king's counsellors*, indeed all who had bowed before the stele in 3:1–7. This is not just the story of Shadrach, Meshach and Abednego, or simply a heroic story about them (Fewell 1988: 81). It aims at the hearts and minds of all the people watching then, and all the people reading or hearing now.

28. Nebuchadnezzar blesses God, much as Daniel does in 2:20–23. He asserts that God deserves high praise, for *he sent his angel and delivered his servants*. He adds that for their part, the three friends *trusted in* God, *set aside the king's command, and gave up their bodies rather than serve and pay homage to any god except their God*. As in 3:16–18, Nebuchadnezzar's speech highlights faith, fidelity and hope above all other commitments. The men could not serve both Nebuchadnezzar and the 'Most High' God. They could not protect their bodies or keep the king's command and serve the 'Most High' God. They had to value their God and their witness more than their lives, their ruler's commands and their hard-won careers.

29–30. Nebuchadnezzar knows no other god can do what he has seen with his own eyes. Borrowing a key word from the men's confession in 3:17, he claims *there is no other god who is able to rescue in this way*. As Redditt (1999: 72) observes, 'Nebuchadnezzar ate his words from v. 15. There he had bragged that no god could deliver the friends from his hands; here he confessed that their God had done just that.' In response, he makes it illegal for any *people, nation or language* (see 3:4) under his rule *to blaspheme* [or *insult*; *speak against*; Montgomery 1927: 219; Lucas 2002: 85] *the God of Shadrach, Meshach and Abednego*. Those who fail to obey face the same penalty threatened in 2:5. He also promotes the three to higher positions *in the province of Babylon* (see 2:49; 3:12).

Meaning

Nebuchadnezzar builds an image he believes will not fall (3:1–7) that represents a kingdom that will avoid the pitfalls described in 2:31–45. He thinks forced unity and worship by his various peoples will hold his kingdom together. The jealousy that arises in the next segment shows how wrong he is.

The Jews' accusers reveal the king's purpose for erecting the stele (3:8–12). It represents his rule over the nations God has given him (2:38; 3:4, 7), a gift he still credits to his gods. For an insecure king trying to circumvent Daniel's interpretation, this non-compliance is extremely unwelcome. It means he does not have the unity he feels he needs.

The malicious men's accusations also remind readers of the continuing harsh realities and hard decisions Jewish exiles faced in Babylon. Religious defilement and potential physical punishment confront them in 1:8–16, and the threat of death hangs over them in Daniel 2 – 3. Faith does not protect them from peril. Martyrdom is certainly possible, though not inevitable (Redditt 1999: 73).

The three men's confession in 3:13–18 is one of the Bible's greatest. It matches John's summary of the martyrs in Revelation 12:11: 'And they have conquered him by the blood of the Lamb and by the word of their testimony, for they loved not their lives even unto death' (ESV). The men's rejection of Nebuchadnezzar's demands provides the greatest resistance to tyranny believers can make (Brueggemann 2010: 142, 145). Nebuchadnezzar can take their home, name and profession from them. He cannot take their faith in God. He cannot take their witness to their God. He cannot remove the wise character they exhibit. Thus, they testify to the kingdom that rises below all manmade images of gods and world leaders, and will eventually make them crumble (see 2:44–45). While types of resistance vary, this one is primary for believers, as faithful persons have shown throughout the centuries. Those of us who have not paid this price honour them, and must be prepared to respond as they have if the necessity arises.

God does not stand aloof from history, refusing to get involved. Having given Hananiah, Mishael and Azariah to Nebuchadnezzar (1:1–2), in 3:19–24 he protects their witness, integrity and dignity, the qualities people like Jehoiakim (see 1:1) cast off. Ernest Lucas (2002: 95) points out that these three men 'are not saved *from* the fiery furnace, but are kept safe *in* it (19–27)'. He adds that the furnace episode connects with other passages, such as where the Old Testament compares the people's time in Egyptian captivity to living in an 'iron furnace' (Deut. 4:20; 1 Kgs 8:51; Jer. 11:4), and where it promises that God will be with them through flood and fire (Ps. 66:1–12; Isa. 43:2; ibid.). In short, God's constant promise is to 'be with' his servants (Exod. 3:12; Josh. 1:1–9; Jer. 1:17–19; Matt. 28:18–20).

This presence emphasizes God's unlimited power. He can protect young trainees in Babylon by giving them wisdom and favour (1:3–20). He can preserve a servant in a foreign court for decades (1:21). He can reveal things hidden in the sleep of a fearful king (2:24–45), and he can use fire however he wishes (3:24). As the God of heaven (2:19), he can send heavenly messengers to protect his faithful ones (3:25).

The whole chapter stresses the importance of loving witness to enemies. Everything that has happened has been for Nebuchadnezzar's benefit. Yet he does not convert. He recognizes the power of the three friends' deity in 3:28–29, but still thinks he controls life and death, and even that he can assign the gods their places in the world (Fewell 1988: 83). He thinks God needs his protection (3:29), so he still has much to learn (Newsom and Breed 2014: 113). The friends have also gone through this ordeal for the sake of witness to the Chaldeans, their accusers, and for that of the mass of officials who bowed without question. They are God's servants, called upon to love their neighbours, some of whom want them dead. They show this servant love by trusting God, denying the king's right to dictate their worship and giving up their bodies if necessary (3:28).

4. GOD HUMBLES THE PROUD (4:1–37)

Human pride is one of the world's greatest dangers. This basic biblical teaching is always needed, but perhaps never more so than in an age when politicians, advertisers, job seekers, business owners, athletes and ministers proclaim and market their importance in every way possible. As technology has developed from writing to print to telegraph to radio to television to the World Wide Web, self-interested voices have grown louder, and seemingly omnipresent. Self-promotion has reached new levels. Thus, it is probably always useful to have an example that interpreters can apply to all people, from the greatest to the lowliest. Daniel 4 provides such an example, for Nebuchadnezzar describes what it finally took for him to 'know that the "Most High" rules the kingdom of men, and gives it to whom he will' (4:25).

Context

This chapter's literary form is unique in Daniel 1 − 6. It is a communication from Nebuchadnezzar to his subjects (4:1).[1] Hartman and Di Lella (1978: 174) deem it an epistle, stating that the passage has 'a standard epistolary introduction' (4:1−3), a 'body of the letter that gives the account of the king's dream and its effects' (4:4−36), 'and finally a conclusion' (4:37) which 'reechoes the praises of God that were sounded in the introduction'. If so, it is an unusual epistle in that Daniel 4:1−18 and 34−37 are autobiographical, but a narrator takes over when Nebuchadnezzar hears from Daniel (4:19−27) and when the king loses his mind (4:28−33). Nebuchadnezzar resumes speaking when he regains sanity. Furthermore, the chapter includes poetry in 4:3 and 4:34b−35. There is a bit of a contest between Daniel and the other wise men in 4:4−18, though not one with the deadly consequences 2:1−45 featured. Thus, many scholars conclude that 'diverse traditions have been woven together in Daniel 4' (see Collins 1993: 216). They also conclude that the material does not fit the second-century BC time period as well as it does earlier settings (see Hartman and Di Lella 1978: 13).

Despite this agreement, experts have found it quite difficult to demonstrate how an editor joined the suggested strands of prose, poetry, autobiography, third-person narration and epistle (Collins 1993: 216). For example, Wills (1990: 114−121) uses the Old Greek version and relevant non-biblical stories to try to reconstruct the original sources a proposed editor possessed, the source material this editor used and discarded, and the words this editor added. While his work demonstrates careful analysis, it may simply show that Daniel's author brought together materials in such a unified manner that it takes extraordinary scholarly knowledge and good fortune to sort them out. It seems more likely that the piece has always been a unified whole, joined, as good literature so often is, by an author blending genres that can only be separated for purposes of discussion. Since Ezra, Nehemiah and other exile literature

---

1. The Masoretic and Greek versions have 4:1−3 as 3:31−33, and thus 4:4−37 as 4:1−34. This commentary will follow the verse numbering in the English Bible based on when the episode begins.

contain similar shifts in content and narration (Lucas 2002: 104), Daniel 4 appears to participate in normal literary practices of the Babylonian-Persian era.

At least three other historical matters deserve mention. First, Eusebius (c. AD 275–339) mentions a tradition that Nebuchadnezzar went to the roof of his palace, predicted the coming of a Persian ruler and wished that ruler to become a beast in the field (see Montgomery 1927: 221; Longman 1999: 117). This account demonstrates that palaces were standard places for a king to be and speak, and that beast imagery was common when discussing kings. Second, in the nineteenth century scholars discovered inscriptions about Nabonidus, the last ruler of the Babylonian Empire (c. 556–539 BC). These included statements about his son Belshazzar, and the fact that Nabonidus left Babylon for ten years to live in Teima (Collins 1993: 217). Third, the discoveries at Qumran in the mid-twentieth century included 'The Prayer of Nabonidus', a document that contains a first-person account of how God struck the king with an illness for seven years while he lived in Teima. God sent an unnamed Jewish magician, who told him that he was suffering for praying to gods of silver and gold, and urged him to repent. The text breaks off, but the account likely ended with the king's acceptance of the message and his renewed health (see Baldwin 1978: 116–117).

This last document has several evident similarities and differences with Daniel 4. After charting these, Hartman and Di Lella (1978: 179) conclude that 'there is no literary dependence of one story on the other'. They add that, taken together, the Nabonidus texts preserve more accurately than Daniel 4 the story of a Babylonian king who suffered illness and gained health through the intervention of a Jewish wise man (1978: 179). This is an extraordinary conclusion, given the lack of any attesting or competing Nebuchadnezzar stories outside the Bible. Thus, it is a much more feasible conclusion that Daniel 4 testifies with other ancient texts to God's work with Babylon's kings. Jeremiah, Daniel, Ezra and Nehemiah convey the same theme, as do extra-biblical works. Of all these texts, Daniel alone presents how God worked directly in Nebuchadnezzar's life. It preserves what is currently unique information, and no known text sets that information aside. The book presents this episode as one of several for which documentary evidence existed when the author wrote the book.

This chapter unfolds in the following manner. In 4:1–3 Nebuchadnezzar addresses his subjects with praise for the 'Most High' God (see 3:26). These verses have a very personal, warm tone. The tense ruler of Daniel 2 – 3 has changed. In 4:4–18 the king states that he recounted a troubling dream to many wise men, and then to Daniel. Daniel explained the dream and counselled the king (4:19–27). Though the dream warned of disastrous consequences for Nebuchadnezzar, it was just that, a warning. Nebuchadnezzar confesses he could have avoided the trouble, but did not. Instead, he suffered madness for 'seven periods of time', until he recognized God's supremacy (4:28–33). Finally, in 4:34–37 Nebuchadnezzar praises God again, and explains to his subjects that all God's ways are right, 'and he is able to humble those who walk in pride' (4:37). The last phrase provides the chapter's theme.

Comment
A. Nebuchadnezzar's letter to his people (4:1–3)

By the end of chapter 3, Nebuchadnezzar has learned that no deity can reveal hidden knowledge (2:47) or deliver his servants (3:26–29) the way the 'Most High' God can. Yet he has not learned that this God rules *him*, the king over the world's 'peoples, nations and languages' (3:4, 7, 29). This letter to his subjects (4:1) indicates that 'the signs and wonders' (4:2–3) God has done in his life have not been in vain.

1. In the standard Aramaic text of Daniel, verses 1–3 conclude chapter 3, thereby making these verses part of the decree 3:29 mentions. However, the giving of the name, the people addressed and the lack of any contents of the decree after 4:3 point to a new segment of the book. No date appears. As in 3:1, the Septuagint places this chapter in the eighteenth year of Nebuchadnezzar's reign, the year he sacked Jerusalem and burned the temple (Jer. 52:29). Nothing in Daniel 4 connects its material to that time, so this date was likely added to the original text (see comments on 3:1). The chapter seems to occur during a peaceful time in Nebuchadnezzar's reign, which would preclude the Septuagint's date.

Nebuchadnezzar was the most powerful king on earth. Gowan (2001: 77) writes that this communication is 'a public pronouncement of a type that is familiar, especially from Assyrian inscriptions'. Royal inscriptions in several languages from the Persian and Greek periods have also been discovered (Collins 1993: 221), and Ezra 4:11 and 7:12 contain similar material. The king uses a common literary form, then, and greets his subjects in a kindly fashion: *May peace be multiplied to you.*

2–3. The king introduces his purpose: *to declare the signs and wonders the 'Most High' God has done with me* (4:2). Signs and wonders 'are events explicable only in terms of divine intervention' (Baldwin 1978: 110). They occur together in 'the exodus tradition, often with specific reference to Pharaoh (Exod. 7:3; Deut. 6:22; 7:19; 26:8; 29:2–3; 34:11; Ps. 105:27; 135:9; Neh. 9:10). Thus, the Egyptian Pharaoh and the Babylonian Nebuchadnezzar are paralleled as monarchs who experience the power of the Israelite God' (Newsom and Breed 2014: 134). Unlike Pharaoh, though, Nebuchadnezzar recognizes Israel's God as the 'Most High' God (4:2; see 3:26), and he gives thanks for what God has done (4:3).

B. Another helpful troubling dream (4:4–18)

Nebuchadnezzar recounts a troubling dream, his second (see 2:1–45). As with the first, God sends this one to help Nebuchadnezzar. The first comforted his fears about a short reign, and revealed events long after his death. This one warns him to change his ways. Failing that, it explains what happens to him in 4:28–33. Nebuchadnezzar asserts that no typical wise man could understand his dream (4:4–7), so he tells it to Daniel (4:8–18).

4–7. The scene begins much like 2:1–2, except this time the king was *at ease, prospering in* his *palace.* Since he was enjoying a peaceful interlude, it may have bothered him even more when he *saw a dream* that *frightened* him. As he considered the dream's possible meaning, he conceived of all sorts of *impure* (see Montgomery 1927: 226; Collins 1993: 222) and hypothetical (*visions of my head*) meanings. Clearly getting nowhere on his own, he summoned *the wise men of Babylon,* the group Daniel's actions saved in chapter 2 (4:6; see

2:12–13, 27). This time they do not have to tell him the dream first, but they still have no success interpreting it (4:6–7).

8–12. *Afterwards, Daniel came* to help the king (4:8), perhaps appearing last due to his status as 'chief prefect over all the wise men of Babylon' (2:48). Nebuchadnezzar notes that he had renamed him *Belteshazzar after the name of my god, but in him is the spirit of the holy god* (or *gods*) (4:8). The king has already noted the 'impure' nature of some of his dream, so he wants a person with a pure spirit to advise him. This description can be a polytheistic statement (*gods*), as it likely is on Pharaoh's lips in Genesis 41:38, or a monotheistic one, as it is on the lips of Joshua in Joshua 24:19 (Collins 1993: 222–223). I have not capitalized the word to reflect that Nebuchadnezzar may not necessarily refer to the God of the Bible. Still, Nebuchadnezzar knows there is something very different about Daniel, and about his God. He knows Daniel serves only one God, and that this deity enables Daniel to interpret dreams no-one else can (4:9).

As he tells it, the dream began pleasantly. A tree grew to a great height (4:10). It *reached to the heavens, and vision of it* [reached to] *the end of all the earth* (4:11). The repetition of 'vision' (4:5) and 'all the earth' (4:1) link the introduction and the body of the letter. The mention of 'heaven' implies that the 'God of heaven' (2:19), the 'Most High' God, has made the tree grow. This is a wondrous tree, for it has *food for all* people, land animals and birds (4:12). The positive image of a large, life-giving tree is a staple in human history (Newsom and Breed 2014: 137; Baldwin 1978: 111), and the Bible adapts it to depict messianic and other themes (Fewell 1988: 94–96). It is a beautiful metaphor.

13–18. But now the dream grows much, much darker. As the king slept, *a watcher* [or *wakeful one*], *a holy one, descended from heaven* (4:13). This is the only time when the Old Testament clearly uses this term for a heavenly being. Gowan (2001: 78) observes that the word 'became widely used in the Jewish literature of the Hellenistic and Roman periods' to describe fallen angels (see 1 Enoch 1 – 36) or holy angels (see 1 Enoch 20:1). Here the being is *holy*, like the spirit that dwells in Daniel. This being comes bearing authority from the God of heaven, for he commands the tree to be chopped down and the beasts scattered (4:14).

Furthermore, the *watcher* orders the stump to be left intact, bound by an iron band, apparently to preserve its shape (4:15a). Then the metaphor shifts. The stump becomes a person, who, like a stump, has no protection from the weather, and becomes wet like the grazing beasts who no longer have the tree's protection (4:15b). This person's *heart will be changed from a man's* to that of *a beast*. Therefore, he will want what an animal wants, just to graze, drink and live, and he will want these things for *seven periods of time*, a phase of undetermined length (4:16). This behaviour is fine for beasts, for God made them this way. For a man or woman, however, it constitutes a twisting of the mind and body. This punishment will happen so *the living may know that the Most High rules the kingdom of men, and he gives it to whom he will, and the lowliest of men he sets over it* (4:17).

Nothing matters more than grasping this truth about God's universal sovereignty, but Nebuchadnezzar does not see what his dream means. Nonetheless, he believes Daniel can help him, for he has in the past (4:18). Daniel has brought him good news before, and the king certainly hopes he will now.

C. A reluctant interpreter and some wise counsel (4:19–27)

Dana Nolan Fewell (1988: 97) observes that the author begins the shift from Nebuchadnezzar's narration to that of a third party here: 'The subtlety of the shift lies in the fact that, though the person shifts from first to third, the perceptual point of view remains the same – at least for the time being. We . . . are still seeing the events from Nebuchadnezzar's point of view because of the use of the name Belteshazzar.' Nebuchadnezzar now begins to lose control of the narrative, however, even as Daniel takes charge of the speaking (4:19). Soon enough, Daniel warns, the king may be the stump, the changed one (4:20–26). He will experience what the watcher has decreed unless he changes his oppressive ways (4:27).

19. This verse demonstrates Daniel's concern, even his love, for Nebuchadnezzar. Like the king, Daniel became *alarmed* (see 4:5). He hesitates, not wishing to give his interpretation. Longman writes that 'God's prophet shows concern for the well-being of the king, not vindictiveness' (1999: 120). Daniel wishes the dream were about Nebuchadnezzar's *enemies*, showing that Daniel is not among them.

20–26. Line by line, Daniel interprets the dream. Nebuchadnezzar is the tree, for his kingdom reaches *the ends of the earth* (4:20–22). Thus, the watcher's orders are about him (4:23–24). He will become like an animal until he knows that God rules the world and gives power to whomever he wills (4:25). The only good news Daniel has to give is that Nebuchadnezzar will recover when he acknowledges God's sovereignty (4:26).

27. Boldly, Daniel urges him: *break off your sins by righteousness, and your iniquities by showing mercy to the afflicted, that there may be a lengthening of your ease.* His counsel unfolds as two parallel phrases concluded by a result or purpose clause. The second parallel line assumes the verb from the first. Dozens of similar constructions occur in the Old Testament.

In this parallel phrase, the governing verb ('break off') occurs in its Hebrew form in Genesis 27:40 to describe Esau eventually breaking Jacob's yoke from his neck, and in Exodus 32:2 to depict the Israelites taking off gold to make an idol (Montgomery 1927: 242; Baldwin 1978: 114). The word for 'sin' is the general Old Testament word for 'missing the established mark'. Thus, Nebuchadnezzar must break with, or put off, his sins.

Consequently, he must replace his old behaviour with something different. The word *righteousness* here indicates 'doing the right thing' as opposed to 'doing the wrong thing' (i.e. 'sin') (Baldwin 1978: 114). The Septuagint translates the word as 'almsgiving', which the book of Tobit equates with 'righteousness', and Matthew 6:1–4 joins the two concepts (see Montgomery 1927: 241–242; Collins 1993: 230). The subsequent parallel phrase, *showing mercy to the afflicted*, explains the preceding one. As a general statement, it indicates that almsgiving to the *afflicted*, which can also mean 'thin' (as in hungry), 'poor' or 'oppressed' depending on the context, would be one thing he could do. Given the breadth of the possibilities of *showing mercy*, however, Lucas correctly comments that 'it seems too narrow to restrict these to almsgiving' (2002: 113). A king can do much more, and in the ancient world no less than in the modern one, it was the king's duty to protect the weak. In short, Daniel may simply tell Nebuchadnezzar to remember his job and do it well, and he may have passages like Psalm 72 in mind. Nebuchadnezzar has been neglecting this basic aspect somehow, and if he wants continued *ease* (see 4:4), he must regain this vital commitment. God has warned him through the 'watcher' and through Daniel. Will he hear and obey?

D. God humbles Nebuchadnezzar (4:28–33)

The author highlights Nebuchadnezzar's foundational sin, the one that causes his others and inhibits his understanding of the 'Most High' God. Daniel 4:27 begins to reveal this sin, for Daniel points out that the king needs to focus on the people who need him to use his power for their benefit. Sadly, this passage reveals Nebuchadnezzar's self-centredness. He boasts of the great kingdom he has built (4:28–30), so the watcher's pronouncement comes to pass (4:31–33). Even this terrible punishment has a good purpose, as 4:34–37 will demonstrate.

28–30. The author reveals that Nebuchadnezzar will not obey (4:28). His downfall happens in stages, not all at once. A full *twelve months* pass (4:29a). God does not carry out the sentence right away. Perhaps the king did what Daniel advised for a while, but the text does not say so. Regardless, he had time to change.

Later, on what could be taken as simply any other normal day, *he was walking on the roof of the palace of the kingdom of Babylon*, as he must have done many times (4:29b). Wiseman writes that Nebuchadnezzar's father left him a palace in bad repair, so Nebuchadnezzar built a magnificent palace, complete with cedar, cypress, painted stone and other luxurious features (1985: 51–55). He adds, 'This palace naturally included the large private residence . . . of the king which overlooked the quay wall and included sleeping accommodations' (1985: 55). Nebuchadnezzar walked on top of the palace he envisioned and had built.

As he looked out, he saw other projects he had completed or wished to attempt: streets, walls, canals, gardens, temples and a ziggurat (Wiseman 1985: 56–73). He built constantly, striving to make Babylon equal or superior to Assyria and other earlier empires. Wiseman (1985: 76–78) also notes that Nebuchadnezzar's workforce included many skilled people taken as prisoners of war. Though treated well by the standards of the time (1985: 76–78), they were not volunteers. Therefore, they were examples of the 'afflicted' people Daniel warned the king to treat with mercy.

Then, in 4:30 he speaks damning, self-praising words: *Is not this 'Babylon the Great', which I have built for a royal residence by power of my might, and for the glory of my majesty?* Note the constant first-person references: *I have built*; *my might*; *my majesty*. He takes complete credit for all that has been done, sharing none with his father, none with his workers, none with his gods and none with the 'Most High' God. When he looks into his heart, his own reflection is all he sees.

31–33. Now, *a voice from heaven* (4:31a), presumably God's or the watcher's, changes his peaceful musings. He has been warned. Now he will be punished. The sentence tolls like a bell: *the kingdom has departed from you . . . you will be driven from among men . . . your dwelling place will be with the beasts of the field . . . you shall eat grass . . . for seven periods of time . . . until you know that the 'Most High' rules over the kingdom of men, and gives it to whom he will* (4:31b–32). And the sentence begins *immediately* (4:33). His whole existence changes in a flash, and the most powerful man in the world can do nothing about it.

Commentators have noted that Nebuchadnezzar's condition is a known illness, lycanthropy (see Baldwin 1978: 109–110; Gowan 2001: 81). Similar afflictions befall characters in other ancient stories (Lucas 2002: 113). Nebuchadnezzar has become a twisted version of himself. God does not expect animals to act with mercy, kindness and humility, but he expects this of human beings, especially of those in authority (see Pss 34:11–22; 72:12–14). Though there is no extra-biblical historical record of Nebuchadnezzar's illness, the Babylonian Chronicles break off in 594 BC, so there are no extra-biblical records for most of what occurred during Nebuchadnezzar's reign. One must also note that *seven periods of time* does not necessarily mean 'seven years', so it is impossible to pinpoint the exact amount of time. Thus, it is not accurate, or it is at least extremely premature, to claim that this account is 'entirely unhistorical', as Hartman and Di Lella do (1978: 178). Officials have various reasons for covering a mad king's duties, as British leaders did during George III's (1760–1820) bouts of madness, or Americans did when President Wilson (1913–1921) suffered a crippling stroke.

E. God heals and restores Nebuchadnezzar (4:34–37)

Nebuchadnezzar resumes his first-person narration. The punishment ends (4:34a), and the king confesses the basic truth of God's just rule (4:34b–35). He returns to his duties, fully aware of the king of heaven's sovereignty over him and over all lands (4:36–37). In short, he has learned that God humbles the proud (4:37).

34–35. These verses restore first-person narration, and take readers from the fields back to the palace. Nebuchadnezzar is himself again. Actually, he is a new man. He is no longer the self he had been, before or during his illness. He explains how this occurred.

First, he reached *the end of the days* of his sentence (4:34a). The 'seven periods of time' had passed. Second, he says, *I lifted my eyes to heaven, and my reason returned to me* (4:34b). This is an interesting phrase, since it implies that the punishment did not simply end and he was well. Rather, he had to look to God, or, having suffered through the seven periods of time, and with his mind intact, he looked to God rather than repeating his prideful comments. Regardless, he had some responsibility in the matter. As Lucas (2002: 113) comments, 'Looking to heaven suggests seeking God's aid, and so implicitly acknowledging his kingship.' Baldwin adds that the fact that he could look to heaven 'proves that he was still human and capable of response to God, despite his derangement' (1978: 115). The text leaves open the possibility that the indefinite 'seven periods' of time could have ended sooner, had he given up his pride more quickly. Third, upon receiving his reason back, he recognized God as *the 'Most High', and praised and glorified him, who lives for ever*. Praise is the appropriate response to healing.

His praise befits a king's interests. Kings have a *dominion*, a *kingdom*, and Nebuchadnezzar states that God's has no end, for it lasts *from generation to generation* (4:34c). Kings have subjects, and God's include *all the inhabitants of the earth* (4:35a), so Nebuchadnezzar is merely God's sub-regent (see 4:1). As such, he now realizes that God, not he, *does according to his will* with all of them. In fact, God does not just rule *the inhabitants of the earth*, he rules *the host of the heavens*, which includes beings like the 'watcher' (4:13). Therefore, *none can stay his hand*, or rebuke his decisions (4:35b).

36. Besides his reason, Nebuchadnezzar received back his kingdom. The aides who had to drive him away when he was ill (4:33) now come and place him back on the throne. What is more, he says, *still more great things were added to me*. Fewell (1988: 109) thinks this phrase indicates Nebuchadnezzar still 'somehow connects God's glory and power with his own'. While always a relevant concern with someone with Nebuchadnezzar's track record, his statements in 4:34–35 and the passive verb in 4:36 ('were given to me') probably indicate his genuine belief that what he has comes from God. In this way, his experience parallels Job's (see Job 42:7–17), for both receive more after their suffering than they had before it (see Collins 1993: 232).

37. This verse summarizes what Daniel 1 – 4 has revealed about God's dealings with Nebuchadnezzar. It also introduces the next chapter by stating what Nebuchadnezzar has learned about *the king of heaven*: *all his works are right, and* [all of his] *ways are just, and those walking in pride he is able to bring down*. Added to his statements in 2:47 and 3:26–29, this one proves that Nebuchadnezzar does not simply view God as Daniel's deity, or the deity who delivered Shadrach, Meshach and Abednego. This God has a personal interest in him, in how he treats his subjects, and in his walking in humility.

Meaning

Nebuchadnezzar praised God for his works in 2:47–48 and 3:26–29, but 4:1–3 demonstrates that now he knows those previous signs and wonders did not exhaust God's power. Now he confesses God's everlasting and enduring nature and authority to all the people he rules. These verses reveal that something startling has happened to Nebuchadnezzar.

This change comes because he learns what pride does to human beings. Pride twists the mind, the heart and the body. It drives Nebuchadnezzar to see only his personal dreams and visions, and none of the afflicted persons around him. Pride flows from the worst mistake of all, which is putting one's self in God's place. Kings are not the only ones to commit this error. It is a common human failing. So it is no wonder that God warns Nebuchadnezzar and every reader about the need to know who rules the world and assigns duties in every walk of life. It is no wonder Jesus said,

'Blessed are the meek' (Matt. 5:5); 'Whoever does not enter the kingdom like a little child shall not enter it' (Luke 18:17); and 'If anyone would come after me, let him deny himself and take up his cross daily and follow me' (Luke 9:23).

Nebuchadnezzar learns because God chastens the proud, whoever they are. God rules monarchs, no less than exiles, wise men and labourers (Towner 1984: 67–68). Every character in the book lives under God's scrutiny and care. This fact transcends racial, national and financial boundaries. No inhabitant of the earth can correct or coerce God (4:35). Like Nebuchadnezzar, all persons are dependent on the 'Most High' (4:34), the holy God (4:8–9, 18), the 'king of heaven' (4:26–27). Confessing this fact of reality is foundational to biblical faith, and thus foundational to peace of mind.

God disciplines through supernatural means. Beings called 'watchers' view the earth and act with full authority from God in 4:13 and 17. This is one of many areas in which interpreters of Daniel ought to proceed with caution. It is easy to get sidetracked from the book's main teachings. Nonetheless, it is also important to note the book's emphasis on God's rule of creation, and in chapters 3 – 4 this sovereignty includes his sending of supernatural created beings who serve him and aid human beings. Daniel runs counter to materialistic worldviews and policies.

This passage also shows God's merciful intentions in disciplining people. As Newsom puts it, God's work with Nebuchadnezzar 'is not merely educative but also transformative' (Newsom and Breed 2014: 148). It is good for him to learn that he is not God, though it is terrible that it took such drastic measures for him to learn this basic truth. As Baldwin writes, 'Thus suffering has a kindly role here (cf. John 11:4), and enables the king to appreciate how frail he is. Having learnt his lesson he is restored to health and to his throne' (1978: 115). It is impossible to know if he acted like a changed man, just as it is impossible to know how anyone will react to such a second chance.

By focusing on Nebuchadnezzar in chapters 2 – 4, the book invites discussion about conversion and worship in every land. Perhaps Nebuchadnezzar never comes to faith in the living God, but I think 4:34–37 indicates that he does. It is no-one's job but

God's to pass judgment on another person's soul, so it is not simply a matter of putting Nebuchadnezzar in heaven or not. The point is to understand that people born in a culture steeped in the worship of many deities may find it difficult to put aside those gods.

At the very least, Nebuchadnezzar's beliefs about God are a long step in the right direction. He holds him as the highest God, the one to whom all must answer, and the only one who can save from a furnace. People who confess these truths may soon see that if the 'Most High' God does all these things, then there is nothing for other deities to do. Then they may find it easier to hold that God is one, and there is no other (Deut. 6:4–9; 32:39). Also, the sooner people see witnesses like Daniel who love people they could hate, the sooner they may understand that true discipleship flows from love of God and love of neighbour.

5. THE HANDWRITING ON THE WALL: THE END OF BABYLON (5:1–31)

Readers take a long historical step between Daniel 4:37 and Daniel 5:1. The author apparently expected the first readers to know Nebuchadnezzar died in 562 BC, and that three kings succeeded him before Nabonidus took the throne in 556 BC. Nabonidus was Babylon's final king, serving until 539 BC, when Persia conquered Babylon. Readers are also expected to recall that Belshazzar (5:1; 7:1; 8:1) served as co-regent in Babylon in his father's absence, and that he was in residence and his father was probably out fighting when the city fell. Most of all, they are expected to recall 4:37, which stresses God's power to bring down the proud, something Belshazzar never learned, at least not until it was too late. Given 1:21, readers are not surprised to find the elderly Daniel still in service.

Context
Though first readers likely did know these things, or an approximation of them, it has taken years for modern scholars to reconstruct many of the events just summarized. For one thing, until 1854 the

Bible provided the only evidence that Belshazzar existed, much less that he ruled in Babylon (see Collins 1993: 217). For another, though called a king in 5:1, he did not have all the power of a king (Collins 1993: 243; Newsom and Breed 2014: 164), but co-regents rarely had such authority. Finally, as Gerhard Hasel demonstrates in a masterly article published in 1977, it was difficult prior to the last sixty years to determine when Nabonidus was away from Babylon, but the years 550–549 to 540 BC are now proven to be the most likely dates (1977: 153–168). Though they vary in their details, several ancient extra-biblical sources describe the circumstances surrounding Babylon's fall, so the event is well-attested (see Newsom and Breed 2014: 163–164). Interestingly, Daniel 5 does not highlight how the city fell. It focuses on why it fell. Pride (see 4:34–37) and blasphemy (see 3:26–29) led God to hand Babylon over to Persia.

By now, readers will recognize certain continuing plot elements. Babylon has conquered Judah (5:1–4; see 1:1–2). A king has a vision that requires interpretation, but his wise men cannot help him (5:1–9; see 2:1–13; 4:1–18), so he eventually appeals to Daniel (5:10–12; see 4:1–18). Daniel explains the situation (5:13–28; see 2:24–45; 4:19–27) and receives honour (5:29; see 2:46–49). Thus, there is a bit of a 'court contest' here (see Introduction: Genre, p. 18). There are also important new features. Belshazzar shows less respect for God than Nebuchadnezzar did (5:1–4), and offers no praise of God (see 2:46–49; 3:26–29; 4:1–3, 34–37) when Daniel solves his problem. Tellingly, Daniel compares Belshazzar unfavourably to Nebuchadnezzar (5:18–23). The passage's tone points towards its purpose, which is to describe why and when God's hand wrote the Babylonian Empire's death notice.

The chapter has a simple structure. In 5:1–12 the king hosts a large feast (5:1–4) that ends when God sends a message through handwriting on a wall (5:4–9) that only Daniel can interpret (5:10–12). In 5:13–28 Daniel explains the writing, comparing Belshazzar negatively to Nebuchadnezzar and declaring Babylon's reign to be over.[1]

---

1. The Old Greek does not have 5:17–23. Collins (1993: 249) suggests that the section is an example of redaction. However, the verses connect to what precedes and comes after ch. 5, so the Aramaic text is valid.

In 5:29–31 the king honours Daniel (5:29) just before the city falls (5:30–31). The ending reveals Babylon's fate, and introduces the new regime.

Comment
A. The handwriting on the wall (5:1–12)

This section includes two of the book's most enduring metaphors: Belshazzar's feasting when the empire is falling, and the handwriting on the wall.[2] The handwriting appears in 5:5 as a result of the king's abuse of the temple vessels taken from Jerusalem (5:1–4; see 1:2). The Chaldean wise men cannot interpret a message from God, whom the king has offended. Eventually, Belshazzar calls for Daniel (5:6–12).

1. As if a long curtain has been pulled back, the passage opens to a great banquet scene like the one in Esther 1:1–9: *King Belshazzar made a great feast for a thousand of his nobles, and he drank wine in front of the thousand.* The word translated *nobles* appears in 4:36 to describe some of those who restore Nebuchadnezzar to his throne. Thus, Belshazzar has gathered the people whom kings must please in order to stay in power. He has not gathered them to increase his power, as Nebuchadnezzar did in 3:1–7. As 5:30–31 eventually discloses, Belshazzar is in a precarious position. Nabonidus is out fighting Persia. Belshazzar does not know that the enemy is about to capture Babylon. Unsuspecting, Belshazzar rallies his people, albeit with feasting rather than with preparation. He sits before them in the manner he thinks befits a great leader.

Many scholars have criticized Daniel's author for inaccurate terminology in 5:1. For instance, Holm (2013: 46) writes that despite what the text says,

> Belshazzar was not the last king of Babylon. In fact, he was never a king
> of Babylon at all, nor was he a son of Nebuchadnezzar as the Book of
> Daniel presents him; he was instead the son of Nabonidus, the last king

---

2. For these images' continuing significance, see Breed's excellent summary of the history of their reception in Newsom and Breed 2014: 179–186.

of Babylon, and he served as Nabonidus's vice-regent when his father was *in absentia* but never ruled independently. This tradition in Daniel has been transposed from Nabonidus to Nebuchadnezzar, much as traditions about Nabonidus's self-imposed exile in Teima are behind part of the story of Nebuchadnezzar's madness in Dan. 4.

In a more balanced analysis, Collins (1993: 243) writes,

> In brief, it is now established that there was a Babylonian prince by the name of Belshazzar and that he acted as vice-regent in Babylon while his father, Nabonidus, was absent in Teima. Nabonidus is said to have entrusted the kingship . . . to him. Yet the annual *akitu* festival was suspended during the absence of Nabonidus, suggesting that Belshazzar was not regarded as king. The *Nabonidus Chronicle* consistently distinguishes between 'the king' (Nabonidus) and 'the son of the king' (Belshazzar). It is supposed that Belshazzar continued as coregent until the fall of Babylon, but this is not actually confirmed in the sources. His status when Nabonidus returned is uncertain.

It is useful to add that, as Hasel (1977: 153–168) argues (see above), Nabonidus left Belshazzar to rule in Babylon for ten years (550/549–540 BC). He 'entrusted the kingdom' to Belshazzar during this period (Dougherty 1929: 65). For all practical purposes, then, Belshazzar was king in the capital city. In several records related to normal royal business matters, he 'was accorded the obedience due to royal command' (Dougherty 1929: 129–134). Furthermore, Nabonidus was away with the Medes and Persians when Babylon fell in 539 BC. Thus, Belshazzar probably had his old task back (Dougherty 1929: 65). True, Belshazzar was not king in the sense that Nabonidus was, and this is a reasonable and helpful historical point, but it seems unfair to criticize Daniel for inaccuracy, given the actual situation and the ancient practice of co-regency.

Furthermore, it is true that Nebuchadnezzar was not Belshazzar's literal father. It is quite possible, though, that he was his grandfather (Wiseman 1985: 10–11; Dougherty 1929: 60–63). Regardless, the term is not just one of blood relationship, but of claims to royal legitimacy or affinity. David's great-grandchildren were not technically his 'sons', but the term applied to them. Elijah was not literally Elisha's father, but he called him that (2 Kgs 2:12). Again, it seems questionable to critique the author over such a matter. True, Daniel does not mention Nabonidus, but ancient history indicates that after 550 BC he was out of Babylon most of the time (Dougherty 1929: 64, 66). Daniel deals with the reality on the ground.

2. As he sits drinking wine in the presence of the kingmakers, Belshazzar makes an odd request for a Babylonian ruler. Normally, Babylonians avoided offending foreign deities, and what Belshazzar does next was viewed as offensive (Montgomery 1927: 251). Perhaps a bit drunk (see Charles 1929: 115), but more likely as a calculated act intended to unite his people, he calls for *the vessels of gold and silver which Nebuchadnezzar his father had taken from the temple in Jerusalem*, and the group drinks from them. Montgomery (1927: 251) notes that 'as the only tangible remains of Israel's ancient cult, [the vessels] were uniquely sacred to the Jewish mind; cf. Isa. 52:11, Ezr. 1:7ff., Bar. 1:1–8'. They went into exile with the people, and eventually went back with them (see Ezra 1:7–11; Newsom and Breed 2014: 167).

They were also powerfully symbolic to the Babylonians, since they represented victories Nebuchadnezzar had achieved during Babylon's not-so-distant glory days (see 1:1–2). Fewell (1988: 118–119) suggests that Belshazzar drinks from them to show that he is more audacious and venturesome than his predecessor, the mighty Nebuchadnezzar. This makes sense, given the current king and co-regent's need to keep city leaders on board with the government's war plans. Such bravado often accompanies wartime sword rattling.

3–4. The king, the nobles and his wives and concubines all drink from the cup, thus enacting a covenant of hubris (5:3). The whole power structure of the tottering city of Babylon is in this together. Perhaps to show the power of the deities they served compared to the victories Nebuchadnezzar achieved by his gods, *they drank and praised the gods of gold, silver, iron, wood and stone*, the idols they venerated. They even insult Babylonian gods. Thus, Belshazzar combines pride, sacrilege and profanation in his revelry (Hartman and Di Lella 1978: 187). He clearly does not understand the power of the 'Most High' God, 'the holy God', the 'king of heaven' (see 2:19; 3:24–25; 4:1–3, 9–10, 34–37). Though his power does not equal Nebuchadnezzar's, his arrogance may exceed his, so some punishment is sure to follow.

5-6. Things change in an instant. His fingers still curved around the temple vessels, Belshazzar sees *the fingers of a man's hand writing before the lampstand*, a well-lit place he could see plainly. Any wine-induced ruddiness left his cheeks, for *his colour changed*. All bloated opinions of himself fled, *and his thoughts alarmed him*. Cup hoisting ceased, *for his limbs gave way*. Pretensions of marching to war evaporated, for *his knees knocked together*.

7-9. Calls for more wine to be poured into Jerusalem's treasures stick in his throat. Instead, *he cried out* like a child calling for help (5:7). He summons the types of wise men who appeared earlier in Daniel: *enchanters* (1:20; 2:2, 10, 27; 4:7), *Chaldeans* (2:2, 4, 5, 10; 3:8; 4:7) and *astrologers* (2:27). He wanted people able to discern illness and suggest a cure (enchanters), historians of the records (Chaldeans) and people who could read signs based on astronomical calculations (astrologers). In short, he needed the writing deciphered, its implications understood and his sudden physical ailments gone.

The king promises great reward for solving the riddle. The highest honour is being *third in the kingdom*, though this honour will be extremely short lived, as the story turns out. As readers have come to expect (see 2:1-12; 4:7), none of these experts can help him (5:8). This being so, he becomes *greatly alarmed, and his nobles perplexed* (5:9).

10-12. It is time for older, wiser heads to keep the young people from floundering. *The queen*, whom commentators since Josephus (first century AD) have identified as the queen mother or grandmother, enters (5:10a). Longman suggests that she 'may have been Nebuchadnezzar's wife, Nitocris, still exerting her influence more than two decades later. Herodotus, the Greek historian, celebrates her wisdom' (1999: 139; see the survey of options in Collins 1993: 248-249). She has not been banqueting, or drinking from the temple vessels. She counsels calm, for she knows how to comfort him and bring the colour back to his face (5:10b).

She suggests that he does not need all these counsellors. Rather, he needs just one man (*There is a man in your kingdom . . .*), a person Belshazzar maybe does not know or has perhaps forgotten. Or has Daniel been downgraded, like the temple vessels? Regardless, she asserts that *a spirit of the holy gods* resides in him (5:11a), reminding readers of 4:8–9 and 4:18, as if they have aged with the queen. She recalls with some detail and perhaps fondness that *King Nebuchadnezzar, your father, raised him up* over the groups that have just failed (5:11b; see 2:48). She emphasizes the importance of this precedent by repeating *your father* as she continues her recommendation.

She shares Nebuchadnezzar's absolute confidence in Daniel (5:12). She says Daniel possesses *knowledge* (see 1:4) and *skill* (see 1:17) to *interpret dreams* (see 1:17), *explain riddles* (see Judg. 14:14, 15, 19; Charles 1929: 130) and *solve problems*. Collins writes, 'Resolution of riddles and problems is precisely the skill called for in this situation' (1993: 249). As Montgomery (1927: 259) explains, certainly 'the mystery of the supernatural script fell into' the category of riddles and problems. Thus, without hesitation, the queen mother believes Daniel *will show you the interpretation*. Rather than repudiating Nebuchadnezzar's ways, she implies that the king ought to emulate them. After all, Nebuchadnezzar had learned the true source of knowledge and wisdom.

B. Daniel interprets the writing (5:13–28)

Always ready, no matter how long since the last time he was needed, Daniel comes as commanded. Belshazzar seems to know more about him than 5:1–12 may imply (5:13). The king repeats the situation (5:14–16), and Daniel provides a theological analysis of the differences between Nebuchadnezzar and Belshazzar (5:17–23). He then interprets the strange words to mean that God has weighed and counted Belshazzar, and has decided to end his rule (5:24–28). Daniel proves as able as the queen mother promised, but not in the way Belshazzar had hoped.

13–16. Nebuchadnezzar's counsellor faces the king's grandson. Daniel sees no reflection of his old monarch, or none that pleases him. Belshazzar recognizes Daniel's presence, and highlights the fact that Daniel is *one of the exiles of Judah whom the king my father brought from Judah* (5:13). Fewell notes that the queen did mention Daniel's ancestry, and suggests 'Belshazzar has overtly shunned Daniel because Daniel is a symbol of his father's regime' (1988: 124). This makes sense, given the misuse of the vessels and the speech Daniel is about to give. Belshazzar wants to lead without reference to the past, and, sadly, the past contains all the glory that is now or ever will be left. Compliments (5:14), challenges to outdo other wise men (5:15) and promises of glory (5:16) cannot change this fact.

17. Daniel's tone is brusque (see Collins 1993: 249; Lucas 2002: 131): *Keep your gifts, or give them to someone else.* He offers to interpret the writing, but not for personal gain. This wise approach may make his interpretation more believable because of its lack of self-serving motives, but it is not a calculated statement. His humility is not a plan for success.

18–19. Daniel does not interpret the writing immediately, as Belshazzar probably expects. Daniel first gives witness to God's work with Nebuchadnezzar. Belshazzar has mentioned 'the king my father', and Daniel wants to talk about him (5:18). Belshazzar has just compared himself quite favourably to Nebuchadnezzar in the banquet hall, and Daniel will have none of it. Daniel returns to the book's premise: that God gave Judah to Nebuchadnezzar (5:19; see 1:1–2). Moreover, he states explicitly that God gave Nebuchadnezzar *all peoples, nations and languages* (see 3:4, 7, 29; 4:1–3) in the empire. Daniel may also know that Jeremiah taught this same point, and that he had predicted Nebuchadnezzar's lineage would end with his grandson (Jer. 27:5–7), since 9:1–2 shows Daniel's familiarity with Jeremiah. Belshazzar rules in the wake of God's gift to Nebuchadnezzar.

20–21. Continuing this prelude to interpreting the writing, Daniel recounts Nebuchadnezzar's madness. Verse 20 includes some new phrases that convey Daniel's interpretation of Nebuchadnezzar's problem. Daniel claims that Nebuchadnezzar's pride occurred when *his heart was raised and his spirit hardened so that he acted proudly.* To be clear, Nebuchadnezzar did these things to himself. Given Daniel's warning to Nebuchadnezzar in 4:27, this probably means that he gave himself credit for his kingdom and mistreated the afflicted people in his realm. He ceased to reverence God, and thus ceased to treat people with respect. Therefore, he was like a beast *until he knew that the 'Most High' God rules the kingdom of men and sets over it whom he will,* as 4:17, 32 and 34–37 have asserted (5:21). Most importantly, he learned this lesson (see 4:1–3, 34–37).

22–23. But Belshazzar, *his son*, has not. Daniel divulges a key piece of information. Belshazzar *knew all this*, that is, the story of

Nebuchadnezzar's humbling by God. He knew that God can 'cast down those who walk in pride' (4:37), but, Daniel tells him, *you have not cast down your heart* (5:22). Rather, he continues, *you have raised up yourself against the Lord of heaven* (5:23). Belshazzar has done so by defiling God's vessels, and by acting as if gods made of metal, stone and wood rule the nations of the world (5:23).

Edging closer to the interpretation of the words, Daniel offers one final rebuke: *but the God in whose hand are your breath and all your paths you have not honoured* (5:23). Nebuchadnezzar finally learned who rules nations, kings, life, minds and governments. Nebuchadnezzar, whose lineage Belshazzar claims and whose legacy he professes to surpass in boldness and leadership, left a humble letter (4:1–37) and a specific example for 'his son' to follow. Belshazzar has not followed the example Nebuchadnezzar set in 4:1–37. Instead, he has basically followed the example Nebuchadnezzar set in 3:1–23. Belshazzar is on the wrong side of Nebuchadnezzar's history.

24. God saw how Belshazzar dishonoured him (5:1–4). Thus, *from his presence*, from his very person, *this hand was sent, and this writing inscribed*. Like the tablet of the Ten Commandments, this writing comes from God's own fingers (see Exod. 31:18). The difference between the living God and the gods of metal, stone and wood becomes clear. As Lederach (1994: 118) writes, 'This God is living and able to act. His works are in stark contrast to the gods . . . that are carried into the city to provide protection. In the great hall, the idols sit where they have been placed. They cannot see, hear, or respond.' Therefore, their worshippers cannot interpret the words on the wall.

25. Daniel finally reveals the words (5:25) and their meaning (5:26–28). After the long wait, these verses proceed swiftly, inexorably. The words are few: *mene, mene, tekel, and parsin* (5:25). Given the words' obscurity, scholars have proposed numerous ways in which the original text may have read (see the excellent summaries in Bevan 1892: 105–106; Montgomery 1927: 262–264; and Collins 1993: 252). These analyses show the writing involves wordplay based on numbers, weights, measures, root words and the word for Persia (see Lucas 2002: 133–134). Perhaps the wise men could read the words, but could not grasp their importance (see Baldwin 1978:

123–125). Still, Collins (1993: 252) is most likely correct when he comments,

> The range of possible meaning is extended by the fact that Daniel does not directly interpret the words, but uses related verbal forms in new sentences. The element of tension between the writing and its interpretation confirms the mysterious character of the writing and helps explain why the Chaldeans could not decipher it.

In short, the author has related terms too hard for readers or the Chaldeans to grasp on their own. All are helpless without Daniel's interpretation.

26–28. The meaning is that God has *numbered . . . weighed . . . found wanting . . . and given* Belshazzar's *kingdom to the Medes and Persians*. The pace and finality of this verdict reads like God's sentencing of Nebuchadnezzar in 4:31–32. Time is up, for nothing in Belshazzar's actions indicates that he will ever learn the lesson Nebuchadnezzar did. Therefore, God, who gave the nations to Babylon, will now give them to someone else.

C. Honours at the eleventh hour (5:29–31)

Belshazzar keeps his word to Daniel without delay (5:29), and God gives Babylon to the Medes and Persians without delay (5:30–31). Babylon's rule ends in a rush, as swiftly as it began in 1:1–2. God's decisions do not tarry.

29. Lying about bestowing honours is not one of Belshazzar's many faults. As the empire expires, he makes Daniel *third ruler in the kingdom*. This seems a meaningless gesture at this point, but turns out to be a very timely promotion. When the Medes and Persians took over Babylon, they left most local leaders in place. Daniel will thus be positioned to give further witness in 6:1–28.

30–31. Belshazzar does not fare as well: *That very night Belshazzar the Chaldean king was killed*. Neither this passage nor ancient records disclose exactly how this occurred. It may have happened the night Cyrus's army, led by Gobryas, marched unhindered to Babylon and took the city (see below on 6:1). Perhaps someone killed him before the enemy arrived. The result is the same: *And Darius the Mede* *received the kingdom, being about sixty-two years old.* I will delay comment on 5:31 to the introductory comments on chapter 6.

Meaning

Daniel 5:1–12 reinforces Jeremiah's messages about Nebuchadnezzar and his lineage. Jeremiah 25:1–12 and 27:5–7 stress that God has been working through Nebuchadnezzar in a particular way for a particular time. His mission is to carry out God's punishment on his disobedient people and their monarch (see 1:1–2). His successors must meet God's standards if they wish to stay in power. Likewise, Belshazzar's successor must recognize God's authority or face the consequences.

Daniel 5:13–28 illustrates God's opposition to arrogance that leads to idolatry. The passage thus agrees with Isaiah 10:5–11; 14:12–14; and 47:10 that God will judge kings and nations who exalt themselves as if God had not given them their power. An adherent of another religion should know that he or she is not the world's creator. In response to Belshazzar's pride, Daniel stresses that God is sovereign, holy, just and eternal. No idol or emperor has these characteristics, so none deserves worship. God still reigns, as the exiled Daniel understands. His witness to Nebuchadnezzar and Belshazzar makes God's universal reign more evident. It affirms that God's kingdom does not depend on Jerusalem, Babylon or any place having a particular political leader on the throne.

Daniel 5:29–31 demonstrates once again that empires rise and fall at God's command, not at the decrees of human rulers. Monarchs come and go. Each seemingly receives the kingdom from other human beings, but in fact from God. Daniel's faithfulness to God gives him a position of great authority. He survives when Babylon does not (see 1:21).

6. GOD SAVES DANIEL FROM THE LIONS (6:1–28)

Daniel 6 is among the Bible's best-known accounts. Like chapter 3, it has comforted suffering believers for over 2,000 years. For instance, 1 Maccabees 2:59–60 mentions Hananiah, Mishael, Azariah and Daniel as individuals who stood firm against idolatry. Hebrews 11:33 references believers who by faith 'stopped the mouths of lions', though it does not mention Daniel's name. Fourth-century Christians decorated their graves with images of Daniel standing among the lions, and dozens of artists have depicted the scene since. Daniel's steadfastness is impressive, but he credits God with preserving him (6:21–22). God's kingdom rises in unexpected historical moments before it comes in its fullness.

Context

Some details of Persia supplanting Babylon deserve mention. Unfortunately, the ancient records are far from complete. For instance, Briant (2002: 34) writes that 'the chronology of the reign of Cyrus remains uncertain, to say the least', since 'only two events are precisely dated: the capture of Babylon (539) and the death of

Cyrus in Central Asia (530)'. Nonetheless, some known general dates illuminate Cyrus's rise to world prominence.

Born to a Persian father and Median mother (Yamauchi 1990: 79), by 559 BC Cyrus had become king of the Persians, who served the Medes at that time (Olmstead 1948: 34). By 550–549 BC Cyrus had led a successful revolt against the Medes, partly due to Nabonidus of Babylon's assistance (Briant 2002: 31–32; Olmstead 1948: 34–38). Having united the Persians and Medes, Cyrus fought successfully against Greek forces led by Croesus in c. 547–546 BC (Briant 2002: 33–38; Olmstead 1948: 38–44). Cyrus's exact movements during 546–540 BC are unclear, but he probably consolidated earlier gains in Asia (Yamauchi 1990: 84–85; Briant 2002: 41; Olmstead 1948: 50). By then his aims and those of Nabonidus no longer matched, so he sought opportunities to defeat Babylon (Briant 2002: 41–43).

In 540 BC Cyrus began attacking the land of Babylon. Nabonidus returned to the city of Babylon to celebrate the New Year Festival in April 539 BC (Yamauchi 1990: 85; Briant 2002: 41). In early October 539 BC the Medes and Persians captured Opis and Sippar, river cities north-east of Babylon (Olmstead 1948: 50). Cyrus's forces, led by Gobryas, entered Babylon two days later, apparently encountering little or no resistance (Yamauchi 1990: 86; Briant 2002: 42; Olmstead 1948: 50). Nabonidus had fled, but was eventually captured and exiled (Yamauchi 1990: 87). Cyrus came to Babylon a few days after the city had capitulated, but did not live there continuously, having other battles to fight. Moreover, he did not proclaim himself king of Babylon during most of his first year in power (Yamauchi 1990: 89).

Cyrus's swift victory left him little time to settle affairs in Babylon. Thus, he left most of the city's ruling class in place, probably to make the new government more palatable to the vanquished people (Briant 2002: 43–44; Olmstead 1948: 51–56). But Daniel 5:31; 6:1, 28; and 11:1 indicate that he did not put a Babylonian in charge. Rather, those texts claim that 'Darius the Mede' was king, and mention only his first year in power. Daniel 6:28 references Darius and Cyrus together. Daniel 1:21 and 10:1 mention only Cyrus, and no existing Babylonian record includes Darius the Mede. Thus, it is difficult to determine Darius the Mede's identity and role in relationship to Cyrus. Scholars have offered three basic explanations, two of which take Daniel as a credible historical witness.

First, Cyrus granted Gobryas or another official the type of authority Belshazzar had, and gave this person the title Darius the Mede (Olmstead 1948: 50–51). This situation only lasted until Cyrus decided how to rule Babylon permanently. Second, during an interim period Cyrus could have ruled using the name 'Darius the Mede' for political reasons (Wiseman 1965: 12–16; Baldwin 1978: 26–28). Kings sometimes had both personal and throne names, as Solomon (2 Sam. 12:24–25) and Tiglath-pileser III of Assyria (2 Kgs 15:19) attest. Also, Daniel 5:31 gives the new ruler's age as sixty-two, which was close to that of Cyrus when Babylon fell. Furthermore, Cyrus's mother was a Mede, Cyrus ruled the Medes, and external sources called his realm the kingdom of the Medes for some time (see comments on 2:24–45). Finally, Darius the Mede exercised empire-wide authority from Babylon (6:2, 25). Third, many experts conclude that Darius the Mede is fictional, which Collins calls 'the consensus of modern scholarship' (1993: 1), or has been confused with a story 'told about the third monarch of the Persian Empire, Darius the Great, son of Hystaspes, 522–486 B.C.' (Newsom and Breed 2014: 192; see Collins 1993: 29–31).

The second option fits most of the necessary criteria, but both of the first two options provide reasonable historical solutions. In these scenarios Daniel lived through a rapid transition from Nabonidus and Belshazzar, to an interim period that may have included a governor-king, followed by Cyrus's clear rule. Therefore, Daniel 6 unfolds in this transitional time. Again, the records currently known are fragmentary, so certainty is impossible.

Though such discussions help orient readers, the book does not deal with them. The author had other goals in mind, and expected initial readers to know the historical setting, or to recognize that available records portrayed an interim period of the type just described. The author highlights God's dealings with Daniel and foreign leaders in the new situation. This emphasis encourages readers to believe that God does not forsake his people when friendly foreign kings die or when new foes emerge.

As for genre, the author returns to the basic 'court conflict' plot that marks Daniel 3. In Darius's early days (6:1–2), opponents try to remove Daniel from power through cunning and deadly means. They realize that Daniel's only 'weakness' lies in his adherence to his God (6:3–5), so they trick the new king into passing a law requiring that all supplications go to him, with death as the penalty for disobedience (6:6–9). Readers learn that Daniel is a man of regular prayer. Undeterred by the new law, Daniel prays three times a day as usual (6:10), and his opponents use his piety as a pretence for his execution (6:11–13). The new king finds there is nothing he can do to override the sentence (6:14–18). When morning comes, he discovers God has delivered Daniel from harm (6:19–23), whereupon he sends Daniel's foes to their death (6:24). In response to this miracle, the king praises God in greater measure than his predecessor Nebuchadnezzar had done (6:25–27). Daniel prospers during the new regime (6:28).

Comment
A. New regime, new dangers (6:1–9)

As Daniel 5 indicates, Belshazzar did not utilize Daniel during his rule until the last moment, despite Daniel's usefulness to Nebuchadnezzar. Whatever had caused this animosity apparently carried over into the new era. As noted above, Cyrus and his lieutenants kept the local leadership intact (6:1–2), and 5:29 indicates that this leadership included Daniel serving as third in the kingdom. The other continuing officials wanted him gone, and plotted to use his faith against him, treating the new ruler as a fool in the process (6:3–9). This proves a very poor course of action for them.

1–2. The swiftly gained kingdom required a quickly chosen new government. Olmstead (1948: 56) notes that Babylon was placed in a *satrapy* (broadly speaking, a district of the empire) with Syria, Phoenicia and Palestine, thus making 'one huge satrapy' that 'Gobryas ruled almost as an independent monarch' (see Briant 2002: 44–45). Given its geographical scope, one can easily see why the ruler needed *120 satraps . . . and three high officials* to oversee them *so that the king might suffer no loss*. The list of officers in 6:7 demonstrates that there were various levels of servants within this broad structure. The term *loss* can mean 'anything that would damage the kingdom. See Ezra 4:13, 15, 22' (Lucas 2002: 143). Daniel would be a good choice for one of the three senior positions because of his long service, his position when Babylon fell and his knowledge of Judah and other southern environs.

3–4. Moreover, besides these qualifications, his integrity and capability were obvious. Though the text does not say how, the new ruler could discern *an excellent spirit* in Daniel (6:3). This phrase could simply mean that Daniel had high character. It could also mean that, as in 4:8, 4:18 and 5:12, he had 'the empowerment of God to perform the tasks of office' (Redditt 1999: 105). If so, then, like Bezalel and Oholiab (Exod. 35:30–35), he had God's Spirit within to guide him in his everyday work. The Holy Spirit does not wait until the New Testament to gift workers with his presence, aid and direction. Given God's help, not even his opponents could find any *error or fault* in him related to how he did his work (6:4).

5. So they look elsewhere for a *ground of complaint*, a phrase that can include real or baseless charges (Montgomery 1927: 271). They decide to use Daniel's faithfulness to *the law of his god* against him. The word translated *law* here is the same as in Esther 3:8, where Haman describes the Jews as following different laws from the rest of the king's subjects. It appears that they want to make Daniel look like an enemy of the king. Thus, they seek a way for civil law to conflict with how Daniel follows God's law. Daniel navigated a similar conflict of interest in 1:8–16. In that instance, however, he did not have determined foes out to destroy him.

6–9. The text does not say how many, but some of the *high officials and satraps came by agreement* to see the king (6:6). The phrase translated *by agreement* indicates collusion (Montgomery 1927: 272), separateness from other officials and satraps (Hartman and Di Lella 1978: 294), and giving the appearance of a unified earnest throng (Collins 1993: 265–266). Such actions are timeless tactics in divisive administrative conniving. The conspirators lie without hesitation, telling the king that all the low and high officials, which of course at least excludes Daniel, but probably many others as well, have decided on some counsel for the king (6:7a). This advice has three parts.

First, they suggest *an ordinance that cannot be changed, according to the law of the Medes and Persians* (6:7–8). Esther 1:19 and 8:8 include a similar description of the laws of the Medes and Persians. Like any system of law, this one had flaws that experienced officials knew. Collins (1993: 268) notes helpfully,

> Two factors may have contributed to the belief that Persian laws were immutable: one is the obvious insistence that no subordinate officer could change what was decreed by the king and marked by his seal; the other is that the laws were to be preserved (in some cases by public inscription) so that they should not . . . be lost or go out of effect.

Daniel's enemies want an unchangeable law written down, to guard their desired outcome.

Second, they suggest a temporary law (*thirty days*) that prohibits *petition to any god or man* except the king (6:7). The word translated *petition* can mean 'prayer', but it simply means 'sought' in 2:13, and 'requested' in 2:16. Several scholars rightly note how odd it would have been for a Persian king to sign a document that made him the sole deity (e.g. Hartman and Di Lella 1978: 198; Collins 1993: 267). Darius may have thought they were proposing a symbolic way to secure the kingdom. He may have considered a thirty-day period that stressed his authority a show of good faith by the leaders whom the new regime sought to pacify. In any case, the law would expire soon enough. It was not a law that established long patterns of practice.

Third, they advise a harsh punishment; those who disobey *will be thrown into a pit of lions*. Assyrian and Babylonian kings kept lions to 'hunt' (i.e. slaughter) in royal preserves. Assyrian reliefs in the British Museum in London portray such lions in cages, released from cages and dying with spears in their hindquarters and upper body. Lions may also have been held for other purposes. These lions obviously had to be kept somewhere. Here it appears they stayed in a cistern-shaped pit sealed with a stone (Montgomery 1927: 273). Both the king and the officials seem to know exactly where one could find such beasts. Newsom writes, 'No record exists of such a punishment in the ancient Near East', and adds that earlier Assyrian texts include the metaphor of an individual praying from a lions' pit (Newsom and Breed 2014: 195). Taking these two observations together, perhaps the opponents want to make Daniel a living metaphor. They want him to pray amidst real lions. Given the unique punishment for this short-lived law, perhaps the king may have thought that no-one would violate it.

The king clearly did not know what the counsellors were plotting, and he signs the ordinance quickly (6:9). The whole scene portrays the king being utterly fooled, as he soon realizes. He has misread the advisors, and as the story unfolds, it becomes apparent that they have also misread him.

B. Daniel's faithfulness and the king's anguish (6:10–18)

This section highlights Daniel's calmness and the king's anguish. Daniel offers his petitions to God, as he has always done (6:10–11). His enemies seize their opportunity (6:12–13), and the crestfallen, conscience-stricken king carries out the law (6:14–16a). However, he hopes Daniel's god can deliver him (6:16b), and spends an uncomfortable night waiting for daylight (6:17–18).

10–11. This simple scene conveys one of the Bible's best examples of profound faith. The author makes sure readers follow the time-frame. After an unspecified period of time, when he *knew that the document had been signed*, Daniel went home (6:10). Abstaining from prayer will keep him safe, and in power. He chooses another path, the one he has walked since he came to Babylon. At home, he had *windows in his upper chamber open towards Jerusalem*. He has been exemplifying the portion of Solomon's temple dedication prayer that focuses on exiles praying towards the temple (1 Kgs 8:48). He has been following Psalms 137:5 and 138:1–2, where exiles pledge to remember Jerusalem (137:5), and promise to testify to God in the presence of other gods (138:1–2).

With death hanging over his actions, he does nothing different. He does not close the windows. He *got down on his knees three times a day and prayed* (6:10). Kneeling 'implies intensity, humility, and submission. Daniel prays . . . at dawn, midday, and evening . . . in harmony with Psalm 55:16–17' (Lederach 1994: 133). He does not pray to 'be seen by others' (Matt. 6:5, ESV), but does not fear others seeing him.

His enemies spy on his prayers (6:11), which violates sacred privacy and human decency. Their knowledge of his habits shows the consistency of his prayers. He violates the new law as surely as

Hananiah, Mishael and Azariah disobeyed Nebuchadnezzar's declaration in 3:1–18. While it is possible that he did not know the law targeted him, it is more likely that a veteran wise man like Daniel knew all about the conspiracy. The text does not divulge if he prayed specifically about the situation.

12–13. The conspirators seize their moment. They make sure the king remembers the law (6:12), and then condemn Daniel (6:13). They use the same derogatory (to them) term to describe Daniel that Belshazzar did: *one of the exiles from Judah* (6:13; see 5:13). The trap has sprung; the pit of lions will be opened.

14–15. Or will it? The king sees their malevolence and his own irresponsible gullibility. All day (*until the sun went down*) he *set his mind* [on finding a way] *to deliver him* (6:14). He could not find one, for it may have appeared to him that Daniel's opponents had expertly manipulated the law. Or perhaps he realized that signing this law made him look foolish to Babylon's leaders, and it would make him look weak to his new subjects. Regardless, he felt trapped when the conspirators reminded him of the law (6:15). At the moment he has lost control of his realm.

16–18. He carries out the letter of the law: *Daniel was brought and cast into the pit of lions* (6:16a). The author leaves no doubt that Daniel went to the pit and stayed there, noting that the king sealed the *mouth of the pit* with his own insignia (6:17). Before doing so, he tells Daniel that he hopes his God, whom he *serves continually*, will *deliver* him. Thus, he uses the same word ('deliver') as Nebuchadnezzar does in 3:15, but with none of the animosity that Nebuchadnezzar showed towards Daniel's friends. The text records nothing Daniel may have said. He goes quietly into the pit at the time for evening prayer, and stays there while the king goes home and spends the night without food, entertainment or sleep (6:18). This scene creates suspense, and lets readers know that this king recognizes his mistake.

C. God delivers Daniel (6:19–24)

God's power prevails. The anxious ruler (6:19–20) rises and learns that his hope has been realized. The living God has saved Daniel by sending an angel (6:21–22), so the king releases Daniel (6:23). God has miraculously spared Daniel, as he spared Shadrach, Meshach and Abednego in 3:24–25. Daniel and the king are both off the hook, but the conspirators are not, for they end up dead in Daniel's place (6:24).

19–20. When day breaks, the king hurries to the mouth of the pit (6:19). As *he drew near*, he called out *in a pained voice . . . to Daniel* (6:20a). He asks if *the living God* has *been able to deliver* his committed servant (6:20b). In the Old Testament the term 'the living God' is 'normally in the mouth of an Israelite, often in contexts of tension between Israelite and Gentile powers or idols (e.g. Josh. 3:10; 1 Sam. 17:26; 2 Kgs 19:4, 16; Jer. 10:10)' (Newsom and Breed 2014: 199). Rather than being premature or a sign of editing (see Collins 1993: 270), this question reflects awareness of Jewish claims for their God, and acknowledges these claims are true if Daniel has survived.

21–22a. Daniel's reply conveys respect and comfort: *O king, live for ever* (6:21; see 2:4; 3:9; 5:10). Unlike his opponents, who used the phrase before lying to the king in 6:6, Daniel speaks for his benefit. Daniel testifies, *My God sent his angel and shut the mouth of the lions* (6:22a). God used the same method to deliver Daniel's friends, though this time the ruler did not see the angel (cf. 3:24–25).

22b. Daniel interprets his deliverance in 6:22b. God delivered him because he *was found blameless* before his God (see 1 Macc. 2:60). The word *blameless* does not mean 'sinless throughout his life', as his confession in 9:1–19 proves. Rather, it means he has not wronged God in the matter at hand. Furthermore, he claims that *also before you, O king, I have done no harm* (or *wrong*). He did not break the thirty-day law because of a rebellious spirit or a desire to hurt the king. His obedience to God did not preclude loyal service to his ruler. God has shown Darius who is innocent in this case, and has given him a way to regain control of his realm.

23. Relieved and *extremely glad*, the king releases Daniel. The author now summarizes the whole scene. Using the same word as in 6:22, the text states that *no kind of harm was found in him*. In this instance, the term can mean that he suffered no ill effects physically, or that he was found innocent. In fact, both are the case. He was unscathed and exonerated because *he had been firm* [or *trusted*] *in his God*.

24. Daniel's deliverance continues when the king eliminates the enemies. Using the phrase found in 3:8 to describe the motives of earlier foes, the author calls Daniel's opponents *those men who had maliciously accused Daniel*. Having eaten 'pieces of Daniel', as the phrase more literally reads, the lions will chew on them (see comments on 3:8). Their actions get them and their families killed. The king commands them all to be thrown into the pit, and the lions crush their bones before they reach the bottom. The families were either complicit, or fell victim to the negative side of the ancient world's view of family solidarity (Owens 1971: 417; see Josh. 7:10–26).

D. Darius's decree and Daniel's security (6:25–28)

Darius makes a decree in 6:25–27 that parallels Nebuchadnezzar's in 3:26–29; 4:1–3; and 4:34–37. Like Nebuchadnezzar, he learns from his mistakes (4:34–37), something Belshazzar failed to do (5:17–28). His respect for Daniel's God leads to security for Daniel (6:28), who lives at least until the third year of Cyrus (10:1), before dying at an advanced age.

25–26. Like Nebuchadnezzar in 4:1, Darius writes to *all the peoples, nations and languages that dwell in all the earth* (6:25). The heart of the decree is that *people are to tremble before the God of Daniel* (6:26). This instruction exceeds Nebuchadnezzar's declaration that no-one may speak against God (3:26–29). As Goldingay writes, this edict means 'Daniel's God is not merely to be tolerated but to be worshiped with reverence and awe' (1989: 135).

Darius also adds three affirmations to Nebuchadnezzar's confession that God's kingdom is everlasting (4:3, 34). First, he calls Daniel's God *the living God*, the God who acts in history on behalf of his people. Daniel's deliverance has proven this to him (see comments on 6:16b and 6:20). Second, he confesses that God's *kingdom will not be destroyed*, thus linking God's kingdom to the one described in 2:44. Third, he affirms God's *dominion will be to the last*. When all else has gone, God and his kingdom will remain.

27. He concludes with claims Nebuchadnezzar made. God *delivers and rescues* (see 3:26–29). God does *signs and wonders* (see 4:2–3). This is the nature and power of the God who *delivered Daniel from the power of the lions*. He does what he has done in the past, and does greater deeds as history requires them.

28. In short, the same God who made Daniel prosper during old regimes does so during new ones. God has guided and protected Daniel for over six decades. The final phrase can be translated as *during the reign of Darius and the reign of Cyrus the Persian*, or as *during the reign of Darius, that is, of Cyrus the Persian*. In short, the words may refer to two persons, or to one with two titles (see above). Wiseman (1965: 12−16) cites 1 Chronicles 5:26 as a parallel passage that has two names for the same ruler joined by a conjunction that does not mean 'and', but 'even', or 'that is'. This verse, like 5:31; 6:1; 9:1; and 11:1, demonstrates the author's commitment to handing on the best accurate information available.

Meaning

Daniel 6 completes the book's narrative section, having thoroughly introduced the setting, visions, interpretations and prayers in Daniel 7 − 12. Readers have been taught to understand exile historically, theologically and imaginatively. They have learned that exile will not end quickly (see 1:1−2, 21; 2:24−45; 6:28).

Thus, exiles must learn to trust and serve God (1:8−16; 2:17−19; 3:16−18; 6:16−23) amid personal and community peril (1:8−16; 2:13−19; 3:8−23; 6:10−23). They must learn great wisdom (1:8−16; 2:13−16; 4:19−27; 5:13−28; 6:21−22) through consistent devotion (1:8−16; 2:17−19; 3:16−18; 6:10−11), divine enablement (1:9, 17; 2:19; 3:24−25; 4:8, 18, 19−27; 5:13−28; 6:3) and readiness to praise the God who rules, protects and saves (1:1−2; 2:20−23; 3:26−29; 4:1−3, 34−37; 6:25−27). Their witness will have a positive impact on some people outside their faith (2:46−49; 3:26−29; 4:1−3, 34−37; 6:25−27), though not on others (3:8−12; 5:1−30; 6:3−9). Regardless, all peoples are welcome in God's kingdom.

The future belongs to their God, and thus to those who trust him (2:24−45; 6:25−27). Visions that stagger the minds of their recipients indicate God's sovereignty. They show his power to use symbols to open the minds of persons focused on this world in the wrong ways (2:1−45; 4:4−33; 5:1−12). The faithful life has many dangers, but it is the life worth living, whatever happens as a result (3:16−19). God's kingdom is rising (2:44), however slowly, and however hard world leaders try to make themselves the centre of the universe (4:30).

7. THE ANCIENT OF DAYS AND THE SON OF MAN (7:1–28)

Daniel 7 begins with familiar characters, but soon opens to new vistas. Readers discover that Daniel did not just interpret dreams and visions. He had visions of his own, which the book describes in chronological order in Daniel 7 – 12. Since this chapter closes the book's Aramaic section and begins the vision sequence, it provides a bridge to God's continued work with Daniel, other faithful persons and humanity as a whole. This chapter includes two of the Bible's most vivid characters: the Ancient of Days and the Son of Man. Humanity's future depends on a right relationship with these two, for only God's 'holy ones', the ones 'set apart for his service', have a place in his permanent kingdom.

Context

Daniel receives this vision in Belshazzar's first year (7:1). As noted above (see the commentary's Introduction and comments on 5:1), the date is most likely 550–549 BC. This was a momentous year in two respects. First, Nabonidus gave rule over Babylon to his co-regent, Belshazzar. Second, Cyrus defeated the Medes, thus forming the kingdom of the Medes and Persians. Change is in the air.

The chapter has a clear structure. In 7:1–14 Daniel reports a multifaceted vision that features four beasts (rulers with kingdoms) rising from the sea (7:1–8), and the Ancient of Days and the Son of Man, the world's true co-regents (7:9–14), ruling in the clouds. In 7:15–28 Daniel receives authoritative information about the four beasts (7:15–18), the special nature of the fourth one (7:19–25) and God's final victory on his people's behalf (7:26–27). This experience staggers Daniel (7:28), even though Daniel 1 – 6 has shown his strength.

Comment
A. Four beasts from the sea (7:1–8)

In this transition year, Daniel has night visions (7:1), much as Nebuchadnezzar did in 2:1 and 4:5. Winds stir the sea (7:2), and four beasts with various qualities emerge, with the fourth having particularly disturbing features (7:3–8). These beasts represent twisted human rulers and their realms. Efforts to use these beasts as guides to the end times have always run into serious difficulties (see the excellent survey of attempts to do so in Owens 1971: 421–423; see also Goldingay 1989: 179–180). As the comments on 2:24–45 demonstrate, the four-nation scheme is a flexible format by design.

1. In *the first year of King Belshazzar*, the veteran wise man *Daniel saw a dream and visions of his head as he lay in bed*. This phrase comes from a narrator, not from Daniel, since it describes him in third-person terms. This narrator writes that *Daniel wrote down the dream, and the sum* [or *beginning*, see BDB 1112] *of the matter*, and then reports Daniel's first-person description of his experience. Therefore, the author indicates possession of a document that recounts what Daniel wrote. The phrase is so evident that any later editor seeking to make the passage appear to come from Daniel would probably not have included it.

2–3. As 2:24–45 has shown, the number four has special importance to Daniel. The author uses it numerous times in various ways (see comments on 2:39–45). Here, Daniel dreams of *the four winds of heaven*, in other words, winds coming from every direction. They are *stirring the great sea*, the Mediterranean, the centre of shipping, trade, wealth, power and politics in Daniel's day. From these troubled waters come *four huge beasts*, representing kings twisted into un-natural shapes, as Nebuchadnezzar experienced in 4:31–33. Lucas (2002: 167–176) notes that several ancient nations had literature that featured such beasts, so Daniel's author participates in that general symbolic environment (also see Collins 1993: 280–294). Lucas observes that Hosea 13:7–8 and other biblical texts include aspects of at least three of these beasts, which demonstrates that this passage uses well-known symbols (2002: 171–172).

4. The first beast resembled a *lion*, and had *eagles' wings*. Lions and eagles are fierce predators. An eagle has more range than a lion because it can fly. Thus, a flying lion would be a terrifying prospect, so perhaps one could take comfort in the beast having *its wings . . . plucked off*. However, it is not so comforting that the beast can *stand on two feet like a man*, and that he receives *the mind of a man*. Now the predator has been disguised, but is still a predator.

5–6. The second beast is *like a bear* that has already eaten enough to have *three ribs in its mouth*, and is then told to go *devour more flesh* (7:5). This predator has no disguise, but has a mandate to kill. The third beast is also predatory. Speed is its great virtue. It is swift *like a leopard*, and also has *four wings of a bird on its back* (7:6). It has great vision, for it has *four heads*. With more speed and vision than the bear, this beast captures ample territory (*dominion*).

7. Frightening as the first three have been, they do not match the fourth beast. As is standard in the ancient lists of four kingdoms (see comments on 2:39–45), the fourth is the strongest. The first three beasts' characteristics thereby highlight how *terrifying and surpassingly strong* their successor looks. Worse than all the rest, it has *large teeth of iron*, so it can chew up its prey and step on *what remains with its feet*. It has more strength, more ways to destroy and greater longevity than the others, for it has *ten horns*, with *horns* symbolizing power, and *ten* symbolizing fullness (Goldingay 1989: 164).

8. As is usually the case in fierce, predatory nations, a division occurs. A *little horn* grows, uprooting three existing horns in the process. It supplants other leaders, as is almost always the case in political manoeuvring. For example, Nabonidus displaced Labashi-Marduk to take control of Babylon in 556 BC, thereby

becoming the fourth king to rule after Nebuchadnezzar. This horn
has *the eyes of a man*, so it has great vision, like the beast in 7:6, yet
specific vision that aids predatory human rulers.

Finally, the horn has a *mouth speaking huge* [see 7:3] *things*. In 7:25
this beast speaks against the 'Most High' God. Later, 'Arrogant
speech is again emphasized in Dan 11:36. Compare the behaviour
of Sennacherib in Isa. 37:23 and, for the motif in general, Ps. 12:3;
Obadiah 12' (Collins 1993: 299). Daniel 4:30 and 5:1–12 have already
stressed the dangerous nature of exalting self over God. Belshazzar
spoke like a 'little horn' trying to be a 'big horn' (better than
Nebuchadnezzar) in 5:1–4. The results were dire for him and his
people.

B. The Ancient of Days and the Son of Man: earth's true co-regents (7:9–14)

The next scene is wonderful, contrasting perfectly with the preceding one. A permanent and pure ruler replaces the twisted beasts
(7:9–10). He judges the mouthy little horn (7:11–12), and gives a
kingdom that will never pass away to a humble co-regent. Unlike all
co-regents and sub-regents in human history, this one rules for ever
(7:13–14; see 7:11–12).

9. Another scene grabs Daniel's attention, though 7:11–12
indicates that he can still view the four beasts. He sees a courtroom,
where *thrones were placed*. Only one takes a seat (7:9), so he is the
supreme judge (Owens 1971: 423). His name is *the Ancient of Days*,
the deity the book has identified as the everlasting God (4:1–3,
34–37; 6:25–27), the God who changes seasons and rulers as he
wills (2:21; 4:4–37; 5:24–28). His white clothing and hair represent
purity and longevity, respectively. He sits on a throne of flames that
has wheels of flame. These flames represent the purity of the king's
governing (Gowan 2001: 107). The wheels represent the kingdom's
far-reaching authority (Owens 1971: 424).

10. Millions serve him, and even more stand before him to
receive his verdicts. As Daniel watched, *the court settled, and the books
were opened*. The 'Most High' God, who weighs kingdoms (5:24–28)
and dispenses them according to his wisdom (4:4–37), has convened
the heavenly court.

11. The verse begins with a reference to timing that is very difficult to translate. Daniel says that he had been looking intently at the throne room scene either since he heard the fourth beast speaking (7:8), when he heard the beast resume speaking (7:11), or while the beast spoke without ever stopping (see the discussion in Montgomery 1927: 301). Though all are possible, the major verb in 7:8 is a participle (*speaking*), so the little horn's big talk probably never stops while Daniel looks at the throne room. It chatters in the background, never stopping *until the beast was killed and its body destroyed and given over to be burned with fire*. Holy fire flicks out from the throne like a lizard's tongue, consuming his corrupt body, mouth and all. Still, the little horn brags on for an unspecified amount of time. God does not silence him immediately.

12. The noisy blasphemous beast makes his charred exit, but the other beasts continue for a while (*their lives were prolonged for a season and a time*), though they lose their *dominions*. History does not stop. Since the little horn and the other beasts survive, they represent types of kingdoms, not necessarily specific ones at a particular point in time. As the book proceeds, there will be more like them.

13. The stage has been cleared for a new figure. Instead of seeing something from a troubled sea, Daniel views *one like a son of man* coming *with the clouds of heaven*. Though like Daniel, then, he is still different. He is at home in the heavenly courtroom, and is also fit to live among human beings. Since cloud imagery often depicts God (Exod. 19:9; 34:5; Num. 11:25; Lucas 2002: 184),[1] this individual has high status, and will receive higher still. Unlike the brash little horn, this person is humble. He waits *to be presented* to the Ancient of Days.

14. At first, it appears that the Ancient of Days grants him the same *dominion and glory and kingdom* that God 'Most High' gave Nebuchadnezzar (4:1–3) and Darius (6:25): *all peoples, nations and languages*. This was indeed a great gift bestowed on magnificently favoured rulers. The second half of the verse, however, reveals that God's gift to him exceeds the ones given to those significant

---

1. See also Exod. 14:19–20; 16:10; 24:16, 18; 1 Kgs 8:10–11; Job 22:14; Ps. 18:11; Isa. 19:1; Jer. 4:13; Lam. 3:44; Ezek. 1:4; and Nah. 1:3.

monarchs. Unlike their temporary reigns and vulnerable realms, *his dominion is an everlasting dominion which will not pass away, and his kingdom one that will not be destroyed*. In short, he receives the kingdom 2:44 describes. Furthermore, he must be everlasting to rule for this length of time, so he has attributes and prerogatives that God 'Most High' possesses in 4:1–3; 4:34–37; and 6:25–27. Nabonidus and Belshazzar had a significant co-regency, but theirs pales in comparison to the one the Ancient of Days and Son of Man share.

Who is this 'one like a son of man'?[2] The phrase can refer generally to a member of humanity (Job 25:6), or specifically to a particular person within humanity (Ezek. 37:11; Dan. 8:17). Context determines the person's identity by divulging his role. Here, this character is 'like a son of man', which indicates that he resembles a human being, whereas the four rulers in 7:1–8 resemble malformed animals (Baldwin 1978: 142–143). Also like the beasts, the 'one like a son of man' has a kingdom that spans the nations, yet theirs is temporary, and his is permanent.

Though 7:14 does not mention David, the Davidic messiah is the only one to whom God gives the world's kingdoms permanently in the Old Testament (see 2 Sam. 7; Pss 2; 110; Isa. 11:1–9, etc.). No angel receives this honour.[3] Gerhard von Rad correctly asserts that only a messianic figure fits this description (1965: 312). Walter Kaiser (1978: 246) states that the Son of Man combines 'the high calling of humanity and the position reserved alone for God'. This interpretation connects the Son of Man's heavenly and human aspects, and fits the vision's interpretation in 7:15–27.

C. The vision's interpretation and Daniel's reaction (7:15–28)

Like Nebuchadnezzar (2:1–16, 26; 4:4–18) and Belshazzar (5:6–16) before him, Daniel needs help understanding what he has seen. He

---

2. For short discussions of the history of interpretation, see Collins 1993: 304–310; Baldwin 1978: 148–154; and Lucas 2002: 185–187. For comprehensive studies of the concept, see Casey 2007 and Casey 1979.

3. Contra Newsom, who, following earlier scholars, suggests that an angelic being receives the kingdom (Newsom and Breed 2014: 236).

asks someone standing nearby for assistance, and the individual obliges (7:15–18). Still fascinated by the fourth beast, Daniel requests more information (7:19–20), and then notices the horn battle against God's faithful ones (7:21–22). The interpreter starts from the beginning, and explains the whole vision and its importance for understanding the future (7:23–27). The experience leaves Daniel shaken (7:28).

15. Though Daniel has a reputation as a great dream interpreter (see 2:47; 4:8–9; 5:10–12), he knows his insights come from God's 'spirit' (2:20–23, 47; 4:8–9, 18; 5:12, 14). Therefore, when his *spirit* becomes *anxious*, he seeks God's help.

16–18. Needing assistance, then, he *drew near to one standing there*, one of the multitude in the court (7:16a). A request for help often occurs in heavenly visions (see Zech. 1:9, 14, 19), and in subsequent literature 'becomes a distinctive feature of apocalyptic visions' (Collins 1993: 311). Daniel talks with more interpreters as the book proceeds, and they provide varying amounts of information (cf. 12:9–13).

This interpreter happily obliges (7:16b). First, he appears to state the obvious: *these four huge beasts are four kings* (7:17a). Obviously, kings have kingdoms (see 7:23). Daniel knew the four-kingdom scheme from 2:24–45, and most likely from earlier historical sources. As the comments on 2:24–45 indicated, this scheme depends on the identity of the first and fourth kingdoms, since this is a periodization device one can adapt to continuing history. The nature of this symbolic scheme allows it to be adjusted as time passes, and fifty years have passed since Nebuchadnezzar's statue dream. Collins writes, 'There is general agreement that the kings in question correspond to the four kingdoms of chap. 2, which are identified in modern scholarship as Babylonian, Median, Persian, and Greek. The prevailing traditional interpretation identified the fourth kingdom as Rome' (1993: 312). Good cases have been made for both interpretations, since the first and fourth kingdoms can be fluid. However, Daniel 2 and 7 do not identify four nations, in contrast to chapter 8.

Second, Daniel's helper says these kingdoms *will arise* (7:17b), which means the four kings and kingdoms are not the same as in 2:24–44. Charles finds the Aramaic text's future orientation 'incongruous' with 2:24–45, so he argues that the Septuagint reading, 'will be destroyed', is superior to the Masoretic Text reading, 'will arise' (1929: 189–191). Few scholars have followed his suggestion, partly because few sense the problem with the future-oriented timing of all four rising kingdoms. Nonetheless, he has a valid concern. Therefore, it is important to recall the context. Taking 7:1 as a valid setting, readers should note that in 'the first year of Belshazzar', the Babylonian Empire was declining, yet intact, and Persia had taken over the Medes. Greece was a foe worth fearing and fighting. A worse threat to God's people loomed. The author is already treating Babylon as a spent force.

Third, the interpreter states the most important point in all Daniel's fourfold lists: who or what comes *after* the fourth kingdom is the most dangerous. The *holy ones of the 'Most High' will receive* [see 2:6; 6:1] *the kingdom and possess the kingdom for ever.* This declaration coincides with 2:44, regardless of the identity of any set of four kingdoms. God's kingdom always prevails.

Lucas (2002: 191) writes that in the Old Testament God's 'holy ones', individuals 'set apart for his service', can refer to heavenly beings (4:13, 17, 23), angels (Wis. 5:5; 10:10) or human beings (Ps. 34:9; Wis. 18:9). Newsom notes that several Qumran texts use the term to describe angels (Newsom and Breed 2014: 237). As always, the book's context within the whole of the Old Testament must decide. Daniel, a human being in exile, receives this vision. These *holy ones* will suffer persecution before they receive the kingdom (7:25). They will not triumph until the Ancient of Days comes (7:22, 26–27). Consequently, it seems likely that the *holy ones* are God's people, the ones he declared 'holy' in Exodus 19:5–6 (see Hartman and Di Lella 1978: 91; Casey 2007: 83; and Casey 1979: 40–48).

19–22. In 2:31–35 Nebuchadnezzar probably wanted to know if his kingdom was the fourth, the one falling. If so, he was relieved to learn that his was the first kingdom, not the last (see 2:36–49). Daniel also has an interest in the fourth kingdom. Thus, he asks about the fourth beast, repeating the description in 7:7–8, with one addition: *claws of bronze* (7:19–20).

While he keeps looking at the scene, *this horn engaged in war with the 'holy ones', and prevailed against them* (7:21). Given 7:11–12, the little horn is not like Nebuchadnezzar, to whom God gave Judah (1:1–2) due to their covenant breaking (see 9:1–19). Rather, he is a blasphemer like Belshazzar (see 5:1–4). He opposes God's people like the men in 3:8–12 and 6:3–9, and like Belshazzar (5:1–4, 10–12), yet with more power.

This development is hardly surprising. Daniel and the other Babylonian exiles certainly suffered. Mordecai and Esther faced death in Persia. God's 'holy ones' in Judea suffered terribly under Antiochus IV (175–164 BC), and under Roman rule before, during and after the destruction of Jerusalem and the temple in AD 66–70. God's people have suffered multiple times since, and many of them live in real danger now. Other oppressors have taken the place of Greece and Rome.

Daniel sees a comforting sight in 7:22. After an unspecified time, the Ancient of Days *came, and judgment was given for the 'holy ones' of the 'Most High', and the 'holy ones' received the kingdom.* This verse confirms what 7:1–12 and 7:18 have declared: the *holy ones* will receive what the Ancient of Days presents to the one 'like a son of man' in 7:13–14. Given this promise, Casey (2007: 85, 114–115) argues that 'the holy ones' are the 'son of man'. To his great credit, Casey strives to determine this issue and others related to the son of man concept through linguistic-contextual-historical means. Given the context, however, the 'son of man' and 'holy ones' are separable characters as the text proceeds, but inseparable in what the Ancient of Days gives them. Just as Babylon received Judah when God gave Judah to Nebuchadnezzar, so the holy ones receive God's kingdom when God gives it to the son of man.

23–27. The interpreter repeats with slight variations what the passage has already divulged. Thus, he confirms the accuracy of Daniel's description of the vision. A fourth kingdom will arise. It will be different from the other three kingdoms 7:1–6 describes. It will be more extensive and more destructive (7:23; see 7:7–8). Ten kings, a general number that signifies completion (7:24a; see 7:7), will rise from it. Then another monarch will take power, displacing *three kings* in the process (7:24b; see 7:8). He will fight successfully against the 'holy ones' for *a time, times, and half a time* (see 7:21; 4:32), an unspecified amount of time. His tactics will include altering *the times and the law*, which refers to how and when worship occurs (7:25). This attempt also figures in 8:9–14, 23–26. Finally, the heavenly court will condemn and execute this enemy (7:26; see 7:11−12, 22). It is worth recalling that when the fourth kingdom falls, the other three will still exist (7:12). Sometime after this creature falls, God's 'holy ones' will receive an everlasting universal kingdom that *all dominions will serve* (7:27; see 7:11−14, 21−22). Though the interpreter confirms what Daniel saw, he does not reveal more, as most readers would like him to do.

28. Daniel confesses that he still does not understand all the vision could mean for himself or for others. Nonetheless, he *kept the matter in* his *heart*. He did not just forget about it. He wrote it down and kept a copy (see 7:1). Having recounted what he saw, and had it confirmed, he can do nothing more except wait.

Meaning

This tremendous passage has inspired hundreds of books, articles, sermons, lectures and media presentations. It has been treated both honourably and unethically, as most symbol-heavy biblical passages have been. Many interpreters have heard good and bad readings of this passage. Thus, one ought to be cautious and humble when drawing conclusions from it.

First, this passage does not specifically name the nations in the four-kingdom scheme it utilizes. Daniel 2:24−45 explicitly begins with Babylon, and ends with God's kingdom rising as the successor to the fourth kingdom. Daniel 7:9−27 also makes God's kingdom the final one. It promises persecution for God's people before that victory, without stating all the specific aspects or timing of that suffering. It leaves previous kingdoms existing even after God removes the little horn (7:12), so it does not equate his death (7:21, 25) with the final judgment day. Therefore, the passage warns Daniel that many hard days remain for God's people. They must persevere, knowing God's kingdom will belong to them. Jesus teaches his followers the same principle. He tells them the Son of Man will come after Jerusalem and the temple have been destroyed, and after much persecution (see Luke 21:1−28 and the comments on Dan. 9:24−27 below). His disciples will therefore need watchful perseverance (Luke 21:29−36).

Second, the New Testament includes several passages that link Jesus' life and ministry to 7:13−14. Maurice Casey has produced a masterful historical summary and personal analysis of the history of interpretation of the term 'son of man'. He quite rightly demonstrates that not every New Testament passage that uses the phrase 'son of man' refers to 7:13–14 or links Jesus with the heavenly figure in 7:13–14 (2007: 318). As I stated above, however, I do not think he is right to equate the 'son of man' in 7:13–14 with 'the holy ones' in 7:18–27. Thus, I do not believe Mark 13:26 and 14:62 are reinterpreting 7:13–14. Rather, both passages connect Jesus the Messiah with the messianic figure in 7:13–14. They assert that Jesus the Messiah is the Son of Man, who comes to give his life for many, to whom the Ancient of Days gives the world's kingdoms. This is how Jesus identifies himself in Mark 10:45; 14:62; Luke 22:69–70; and John 3:13–15. This is also the way in which the Jewish leaders understood his statements. Jesus used the whole Old Testament to interpret the role of the Son of Man without bypassing the original context of Daniel 7:9–14, and it is important to follow his example.

Third, it is wise for every generation of believers to examine the nature of rulers and their kingdoms, as Daniel has in the book's first seven chapters. In particular, believers should see that when rulers devour, break down, persecute and oppress anyone, believers or otherwise, they become twisted human beings. Nebuchadnezzar discovers this principle in Daniel 4. Belshazzar and the beasts in 7:1–8 do not. They remind readers that regimes are often brutal. The little horn reminds readers that oppressive regimes may oppose God, and often kill his people. Shadrach, Meshach and Abednego recognized this possibility in 3:16–18. Nonetheless, God's kingdom continues to rise.

8. A RAM, A GOAT, A HORN AND A TEMPLE (8:1–27)

Two years pass between visions, and the book reverts to Hebrew. Unlike the transition from Hebrew to Aramaic in 2:4, the author gives no reason for doing so. Nonetheless, readers may sense they are being prompted to expect that something important will follow. Daniel 8 takes readers to where ageing Daniel's mind increasingly goes while he lives on and on in exile – back home, to Judah. Back to its language, back to its temple, back to its people and back to its future. But to make this mindful journey, Daniel must envision another foreign place, one outside Babylon. He must also never lose sight of the importance of God's rule of the whole world while he thinks more about his roots. His next vision combines these interests. It portrays a ram, a goat, the dreaded little horn from chapter 7, the temple's sacrifices and a new version of the four-kingdom pattern found in chapters 2 and 7. As before, God's kingdom will rise, yet only amid much travail for God's people.

Context

The stated setting places the vision near the time of significant battles that took place between Cyrus's armies and Greek forces in *c.* 547–546 BC (see the introductory material on Dan. 6). Cyrus prevailed. This vision reveals that such will not always be the case. The day is coming when these roles will be reversed. Some day a great king will lead Greece to overcome and rule the Medes and Persians. History reveals this man as Alexander the Great (*c.* 356–323 BC), who ruled Greece from 336 to 323 BC. The vision then traces what occurs after his time down to the little horn's era, before noting that other kingdoms will follow. Time will march on, always under God's authority.

Like Daniel 7, this chapter's vision has a simple structure with some difficult internal parts. Repetition helps readers maintain focus as the passage's symbols stimulate their imaginations. Daniel 8:1 introduces the vision, Daniel 8:2–14 reports it, Daniel 8:15–26 interprets it and Daniel 8:27 describes Daniel's reaction to it. Welcome and unwelcome characters from previous chapters appear alongside new ones, thereby providing unity within the chapter and book.

Comment

A. A ram, a goat and a temple: Daniel's vision (8:1–14)

Having prepared readers by describing four kingdoms twice (2:24–45 and 7:1–27), this vision begins with only two kingdoms, the ones following Babylon. Daniel's second vision (8:1; see 7:1) opens with a mighty two-horned ram, the king of the sheep, who does as he pleases (8:2–4). Eventually, a speedy one-horned goat blasts the ram, breaks his horns and tramples him (8:5–7). Later, the goat's horn breaks (8:8). Four horns form, one of them the little horn introduced in the previous chapter that harms God's people (8:9–14; see 7:23–27).

1. Daniel speaks throughout the chapter. There is no third-person voice as in 7:1. Daniel probably wrote down this vision in response to the command in 8:26. Daniel's previous vision (7:1–27) left him 'greatly alarmed' and with his 'colour changed' (7:28). In short, it left him in the same condition as Belshazzar after he saw

the writing on the wall (5:6, 10). Thus, he is not seeking more visions. Nonetheless, one assaults him in *the third year of the reign of King Belshazzar*, a year when Cyrus successfully battled against Greece (see above).

2-4. These verses reveal a place (8:2), an important person (8:3) and that person's activities (8:4). In *the vision*, not in his body (Miller 1994: 220–221), Daniel goes to *Susa the citadel, which was in the province of Elam*. More specifically, he had a vision of being *at the Ulai canal*.

Susa already had an ancient and glorious history in Daniel's time. It was one of the central cities of the Elamite kingdom, which was located between Babylon and Assyria. Elam was a strong supporter of Babylon during the Assyrian era (see Isa. 21:2; Vallat 1992: 427). By 547 BC, Elam and Susa had fallen on hard times. Assyria destroyed Susa in *c.* 646–640 BC, but the city was rebuilt *c.* 625 BC in the waning years of the Assyrian Empire (de Miroschedji 1992: 243). Cyrus conquered Susa shortly before he captured Babylon (ibid.). Under Darius the Great (*c.* 521–485 BC), the city became 'the main capital of the [Persian] empire' (ibid.). Esther 1:2 and Nehemiah 1:1 reflect Susa's later prominence. The *Ulai canal* was 'a huge artificial channel canal (classical Eulaeus), which ran near Susa' (Owens 1971: 430). Susa was a *citadel*, a secure place that stored military materials.

Daniel sees a magnificent *ram standing on the bank of the canal* (8:3). The word translated *ram* can also mean 'leader', and this ram clearly rules his own territory. He has two horns, one higher than the other, with the higher one having grown last. He does not stand for long, for he is anxious to run and butt. He charges *westward and northward and southward* with complete success: *no-one could stand before him, and there was no-one who could deliver from his power, so he did as he pleased, and made himself great* (8:4). One imagines a strong, contented, self-satisfied animal. Such beasts are glorious in their own way.

5. Such beasts are also temporary, however strong during the days of their full vigour. A challenger always arises, as happens here. A *male goat* so speedy that his feet are not *touching the ground* comes *from the west*. He has only one horn, but it is *between his eyes*, in a perfect position to bring down the two-horned ram.

6-7. The two collide. The goat *ran at him in the strength of his wrath* (8:7). This time the ram falls, powerless to stand. He has no deliverer

(8:7; see 8:4), and the goat *trampled on him*. What the ram has done to others has been done to him.

8. Exceeding his predecessor, *the goat made himself very great* (see 8:4). But the vision does not tarry long with this interesting character. When *he was strong, the great horn was broken, and four conspicuous* [lit. *visions of*] *horns came up*. These four horns cover the whole territory that *the great horn* had captured, which included wherever *the four winds of the heavens* blew (see 7:2).

9. An old enemy reappears. From one of these four horns grows the little horn introduced in 7:8; 7:11–12; and 7:19–27. Thus, the visions have important overlapping material. The word translated *great* (see 8:8) appears often in 8:9–11 to indicate the creature's rise in power. The [*most*] *glorious land* is the land of promise, the place God gave to Israel as their home, the home that flows with milk and honey (see Jer. 3:19; Ezek. 20:6, 15; Dan. 11:16, 41). As in 7:7–27, the little horn will threaten God's people.

10. Continuing the enlargement theme, the 'little horn' *became great*, as the ram and goat had (8:4, 8). His growth reveals that his desires are different from theirs (see 7:7–8, 21–22). He expands upwards, towards God, *unto the hosts of heaven*. In the Bible this imagery can depict human armies, armies of angels, stars and planets, or idols, depending on context (Ryken et al. 1998: 372–373). In the rest of this chapter the author uses most of these meanings to construct a connected play on words.

The little horn grows upwards towards the stars, just as he has spread outwards in various lands (8:10a). He gains strange new victories. The horn *made fall to the ground some from the hosts and some from the stars, and trampled on them* (8:10b). He will triumph over his opponents in the same way as the goat did (8:7). Who, or what, does he defeat? Scholars have puzzled over these metaphors for centuries, sometimes offering extremely complex options,[1] but a simple approach works here. The word translated *hosts* means 'armies', and the word translated *stars* can refer to deities. Thus, the little horn will

---

1. For a survey of options, including some that focus on proposed mythological backgrounds, consult Montgomery 1927: 333–335; Collins 1993: 331–333; and Lucas 2002: 215–216.

defeat some armies (*hosts*) fighting for God, and some fighting for
other gods (*the stars*). These human armies represent the cosmic
forces they believe support them. What is most important to Daniel
is that these defeated armies include some of God's people, the
'holy ones' in 7:21–22, 25.

11. The horn grows greater still, making readers glad that they
have already read of his demise in 7:11–12 and 23–27. He becomes
as *great as the prince of the host*, the person in charge of fighting
figuratively or literally for God. The little horn defeats him, and
takes control of the *regular burnt offering*, the morning and evening
sacrifices (Exod. 29:42; Num. 28:3, 10; Lucas 2002: 216), and *the place
of his* [lit. the 'prince of the host'] *sanctuary*. The little horn will
control the temple and its sacrifices by defeating the high priest
(*prince*) in charge of those offerings.

12. Those figuratively or literally fighting for God's sacrifices
alongside the 'prince of the host' will fall with their leader: *a host*
[army] *will be given along with the regular burnt offering*, as 7:25 has already
divulged (Collins 1993: 334–335). Standing for God will not protect
the people then. The horn's motives, methods and means amount
to *transgression*. God's people can suffer for their own transgressions,
as 1:1–2 has shown, but here the text does not reveal why God lets
the little horn afflict them (contra Baldwin 1978: 158). The little
horn will *throw truth to the ground*, because it is his enemy (cf. 8:7). For
a while, whatever he does succeeds.

13. Verses 11–12 present a very dark scene of evil triumphing. It
comes as a relief, then, for Daniel to hear *a holy one speaking*, and for
a second *holy one* to ask *how long* this suffering will last. The holy ones
here could be God's people, as in 7:9–27, but are more likely angelic
beings (see 4:13–33), since 8:14 reveals that one of them knows the
suffering's duration. The questioner repeats the woes the little horn
causes. The *regular burnt offering* will cease, but for *how long*? The
transgression – the motives, methods and means the horn uses – will
make the temple *desolate*, unable to fulfil its proper function. But for
how long? How long will the little horn trample the sanctuary?

14. The answer is enigmatic: *2,300 evenings and mornings*. The days
constitute either a little over three years if each separate instance of
'evening and morning' equals one day (1,150 days), or just over six
years if the phrase refers to both morning and evening sacrifices in

one day (2,300 days). Either way, this will be too long for those suffering through the trampling, but the little horn does not defeat God's followers permanently. Like the number in 7:25, this number symbolizes a reasonably brief period, not an exact number.

B. Gabriel's interpretation and Daniel's reaction (8:15–27)

With the vision's imagery in mind, the interpretation makes better sense. This passage names an angel for the first time in the Bible. As Daniel tries to work out the vision's meaning (8:15), God sends Gabriel to help him (8:16). Gabriel comforts Daniel with the news that these things are not going to happen soon (8:17). He quickly identifies the ram, goat and horn (8:18–24). He then promises that the horn will not triumph (8:25–26), thereby echoing 7:23–27. Daniel has a hard time recovering from what he has seen (8:27).

15–17. Daniel had earned a reputation for understanding hard dreams and visions (1:17; 2:24–45; 4:18–27; 5:13–28). Yet for a second time (see 7:16) he needs interpretive help (8:15a). While he *sought to understand* the vision, he saw *one in the likeness of* [see 7:13] *a mighty man* (8:15b), a soldier. Using a different word for *man* in 8:16 from 'mighty man' in 8:15, *a man's voice . . . called and said, 'Gabriel, make this man understand the revelation'* (lit. *appearance*; see 8:15). This is a playful voice, or at least a friendly one. *Gabriel* means 'mighty man of God' (see 8:15), so the voice orders the mighty man to teach Daniel, who is just a man (8:17), though a fine one. The voice that commands the *mighty man of God* belongs to God himself (Lucas: 2002: 219).

Gabriel's appearance causes Daniel to fall on his face, which Collins (1993: 337) notes is the normal reaction to such visitations in the Bible (see Josh. 5:14; Ezek. 1:28; 3:23; Rev. 1:17). Gabriel gives Daniel the news that *the vision is for the time of the end* (8:17). In the New Testament Gabriel appears to give news to Zechariah, John the Baptist's father (Luke 1:19), and Mary, Jesus' mother (Luke 1:26). In context, the phrase *time of the end* does not refer to 'the end of time'. Rather, it signifies 'the end of the time of persecution of the Jews and the desecration of the temple' (Owens 1971: 433; Miller 1994: 232). Daniel will not live to see these days, but he still cares about what will happen to his people.

18–19. Daniel has stood before kings and high officials and never wavered. In Gabriel's presence, however, he loses consciousness (8:18), as Abraham does in Genesis 15:12. Gabriel revives him, as an angel does for John in Revelation 1:17 (Collins 1993: 338). Gabriel revives Daniel (8:18) to *make known* to him *what will be in the later days of the wrath, for it pertains to the appointed time of the end* (8:19). As in 2:28, *later days*, which here means days after Daniel's, is a better translation than 'latter days', since 'latter days' now almost solely means 'the days of the end of time' to most readers (see Goldingay 1989: 215). Baldwin (1978: 159) writes that the term 'the wrath' refers to 'the sentence of God which must eventually fall on those who rebel against Him and fail to repent. His own people are not exempt (Isa. 10:5–11), but neither are the nations (Jer. 10:10).' In context, this 'wrath' is the little horn's trampling of the temple. Montgomery (1927: 347) notes that God's wrath falls on Israel because of their sins against him, and falls on Israel's foes because they have 'taken advantage of her bitter discipline'. As in 7:25–27, *appointed time of the end* refers to the little horn's end, and to the end of anyone who takes advantage of God's people. God's kingdom will rise for his holy ones. As it does, they persevere in faithful obedience.

20–22. Gabriel does not waste words. He presents his interpretation in an orderly manner, and leaves no time for questions. First, *the kings of Media and Persia* are the two horns of the *ram* in 8:1–7 (8:20). By 550 BC, Cyrus ruled those lands. Second, *the goat is the king of Greece.* More specifically, the *horn between his eyes is the first king* (8:21). By *first*, Gabriel means the first to vanquish Persia. Alexander the Great captured Persia, including Susa, by 331 BC (see Bengtson 1988: 205–212), so he is the individual whom the passage predicts. Third, he is also the broken horn, for *four kingdoms arise from his nation, but not with his power* after he died in 323 BC (8:22). Alexander left no heir, which led to decades of bitter fighting (Bengtson 1988: 225). As Montgomery explains, 'The four kingdoms, represented by the four horns, are apparently . . . Macedonia (under Cassander), Thrace and Asia Minor (Lysimachus), "Asia" or "Syria" (under Seleucus), Egypt (Ptolemy)' (1927: 332). Thus, yet another four-kingdom scheme joins the ones in chapters 2 and 7.

23. Skipping decades to get to the heart of the matter, Gabriel states that Daniel's vision relates to *the later end of their kingship*, the time when Alexander's successors' rule concludes. This is the same time when 'the wrath' ends (8:19; Lucas 2002: 220). This end will come when *their transgressing* [see 8:13] *is complete*, in the sense of both 'finished' and 'done to the maximum level' (Collins 1993: 339). This will occur when *a king brazen of face and who understands problems* comes. The word translated *brazen* sounds like the word rendered 'goat', so he will have some of the first king's boldness. The ability to solve problems is one of the skills the queen mother attributes to Daniel in 5:12. Sadly, this king will misuse this gift (Lucas 2002: 221). These descriptions supplement 7:7–27, and almost certainly refer to Antiochus IV, who ruled Judea from *c*. 175 to 164 BC. Part of the Seleucid dynasty, he was only fourth in line to become king (Collins 1993: 321), so he demonstrated boldness and political skill by gaining the throne. Rome supplanted Greece as the world's great empire during his lifetime. By 168 BC, Rome limited his territory and began to rule parts of Greece and Asia Minor (Bengtson 1988: 306). Thus, Antiochus IV represents *the later end* of Greece's kingdom in Judea.

24. Like the first goat, Gabriel continues, this ruler will succeed to a certain point: *his power will be great, but not with his power* (8:24a). The second half of this difficult phrase echoes 8:22, where Gabriel says that the four kingdoms will not have the first king's power. It also foreshadows 8:25, where Gabriel notes that the king's *cunning* and *deceit* make him prosper. In other words, he will not have the *kind* of power the first king has, for he will not simply overpower everyone. His power will come by guile. Nonetheless, his methods will enable him *to destroy powerful men, and the people of the holy ones*.

By ancient standards, Antiochus IV was an effective ruler. As 8:23 indicates, he knew how to solve problems. By 169–168 BC, he had convinced many Jews in Jerusalem to accept Greek ways, had gained control of their high priesthood, and had taken money from the temple treasury to help finance his wars in Egypt (Collins 1993: 321). Therefore, he controlled the *people of the holy ones*. Taking advantage of Roman intervention in Macedonia, he extended his territory from Syria into Egypt by 168 BC (Bengtson 1988: 306). He did indeed defeat powerful foes. Yet Rome was a problem he could not solve, a power he could overcome. When the Romans ordered him out of Egypt in 168 BC, he had no choice but to go.

25. Having prospered through *skill* and *deceit*, this ruler *will become great in his own heart, and without warning he will destroy many, and he will stand against the Prince of princes.* In other words, he will arrogantly fight God, 'the Prince of princes'. He will put himself in the position only God holds. He will believe he rules the kingdoms of humankind and gives them to whomever he wishes (see 4:34–37). He will stop the sacrifices and make the temple desolate, as 7:25 and 8:1–12 have revealed. He will display Belshazzar's type of arrogance (5:1–16). Thus, he *will be shattered, but by no human hand.* God will end his rule as surely as he ended Belshazzar's (5:17–31), for God gives kingdoms to whom he will (see 4:1–3, 17–23, 34–37).

After Rome forced Antiochus IV out of Egypt, he took out his frustration on the Jews *without warning.* Besides fighting the 'holy ones' (8:24), he exalted himself against God in ways his predecessors had not. As Bengtson (1988: 306) writes,

> The conflict reached its climax when Antiochus IV in December
> 167 BC attempted to carry through the Hellenizing of Jerusalem
> by force. The Jaweh cult was abolished and all Jewish rites
> prohibited. An altar was erected in the Temple to Zeus Olympios,
> the 'Imperial God,' and a statue of the reigning sovereign set up
> beside it, to which the offerings prescribed for the ruler cult were
> to be brought.

Antiochus's scheme did not work; his power did not last. The Jews rebelled. Three years later, after tearing down the image of Zeus, they rededicated the temple (Bengtson 1988: 306). God guarded his temple against the haughty king. Antiochus died *c.* 164 BC. History does not record exactly how that happened (see comments on 11:40–45), but he did not die in Jerusalem.

26. Before his death, *the vision of the evenings and mornings,* the 2,300 days when sacrifices will cease (see 8:14), will take place. This will be a sad and dangerous time. Thus, once again Gabriel emphasizes that the vision *refers to many days from now,* that is, from Daniel's time. Gabriel commands Daniel to *seal up the vision,* which means Daniel must roll up the scroll containing the words of the vision and its interpretation and seal it (Miller 1994: 236; Collins 1993: 341). Readers may protest, wishing for more details, but Gabriel has finished, and 'God's mighty man' does not field unnecessary queries, as Zechariah learns in Luke 1:19–20.

27. Unlike Zechariah, Daniel says nothing. Perhaps he could not, for he *was overcome and sick for days.* Then he *rose and did the king's business,* but remained *appalled, and did not understand the vision.* To this day, interpreters struggle mightily to understand what Daniel saw and Gabriel said. Daniel felt no ecstasy over having had a vision. The experience left him drained, as well it might. He knows his people will face a long series of hardships as they live through the kingdoms he has envisioned. Worse, he knows that trouble lies beyond that fourth kingdom. Whoever suppresses the little horn will be fierce. What comfort Daniel can have now must come from seeking God, which is what he is doing when the next scene begins.

Meaning
Through this health-wrecking vision, Daniel encounters some encouraging truths. First, this passage agrees with Daniel 1 – 7, that God discloses and rules the future. Human events are not self-selecting, not tenuous, not open to chance. God knows and rules the future as readily as the past and present. Second, this text agrees with Daniel 2 – 7 by stressing that God will overthrow arrogant kings and establish his rule. The God who knows and discloses the future owns the future. Persia will rise, and then Greece. Greece's final ruler over Jerusalem will exalt himself above God, but will die, as all men do. Third, the vision indicates that the temple will be rebuilt, for the sacred liturgy will resume. As Deuteronomy 30:1–10, Jeremiah 30 – 33 and Ezekiel 33 – 37 promise, the 'holy ones' will return to repopulate and replenish the land. As Haggai and Zechariah proclaimed, the temple will rise again, and the messiah will come.

However, these positive statements have discouraging aspects. Though God rules, his people suffer for a long time. They endure the wrath of powerful enemies opposed to them and their God. They live faithfully in trust that their God will give his people the victory over oppressors, knowing full well that some later generation of their community will see with physical eyes what they saw only with eyes of faith. Though the temple will be rebuilt, it will suffer the indignity of desecration. Rebuilding will not occur simultaneously with the kingdom of God coming in its fullness. Therefore, wise endurance of the sort Daniel continues to exemplify must become the normal way of life for God's people in Daniel's age, or any other.

Finally, it is important to note where this chapter gives specific information and where it does not. Daniel 8 is clear about general facts. Persia succeeds Babylon, and Greece supplants Persia. A king at the end of the Greek era will fight God's people and exalt himself above God. However, the specific day-to-day details about what Persia and Greece will do in these and following eras are not so clear. Interpreters make good-faith efforts to link textual clues and historical events, as I have tried to do. Yet the details are not clear enough to claim, for instance, that the book must have been written after these events occurred, for example in c. 167−164 BC.

9. DANIEL'S PRAYER AND HEAVEN'S ANSWER (9:1–27)

Daniel recovers from the debilities his second vision caused. By his own admission, he did not understand that vision (8:27). However, he does understand the importance of prayer (see 2:17–23; 6:10–11) when facing puzzling moments (2:17–23) and dangerous foes (6:10–11). Indeed, daily prayer is part of his life (6:10–11). He cannot worship in Jerusalem, but he can pray towards Jerusalem (6:10). Now old, in his own 'later times' he pursues understanding where he has found it in the past. He turns to conversation with the living God. His words contain both confessions of sin and statements of trust in God's unchanging righteous character.

Context

Though a complicated passage, the chapter has a clear structure. In 9:1–3 Daniel prepares to voice a great prayer of confession. About eight years after his last vision (9:1), Daniel reads Jeremiah's prophecies (9:2), which move him to seek God through prayer and fasting (9:3). In 9:4–19 he prays like Moses, Solomon, Ezra,

Nehemiah and others have through the centuries (see Exod. 32:11–13; 1 Kgs 8:22–61; Pss 78; 89; Ezra 9:6–15; Neh. 9:5–38; and Pss 104 – 106). The last four of these texts date after Jerusalem's destruction in 587 BC. The commonalities between these texts and Daniel's prayer make it unnecessary to conclude that a later editor added 9:4–19 to the book, as some experts deduce (e.g. Anderson 1984: 106; Hartman and Di Lella 1978: 245–246; see the arguments for the chapter's unity in Lucas 2002: 232–234). Daniel invokes God's covenant name, Yahweh (9:4), the only time the book does so, to underscore his prayer's emphasis on Israel's covenant with their God. Daniel confesses sin committed against the covenant-keeping God (9:5–15), and asks him to forgive the people, return them to the land and restore the city and temple (9:16–19). As in 2:17–23, Daniel does not have to wait long for an answer. In 9:20–27 Gabriel returns, flying to Daniel while he is still praying (9:20–21) to give the much-loved wise man God's response (9:22–23). He explains that Daniel's people will endure a period of difficulty seven times the length of their current troubles, but that God's 'everlasting righteousness' will prevail (9:24–27).

As for the date, 9:1 states that what follows occurred in c. 539 BC, the first year of Darius the Mede, the royal figure introduced in 5:31; 6:1; and 6:28. The narrative framework in 9:1–3 indicates that it was written down soon afterwards (see Steinmann 2008: 427–429). Thus, like Daniel 5 – 8, this prayer and interpretation occur in a time of transition. Daniel 6 revealed what a turbulent time this was for Daniel. At an advanced age, he undertook new responsibilities that carried new threats. Yet as he read Jeremiah's prophecies, he wondered if this was also a time of renewal for his people. His mind keeps turning to them, as he waits for God's kingdom to rise (see 2:44) and God's people to receive the kingdom along with the Son of Man (7:9–27).

Comment
A. Preparation for prayer (9:1–3)

With all that happens in Daniel, it is easy to overlook the book's emphasis on worship. This is unfortunate, since, as Winfried Vogel (2010: 216–217) contends,

One of the most prominent theological themes in the book of Daniel is that of worship, because it is the issue which is addressed on virtually every page. To be sure, the issue is not so much the style of worship as it is the essence of worship as an expression of loyalty to a particular deity. In the book of Daniel, the very essence is the question of *whom* one worships.

Prayer has definitely been one of the ways in which Daniel shows whom *he* worships (see 2:17–23; 6:1–9). These introductory verses present Daniel as one who prays throughout the years (9:1), prays in response to God's Word (9:2) and prays with humility (9:3).

   1. This verse adds a detail about Darius not present in 5:30–31; 6:1; and 6:28, which is that he was *the son of Ahasuerus*. This statement leads to the same discussions of the book's accuracy that one finds in treatments of earlier verses. For instance, Collins (1993: 348) writes that Ezra 4:5–6 indicates that names of later rulers have been transposed in 9:1, and concludes that this verse is fictitious (see also Newsom and Breed 2014: 289). On the other hand, W. F. Albright (1929: 112–113, fn. 19) suggests that *Darius* was 'an old Iranian royal title'. Wiseman concurs (1965: 15), and others have made similar suggestions (see Goldingay 1989: 239 for a survey). Both approaches are suggestions, and most interpreters, including this one, approach this verse as they have 5:31; 6:1; and 6:28. Thus, I think this verse reflects the period in which Daniel received it, shows that Daniel turned to God in both normal and unusual times during his long personal exile, and continues to present Daniel 7 – 12 in a chronological order that lets each passage build on previous ones.

   2. Daniel read scrolls his entire adult life (see 1:3–7). Here he reads Hebrew scrolls, not Babylonian ones. While doing so, he notes *the number of years* that *Jeremiah the prophet* declared by divine inspiration (*according to the word of Yahweh*) were required *to complete the desolations of Jerusalem*. According to Daniel's reading of Jeremiah, *seventy years* had to pass. Since Daniel was exiled as early as 605 BC (see 1:1–7), and he wrote these words in the tumultuous year 539 BC, he may wonder if the time of punishment is over, or nearly so.

   More than one Jeremiah text may inform his thinking, but only 25:11–12 and 29:10 mention 'seventy years'. Jeremiah 25:1–12 unfolds in Nebuchadnezzar's first year, *c.* 605 BC (25:1; see

Dan. 1:1–2). The prophet announces that God has decided to give Judah and the surrounding nations to Nebuchadnezzar (25:2–11), but also that 'when seventy years are complete' (25:12), virtually the same phrase as in Daniel 9:2, God will punish Babylon. Jeremiah 27:1–11 sets Babylon's punishment in Nebuchadnezzar's grandson's time (see Dan. 5:1–28), but does not mention seventy years. Jeremiah 29:1–23 was on a scroll that Jeremiah sent to exiles in Babylon (29:1). He explains that they should settle down in exile, seek Babylon's 'wholeness' (or 'peace') and seek Yahweh, knowing that God will restore them after 'seventy years are complete' (29:10; see Dan. 9:2 and Jer. 25:12).

Daniel's chief concern is for Jerusalem's *desolations* to end when seventy years have passed. Jeremiah 25:18 warns that Judah's cities, kings and officials will become 'a desolation and a waste, a hissing and a curse' (ESV). As in Daniel 8:13, these *desolations* refer to the fact that Jerusalem is 'not being used for its intended purposes', not just that the places have been razed and empty spaces created. In the 'later days' 8:13 describes, the temple stands again, but proper sacrifices have ceased. Daniel 9:6 and 8 include 'kings' and 'officials', and 9:11 and 16 incorporate 'curse' and 'byword', another version of a person 'hissing'. Thus, Jeremiah 25:1–18 is probably part of what Daniel read about Jerusalem's *desolations*. Furthermore, Jeremiah 29:12–14 states that prayer, seeking God, is the key to God bringing the people back home. Daniel 9:16–19 presents Daniel carrying out that instruction and expecting God to keep his promises. Therefore, Jeremiah 29 is also likely part of Daniel's reading.

Daniel poring over Jeremiah's scroll offers a striking portrait of this wise man. Artists have used his experience in the lions' den as a fine backdrop for their work. One would do well to imagine Daniel with the scrolls, peering into them, the way many painters have depicted Saint Jerome, the translator of the Bible from the original languages into Latin. Daniel's invested reading of God's words leads logically to him talking to God about them.

3. Despite his impressive, decades-long accomplishments as a believer in a hostile environment, Daniel comes to God in total humility. His prayer is personal, not detached. He *turned his face*, the part of him that represents his total recognizable self, *to the Lord God*, whom he has served all his life. He comes *fasting*, thus hungry for God's Word (Deut. 8:3), wearing *sackcloth and ashes*, a mourner's outfit, hoping for comfort. He does not dress this way in 6:10–11, so he has special requests on his mind.

He asks for *mercy*, one of God's chief characteristics (see Exod. 34:5–6). Forsaking any other source of help (see 1:8–16; 2:17–23; 6:10–11), he endeavours to *seek*, to pursue diligently, his God for answers, the way Jeremiah 29:10–14 directs the exiles to do (Lucas 2002: 236). Daniel claims no status but that of a chastened believer before a great God.

B. Daniel's confession of sin and trust (9:4–15)

The Bible includes many examples of individual (see Ps. 51) and corporate (see Lam. 5) confessions of sin. The corporate confessions do not excuse anyone from participation, even those already right with God (see Ezra 9:6–15; Neh. 9:5–38). Daniel includes himself in his community's sins. Lacking fellow worshippers, he still prays corporately, one man for the whole people. He praises God (9:4), admits Israel's sin (9:5–6), praises God's righteousness (9:7–14) and recites God's saving deeds and great name (9:15; see Goldingay 1989: 235).

4. Daniel addresses God as one *great and awesome* due to his unstinting covenant fidelity. Indeed, he says, God's covenant loyalty (*steadfast love*) accompanies all *who love him and keep his commandments*, the standard Moses (see Deut. 6:4–9) and Jesus (see John 14:15) set for God's people. In all these verses, *love* amounts to loyalty, not feeling. God has been faithful to his people. He has been patient with them. They are not in exile because of *his* failures, but because he 'will not clear the guilty' (see Exod. 34:6–8).

5–6. Daniel begins his confession of sin. He admits that he and the people have *sinned, and committed iniquity, and acted wickedly and rebelled, turning aside from your commandments and rules* (9:5). The word for *sin* means missing the target God set; the word for *iniquity* means twisting God's teaching; the words *acted wickedly* are emphatic; and the word *rebelled* indicates actions against their king. They have committed every type of transgression against God through the years. This has been a habitual problem at least since the golden calf incident in Exodus 32:1–6. God forgave them then because Moses interceded for them (Exod. 32:11–14; 34:5–7). God provided sacrifices for their sins in Leviticus, especially the Day of Atonement sacrifice in Leviticus 16.

Furthermore, Daniel observes, God warned the people through his *servants the prophets* (9:6), a phrase that occurs in the Jeremiah passages that Daniel consults (see Jer. 25:4). The second book of Kings (17:7–23) also highlights the role that ignoring the prophets had in Israel and Judah's exiles. Daniel claims that every class of person – *kings . . . nobles . . . fathers* – refused God's servants' help (see Jer. 25:18).

7–8. Given this widespread disobedience, God has been *righteous* – in the right in a legal and moral sense (Montgomery 1927: 364) – to judge them, *because of the treachery* that the people *have committed* against him. But 'righteousness' does not just refer to a legal standing here. As Sinclair Ferguson (1988: 192) explains,

> Daniel sees the righteousness of God both as the basis for God's judgment of the people (v. 7) and also as the basis for his own prayer of forgiveness. How can this be? In Scripture, 'righteousness' basically means 'integrity.' Sometimes it is defined as 'conformity to a norm.' In the case of God, the norm to which He conforms is His own being and character. He is true to Himself; He always acts in character.

In keeping his word, God has sent some of the people *far away* in exile to other lands, in Daniel's case to Babylon (9:7; 1:1–7; see Lev. 26:14–39; Deut. 28:15–68). Since God has been faithful, the people deserve *open shame*, 'the sense of shame that betrays itself in one's countenance and thus brings on the reproach of others' (Hartman and Di Lella 1978: 242), for what they have done (9:8). Exile has occurred. Shame sticks to them, for the time being.

9–10. God has not judged harshly or quickly. In fact, *to the Lord our God belong compassion and forgiveness*. These traits stick to him, and not just for the time being. They are permanent parts of his character. Variations of the words translated here as *compassion* and *forgiveness* occur in God's self-description in Exodus 34:5–7. The first word indicates that the sort of kindness a parent shows for a child (see 1 Kgs 3:26) is the kind of love God shows for Israel, his son (see Hos. 11:8–9; House 2005: 5–6). The second word depicts God 'sending away' sin, as one dismisses a messenger. Taken as a whole, the verse indicates that God did not judge them as they deserved. Instead, he stuck with his people even though they *rebelled against him* (9:9) by disobeying his *voice* (9:10; see Hos. 11:1–7), echoed in his *laws* (or *instructions*) and in the voices of *his servants the prophets*. He has withheld compassion and release from the Babylonians because the people stick with their sins (9:7–8), for the time being.

11–12. This rebellion has included *all Israel*, Judah and Israel alike, for they all agreed to God's covenant (9:11a; see Exod. 24:1–8). Therefore, *the curse and oath that are written in the law of Moses the servant of God have been poured out* (9:11b). According to Leviticus 26:14–39 and Deuteronomy 28:15–68 (also see 1 Kgs 8:46), God's integrity includes keeping his promise to discipline the people for their sins. This includes sending them into exile unless they turn from long-term, ingrained and continuing sin. Exile is God's climactic disciplinary action (*curse*). By 539 BC, God had *confirmed his words* by sending Nebuchadnezzar *against Jerusalem* (9:12; see Jer. 25:1–12; 27:1–11; 29:1–14). Daniel claims that *there has not been anything like this before*. He may mean that Jerusalem's devastation was unprecedented because God had only promised to dwell in Jerusalem (Baldwin 1978: 166).

13. Daniel confesses that despite Moses' warnings, *all this calamity has come upon us* (9:13a). He has lived through the era when Moses' words became frightening realities. Perhaps worse still, the people have not learned from these times. Leviticus 26:40–45, Deuteronomy 30:1–10 and 1 Kings 8:46–53 state that God will restore the people when they confess their sins (Lev. 26:40), return to God (Deut. 30:2) and pray 'towards their land' (1 Kgs 8:48). Jeremiah 29:12–14 promises that restoration will follow true, heartfelt seeking of God. But so far, the people *have not pleaded to the face of* their God; they have not turned from *iniquity*. Therefore, they have not shown signs of *gaining insight*, one of the most valuable traits in Daniel (9:13b; see 1:4, 17; Newsom and Breed 2014: 296), *by* God's *truth* (or *faithfulness*).

14–15. Given this level of covenant infidelity and unwillingness to learn, God has *kept ready* – has been vigilant to keep close at hand (see Jer. 1:12; 31:28; 44:27; Montgomery 1927: 366) – the calamity they continue to experience (9:14). He keeps using it as a tool of

instruction. Daniel believes God has been *righteous* (see 9:7) to do
so (9:14).

He desires for God to change things. Therefore, he confesses
that he and his fellow Israelites have *sinned . . . and done wickedly*.
Nonetheless, he says, Yahweh remains *our God*, and Israel remains
his people, the ones he *brought . . . out of the land of Egypt* and thus
made a name for himself (9:15). As Moses did in Exodus 32:11–14 in
the aftermath of the golden calf debacle, Daniel prays based on
God's covenant fidelity and character (*name*) shown to all nations by
his relationship with Israel. As Jeremiah 29:10–14 urges, Daniel
prays, seeks God and turns from sin. He obeys the words in
Jeremiah's scroll, for he has cultivated the habit of obeying God's
Word (see 1:8–16).

C. Daniel's specific requests (9:16–19)

Daniel has prayed with specific aims in mind, aims that God
approves. He treats God's righteousness as the basis for God to
restore Jerusalem and thereby remove shame from God's own name
(9:16). He desires a sanctuary (9:17) with sacrifices restored (9:18),
and wants this to occur swiftly (9:19).

16. God's righteousness guaranteed Israel's calamity, and it
guarantees Israel's restoration (9:13–15; Ferguson 1988: 192). Since
God keeps his word when speaking of either judgment or
forgiveness, Daniel asks him to set aside his *anger and wrath* over the
people's *sins and iniquities*, because Jerusalem is his city, and Israel
his people (see Gen. 17:7–8; Lev. 26:12). Rolf Rendtorff (1998) has
demonstrated that the formula 'I will be your God and you will be
my people' is fundamental to biblical theology. Daniel believes God
will honour Leviticus 26:40–45; Deuteronomy 30:1–10; 1 Kings
8:48; Jeremiah 25:1–12; and Jeremiah 29:10–14. Currently God and
Jerusalem are both *a byword among all who are around* (9:16; see Jer.
25:18), as 2:25; 3:8–12; 5:13; and 6:13 have made clear.

17–19. Therefore, Daniel asks God to *make your face shine on your
holy place, which is desolate* (9:17). The term *holy place* does not just
mean 'the temple' here, but treats all of Jerusalem as 'set apart' for
God's purposes. It has become *desolate* in that it is not currently
fulfilling those purposes, not just in the sense that it has been torn

apart through invasion. As 8:13 has shown, the temple can both be standing and be desolate. However, there are indeed many empty places (*desolations*) in the land, and Daniel wants them rebuilt (9:18). He longs for God's *great mercy* to move him to *pay attention and act*, and to do so now, without *delay* (9:19). He wants the end of the seventy years to complete (see 9:2) Jerusalem's troubles.

D. Heaven's answer: Gabriel returns (9:20–27)

This is a deeply touching passage. While Daniel is still praying, Gabriel comes to him (9:20–21). This time he does not frighten Daniel (see 8:16–17). As before, Gabriel comes to instruct (9:22). He has uneven news about Jerusalem's future, but he has only high regard for Daniel, calling him 'very precious' to God (9:23). Just as Daniel's vision in 8:1–14 provides details related to 7:1–27, so now Gabriel explains more in 9:24–27 about 8:1–26. In short, Jerusalem will have troubles for a long time. Its desolations will not end when the little horn (7:7–8; 8:9–14) dies. Daniel will be an example of warning and endurance, not a herald declaring the immediate emergence of God's kingdom. The final kingdom still rises slowly (see 2:44).

20–21. While Daniel was still *speaking ... praying ... confessing ... presenting* his *plea for mercy* for *the holy hill* (9:20), *the man-like* [see Hartman and Di Lella 1978: 243] *Gabriel* came to him, at *the time of the evening sacrifice* (9:21). Evening sacrifices were occasions for confession (Ezra 9:4–5), and Daniel was used to praying then in any case (see 6:10–11; Lucas 2002: 240). He recognized Gabriel from the *first* [or *previous*] *vision*, which at least refers to 8:15–26, if not to 7:16. Gabriel came *in swift flight*. He does not waste time.

22–23. He announces his purpose as swiftly as he flew: *I have now come to give insight* [or *skill*; see 1:4, 17; 9:13] *and understanding*. Since Daniel did not have a vision in 9:1–19, Gabriel has come to help him understand God's promises in Jeremiah's scroll. He has also come to let humble Daniel know that he is *greatly loved* or, more literally, *very precious*, like gold, fine garments and excellent food (BDB 326). There are few like him, and God is pleased with him. This is why God sent Gabriel the moment Daniel began praying. Remaining on task, Gabriel commands Daniel to *understand the word* Jeremiah delivered, *and understand the revelation* [or *vision*] he will now reveal.

24. Chapters 2, 7 and 8 have set the stage for 9:24–27. All three previous revelations have included four kingdoms (2:21–48; 7:1–14; 8:1–14). The latter two depicted four beastly leaders (7:1–14; 8:1–14), the last of which fights God's people (7:19–24; 8:22–25a), defiles the temple (7:25; 8:9–14) and dies at God's command (7:11–12, 26; 8:25). History does not end when the fourth leader dies (7:11–12; 8:14, 25). God will eventually give his kingdom to the Son of Man (7:9–14), and God's 'holy ones' will possess that kingdom for ever with him (7:22, 26–27). This four-part division of history and this dreadful fourth beast appear again in 9:24–27.

Gabriel tells Daniel that not just 'seventy years' (Jer. 25:12; 29:10), but *seventy sevens will be divided*[1] *concerning your people and concerning your holy city.* There is no word for 'year' in this passage, as there is in Jeremiah 25:12 and 29:10, though many interpreters assume it. There are seven days in a week, so the concept here may be 'seventy weeks of years'. This is seven times as long as the nearly seventy years of trials Daniel and Jerusalem have already experienced. Since seven and ten are symbols of full and complete amounts in the Bible, multiplying them together and multiplying by seventy simply means a very long and complete time (McComiskey 1985: 18–45). One cannot match this exact number of years to specific amounts of time and particular events, as the numerous failed attempts to do so throughout history have shown (see Montgomery 1927: 390–401 for a survey of attempts up to 1927, and Baldwin 1978: 176–178 and Newsom and Breed 2014: 309–320 for subsequent ones). Daniel understood the symbolic nature of Jeremiah's promise regarding 'seventy years' (Jer. 25:12), since he prays when Babylon falls (Jer. 29:10), not in the exact seventieth year of his exile or Jerusalem's fall. In short, he understood Babylon's 'seventy years' as whatever amount of time God gave Jerusalem to Babylon. Readers can expect him to understand the time-frames Gabriel reveals next in the same way.

---

1. The word translated *divided* appears only here in the Old Testament. Since Gabriel proceeds to divide the seventy weeks into parts, I have translated it this way. See BDB 367.

Though discouraging, the news has some hopeful imagery behind it. It may draw on Leviticus 25:8, where God tells Moses to count 'seven weeks of years', thus 'forty-nine years', to mark a fiftieth year (Jubilee), one of rest and release (Lucas 2002: 241). This signals more years of troubles ahead, but also that these troubles will not be constant (Baldwin 1978: 171). Gabriel may even imply that a tenfold Jubilee lies ahead. Regardless, his answer demonstrates that Daniel has not just asked about the end of exile. By asking for the desolation to end, he seeks the coming of God's permanent kingdom, the one featured in 2:21–45 and 7:9–27.

Gabriel states that this very long period of time will accomplish six positive goals: *to complete the transgression, to seal up sin, to atone for iniquity, to bring everlasting righteousness, to seal vision and prophet and to anoint a holy of holies.* Taking these six infinitives in order, *to complete the transgression* relates to 8:12–13 and 8:23, which feature the 'transgression' of the little horn defiling the temple and stopping its sacrifices (8:12–13).

The expression *to seal up* means 'to close and place a seal on' his people's 'sins' (see 9:5, 8, 11, 15, 16 and 20), as if those misdeeds were a land deed (Jer. 32:10–11) or a prophecy (Dan. 12:4). In other words, he wants God to 'end' their sins. The words *to atone for iniquity* explain how sin becomes sealed up. They echo Jeremiah 25:12 and Daniel 4:27, both of which mention Babylonian 'iniquity', and Daniel 9:16, where Daniel asks God to forgive the 'iniquities of our fathers'. No other atonement language occurs in Daniel or in the relevant passages in Jeremiah. It appears, however, in Leviticus 25:9, the verse after the 'seven times seven' text referenced above, where the Day of Atonement begins the Year of Jubilee. Thus, Gabriel may combine the two great events here as a marvellous final coming of God's kingdom.

The phrase *to bring everlasting righteousness* reminds readers of Daniel's many references to God's righteousness in his prayer (9:7, 14, 16, 18, 24). To bring *everlasting righteousness* means to have God's righteousness prevail at all times. It amounts to God's kingdom coming on earth (see 2:44), and the fulfilment of prophecy, as the next phrase indicates. Gabriel's mention of *to seal up, prophet* and *vision* could refer to Jeremiah and Daniel or, more likely, to prophets and visions in general, since they all focus on God's righteous rule.

Everlasting righteousness will 'seal' prophecy in the sense of authenticating and ending it.

Finally, *to anoint a holy of holies* does not relate to any other verse in Daniel. In the Old Testament the term 'holy of holies' occurs only in passages about the tabernacle, temple or priesthood (Montgomery 1927: 375; Collins 1993: 354; BDB 871–872). Since Daniel 7:23–27; 8:13–14; and 8:23 address the temple's defilement, Gabriel probably references the temple and priesthood.

Gabriel's opening words cover Babylon's seventy years (Jer. 25:12; 29:10–14), God's promises about Israel's return to the land, the end of the four rulers' misdeeds (Dan. 8:13–14, 23), the cleansing and renewing of the temple, and the coming of God's endless righteous kingdom (2:44; 7:9–27). All this will take a long time, given the symbolic number *seventy sevens*. That kingdom will not come simply because Babylon has fallen. Still, it will come in due course. Atonement for sin will occur. The effects of the Day of Atonement and Year of Jubilee will last for ever.

25. Having stated the results of the long symbolic amount of time, Gabriel begins to divide the time itself into four periods that feature four major figures. This interpretation fits the fact that most commentators claim that 9:25–27 depicts three periods, and then discuss how the last 'seven' of the third era divides further (see Bevan 1892: 147; Montgomery 1927: 386–389; Charles 1929: 250–252; Baldwin 1978: 171; and Newsom and Breed 2014, 304–305). There is some overlap between eras, as is always the case in history. Thus, Gabriel presents another version of the four-kingdom scheme utilized in Daniel 2:21–45; 7:1–27; and 8:1–26. Taking Gabriel's statements as the next instance of a common literary trait in Daniel may offer a way forward in understanding this difficult text. The time periods and leaders he mentions are as follows: seven weeks (an anointed one); sixty-two weeks (an anointed one cut off); half a week (the coming prince); and half a week (the desolator).

The first period lasts *from the going out of the word to return and build Jerusalem, until* [the coming of] *an anointed one, a prince, seven weeks.*[2]

There are several opinions about when the first era begins (for a succinct summary, see Newsom and Breed 2014: 304). Is it the date of Jeremiah's prophecy? Is it when Daniel begins praying? Is it the decree of Cyrus? Gabriel does not say, but taking 9:1 seriously may help. Regardless of whether Cyrus and Darius are the same person or not (see comments on 5:30–31; 6:1; 6:28; and 9:1), this reference places 9:25–27 after Babylon's seventy years and before Cyrus's first year (see 1:21), when he decrees that Jews may return to Jerusalem and build the temple. Ezra 1:1 asserts that Cyrus made this decree 'that the word of the LORD by the mouth of Jeremiah might be fulfilled' (ESV). Therefore, the first period of time begins then.

This short period is highlighted by the coming of an *anointed one, a prince*. Scholars have suggested Cyrus, Zerubbabel, Joshua the priest or the messiah fit this context. In the Old Testament, priests (Lev. 4:3, 5, 16), kings (1 Sam. 16:1–13) and prophets (1 Kgs 19:16) are anointed at the beginning of their ministries to stress that their calling and power come from God. The word 'messiah' means 'anointed one'. In the Old Testament the word translated 'prince' (or 'leader') applies to kings of Israel (see 2 Sam. 7:11) and other nations, as well as to Israel's priests (BDB 617–618). Cyrus is significant in the early years of Jerusalem's renewal because he decrees its rebuilding. Zerubbabel, a Davidic descendant, led the earliest returnees back to Jerusalem (see Ezra 2:1–2). Joshua went to Jerusalem with Zerubbabel and became the first high priest in the new era. Jeremiah 33:17–18 promises long-term continuing roles for David and Levi. Though any of these could fit, then, Zerubbabel and Joshua are Davidic and Levite Jews who return to Jerusalem, so they make the most sense.

The second period lasts sixty-two weeks. *During this time* Jerusalem *will be built with squares and a moat, but in a time of distress.* At the end of this era, *an anointed one will be cut off.* This person will have nothing left to rule due to what the third major figure will do. During this second and longest period, the city and temple will rise

---

(note 2 *cont.*) the 'anointed' one comes after sixty-nine weeks, which fuelled later messianic interpretations of 9:25–26, though none in the New Testament.

again. The word *squares* indicates settled living space, and the word *moats* signifies defensive measures. Jerusalem will once again become a legitimate city. Gabriel calls this era of building *a time of distress*. Ezra 2 – 6, Nehemiah, Haggai, Zechariah and 1–2 Maccabees chronicle decades-long difficulties associated with rebuilding.

26–27a. Nonetheless, well before the time of Antiochus IV (175–164 BC), the city and temple operated again. By 167 BC, however, he had cut off any legitimate *anointed one*, whether Davidic or priestly, for he ruled the city and temple (see comments on Dan. 7 – 8). Several scholars think the *anointed one* refers to Onias III, the high priest Antiochus removed in 171 BC (see Collins 1993: 356; Newsom and Breed 2014: 306–307). While possible, given the context of the end of the Greek era and the sixty-two weeks, this text is not that specific. It is also not specific enough to conclude that the *anointed one* is the messiah, as Archer (1985: 113) does.

The third era features a third leader and his armies: *the people of a prince who is coming*. This leader and people *will* either *destroy* or *defile* Jerusalem (*the city*) and the temple (*the sanctuary*). The Hebrew word can be translated either way, so one must choose. Daniel 8:24–25 uses versions of the word to describe destruction, so the closest contextual usage favours *destroy*. In this specific context, however, Gabriel stresses the loss of priestly leader (9:26), sacrifice (9:27) and offering (9:27). Therefore, the context is more like the word's use in Isaiah 1:4, one of defilement by sinful action. Though it is a difficult choice, *defile* is the best rendering here. This defilement (9:26–27a) will occur during a period when people and places will be destroyed, in short, during a time of war (8:22–26).

Furthermore, this leader will end proper temple worship suddenly (*with a flood*), and *until the end, there will be war, desolations being decreed*. War will last as long as this leader does, and well beyond. This leader will co-opt some of Jerusalem's people (*he will make a covenant of warriors*) for *one week*, and *cause sacrifice and offering to cease for half a week*. He will not finish the entire 'week'. Another leader will do that.

Most scholars treat Antiochus IV as the *prince who is coming*, given Daniel 7 – 8 and 11. He ruled Jerusalem, the high priest and thus the government and the temple (see comments on 8:22–26). He waged war against the Jews (see comments on 8:22–26; 11:20–45).

He ended sacrifice and ordered worship of Greek gods. However, he did not 'destroy' the city and temple, though he defiled and oppressed both.[3] Later, the Romans, under Titus's leadership, destroyed Jerusalem and the temple in AD 70 after rebellions that began at least four years earlier. Before then, Titus stopped sacrifices to Israel's God and erected a god in the temple.

Therefore, Antiochus IV and Titus have several traits in common. Both ruled by force ('a warrior covenant'). Both 'defiled' the temple by ending sacrifices and erecting idols there. Both fought wars against the Jews. Both 'decreed desolation' and 'war to the end'. Still, only one destroyed the city and temple. Given what the whole book reveals about Antiochus IV (7:1–27; 8:1–26; 11:20–45), he is the 'prince to come'. Nonetheless, another one will come, as 7:11–12; 8:14; and 9:27b indicate. The kingdom of God does not come when Antiochus IV dies.

27b. The fourth era consists of the half of the final 'seven'. Gabriel presents the fourth era's leader without much detail, in keeping with 7:11–12 and 8:14: *and upon the wing of abominations comes one making desolate, until the completion being decreed pours out on the desolator.* This passage has quite understandably puzzled commentators for centuries. For instance, Montgomery (1927: 387) suggests the wing is part of the temple. Collins (1993: 358) poses a textual emendation.

Though certainly difficult, this imagery is consistent with earlier texts in Daniel. It presents the end of yet another four-part scheme. Also, just as the little horn grew out of a bigger horn in 8:1–14, so this *one making desolate* emerges from a wing, a wing of *abominations*, of desecration of the holy, and remains until God decrees otherwise. In short, the fourth major leader grows out of the same sort of attitudes and actions as the previous opponents of God's people. This desolator may well be Titus, since he destroyed the city and temple. Gabriel does not say. He simply reveals that more suffering will come after Antiochus IV, and history proves that to be the case.

As the chapter closes, Daniel does not collapse, as he did in 8:27, and will again in 10:2–14. He has learned that the end of Babylon's

---

3. Baldwin 1978: 171. See Collins 1993: 357; Lederach 1994: 217.

rule fulfils God's word through Jeremiah. But it does not spell the end of Jerusalem's desolation or the suffering of faithful people like Daniel. Happily, it also does not negate the future kingdom of God led by the Son of Man that 7:9–27 describes. Having prayed, he discovers he must persevere in faith and witness. This answer satisfies him. Gabriel can fly away home.

Meaning

Matthew 24, Mark 13 and Luke 21 present Jesus teaching his disciples about three topics before he faces crucifixion: the temple's destruction, Jerusalem's destruction and the coming of the Son of Man. All three relate to Daniel 9:24–27. Like Daniel 9:1–19, Matthew 23:37–39 puts these in the context of Jerusalem rejecting the prophets, rejecting Jesus, and therefore becoming 'desolate'. Luke may offer the clearest presentation of these subjects. First, Jesus warns his disciples that persecution will accompany the city's fall and the temple's demolition (Luke 21:10–19). It is worth adding that in other texts Jesus identifies his body as the temple (John 2:13–22), and Paul calls believers' bodies God's temple (1 Cor. 6:19) because of their union with Christ. The Christ and his people now constitute the temple. Someone may build a new physical temple and renew sacrifices. Such sacrifices will not please God, since Hebrews 7 – 10 indicates that God has designated Jesus Christ as the full perpetuation and completion of temple, sacrifice and priesthood, and has sent his people to carry on Christ's work. Second, Luke 21:25 states that there will be awful 'distress and perplexity' surrounding the Son of Man's coming 'in a cloud with power and great glory' (see 21:25–28). Third, Jesus identifies himself as the Son of Man in Luke 22:69–70.

Jesus does not give these events a time-frame, but these texts and his command in Acts 1:6–11 of a world mission by a handful of people prior to his return (see Matt. 24:14; Mark 13:10) indicate that the Son of Man would not necessarily come quickly. Thus, Jesus' disciples had to prepare to persevere so they could 'stand before the Son of Man' (Luke 21:34–36). Today's believers take up their mantle of expectant, persevering service, while they pray that Jesus will come quickly, knowing that he is with all his disciples (Rev. 22:20–21). Daniel never seems disappointed in God's decisions, and there is no reason to think that current believers will be disappointed at the timing of the Son of Man's coming. Believers who follow Daniel's pattern of reading God's Word and engaging in serious prayer discover two primary sources of perseverance. Furthermore, Jesus makes two very important comments to his disciples that should be noted in every generation. First, he claims it is not for the apostles (the apostles!) to know the times God has fixed for the end (Acts 1:6–7). Second, and even more startling, he claims that no-one, not even angels or the Son, knows the time God the Father has set for the end (Matt. 24:36). Thus, Gabriel can only tell Daniel so much, and no more. Jesus can only say so much, and no more. If language means anything, these statements prohibit speculation about times, political situations, leaders and dates that goes beyond the expectation of witness, perseverance, persecution and the certain rise of God's kingdom of 'everlasting righteousness' (Dan. 9:24). Space does not permit further discussion, but it is important to note that Paul (see 2 Thess. 2:1–12) and the book of Revelation do not violate these principles.

Based on 2 Thessalonians 2:1–12 and other passages, many popular theories about 'the anti-Christ' have arisen. Though Titus could fit what Paul describes in 2 Thessalonians, and 1 John 2:18–27 states that many anti-Christs have already arisen, speculation continues. To be sure, such a person may arise, and that should not surprise believers given Daniel's view of history. However, Gabriel offers no such information, and the New Testament does not use Daniel 9:24–27 in this manner. Rather, Gabriel implies that there will always be some desolator on the rise until 'the completion' of such persons comes. And their end *will* come, as surely as 'the completion' of Babylon's time came (see Jer. 29:10; Dan. 9:1). God's kingdom outlives all desolators. Beyond that assurance, one can only speculate, something the New Testament specifically warns against (Acts 1:7–8).

10. FROM CYRUS TO RESURRECTION: DANIEL'S LONGEST VISION (10:1 – 12:13)

Daniel 10 – 12 is the book's longest vision in both words and time. It stretches from Cyrus's third year to Daniel's resurrection from the dead. A unified whole, it portrays the travails and victories of God's people in a manner that builds on previous passages. As before, troubles and triumphs give way to the kingdom of God. As before, Daniel can only reveal so much and no more, for the angels who instruct him can only reveal so much and no more. Nonetheless, as the passage develops, it reveals marvellous things old and new in three stages. First, Daniel prepares to receive his final vision from an angelic being (10:1 – 11:1). Second, the revealer of the vision's meaning surveys time from the Persian era, through the Greek era and into an unspecified time of terrible trouble (11:2 – 12:4). Third, two angelic figures close the book by telling Daniel that history will go on for some time, so he should anticipate rest and await resurrection (12:5–13).

Context

According to 10:1, Daniel has this vision in Cyrus's third year (*c.* 537–536 BC). In 1:21 the text states that 'Daniel was there [Babylon] until the first year of King Cyrus' (*c.* 539–538 BC), which discloses that Daniel survived all the years of Babylon's sovereignty over Jerusalem. The earlier verse does not provide the year of his death. Cyrus's third year is a significant one for Daniel and others hoping for the end of Jerusalem's desolations (see 9:1–19). Ezra 1:1–9 states that Cyrus decreed that the Jews could return to Jerusalem in his first year (see comments on 9:25). According to Ezra 3:8–13, in the second year after the Jews had returned, and in the second month, they rededicated the temple. Thus, Daniel may be praying and fasting for that event. If so, then God gives him this vision at a moment of new beginnings.

The issues related to the authorship and date of these chapters are basically the same as in preceding ones (see comments on 1:1; 2:1; 4:1; 5:1; 6:1; 7:1; 8:1; and 9:1). Thus, I will not repeat them here, but will only state my conclusions. In my opinion, the book's author gathered and shaped narratives about Daniel and Daniel's own first-person descriptions of his visions. This likely happened in the Persian era, given the similarities the book has with Ezra and other post-exilic writings. The book encouraged later faithful people, including those who suffered throughout the reign of Antiochus IV.

As for this passage's literary form, Lucas (2002: 269) suggests that it reflects ancient Akkadian prophecies that 'come from various dates between the twelfth . . . and third . . . centuries BC'. The texts 'are purported prophecies that take the form of concise surveys of a series of rulers' reigns' (Lucas 2002: 269). These texts interpret history, then; they do not predict future events (Lucas 2002: 272). Lucas thinks Daniel may borrow this literary form, and if so, readers would have known Daniel 10 – 12 included events that had already occurred, so there would have been no intent to deceive readers into thinking the book predicts events from afar (Lucas 2002: 272).

Given the specific reference in 10:1, however, it seems that the book does indeed present the material as predictive. Thus, this may be another time when Daniel's author uses a known literary form, but bends it to his own purposes, as most good authors do. In this case, the author shows God's superiority by indicating his ability to declare beforehand what other deities can only reveal after the fact. However, Lucas rightly observes that this passage interprets history. It does not deal with every historical situation in the time-frame, and its predictions are often fairly general, though accurate.

Comment
A. Terror and comfort: introduction to the vision (10:1 – 11:1)

This passage is the prelude to the whole vision. Like 8:15–26, it depicts Daniel fearing heavenly messengers and needing comfort, but takes much longer to describe these experiences. The length and detail alert readers that a long and important set of images will follow. After a statement of the setting (10:1), a description of Daniel's terrifying vision of an angel (10:2–9) and a report of his conversation with heaven's messengers (10:10 – 11:1) follow.

1. This verse speaks of Daniel in the third person. Like 7:1, then, it reveals the author's presence. In the *third year of Cyrus*, the Jews who had returned to Jerusalem were getting ready to dedicate the temple (see above). The author reminds readers of Daniel's Babylonian name (*Belteshazzar*) to focus attention on his long service in exile, and then asserts that Daniel received *the word* (see 9:2), the revelation that follows. He did not create it. This *word* is *true*. Its subject matter may be translated as *hard service*, or as *warfare* (see Isa. 40:2). Of course, warfare and hard service often coincide. By now, readers know the book stresses perseverance, not immediate deliverance. Unlike in 8:27, Daniel *had understanding of the revelation*.

2–4. Daniel 9:1–3 reports Daniel reading God's Word, fasting and praying because he knew Babylon's 'seventy years' of rule (see Jer. 29:10) was ending. He sought answers from God about the future. Here he is *mourning*, in the sense of afflicting himself for a particular purpose (10:2). He eats *no delicacies, no meat*, drinks no *wine*, and does not *anoint* his body *until the completion of three weeks* (10:3). This statement indicates that the diet Daniel chose in 1:8–16 was not permanent, but was a witness to the Babylonians of God's power (see comments on 1:8–16). Daniel took these strict measures until *the twenty-fourth day of the first month* (10:4), so he was likely observing Passover (see Lev. 23:4–8), presumably along with the people in Jerusalem. If so, Owens (1971: 445) suggests that he restricted himself to 'the bread of affliction' associated with Passover (see Deut. 16:3). The text does not state why, but he was *standing on the bank of the great river, the Tigris*,[1] fifty miles from Babylon (Owens 1971: 445), when the revelation comes.

5–6. Daniel looks across the river and sees an extraordinary being. He may have been thinking about temple rituals, for this individual was dressed *in linen* like a priest (see Lev. 6:10; 16:4). However, the being wore a ritual loincloth made of the gold of Uphaz, among the finest of its day (Montgomery 1927: 408), which was nothing like how a normal priest dressed (10:5)! The being's body shone *like beryl*, for his *face* was *like the appearance of lightning*, his *eyes like flaming torches*, and *his arms and legs* looked like *polished bronze* (10:6a). Apparently, he spoke to Daniel, but *his words* were *like the noise of a large crowd*, so the volume overwhelmed Daniel (10:6b).

7–9. The vision has not begun, and the men with Daniel do not stay for it. When *great terror fell on them*, they understandably *fled to hide themselves* (10:7). Therefore, Daniel *alone saw the vision*, because, as he admits, he had no strength left to run (10:8), perhaps in part because he was very old. The sound of the being's voice forced Daniel onto his *face in deep sleep* (10:9). In other words, it rendered him unconscious. The combination of the rigours of Passover preparation, age and the intensity of the being's presence leave him helpless.

10–12. Then, he recounts, *a hand touched me and set me trembling on my hands and knees* (10:10). One has to wonder if Daniel wants to rise any higher! Is this the touch of his old friend Gabriel, who raised him up in 8:18? The text does not say, but he calls Daniel *very precious* (10:11), as Gabriel did in 9:23, the last time Daniel prayed about his people's future. The being says that Daniel's *words have been heard* since the day he began his three weeks of setting his *heart to understand*, to gain wisdom (Redditt 1999: 173) about Israel's future

---

1. The Euphrates is normally called 'the great river', so several versions emend the text here (see Collins 1993: 373; Montgomery 1927: 407), though others do not (see Goldingay 1989: 275).

(Charles 1929: 261; Porteous 1979: 152) in light of their fresh start in Jerusalem (10:12).

13. If Daniel is so beloved, why has God's messenger delayed his coming? The angel explains that *the prince of the kingdom of Persia was standing before me twenty-one days*, the length of time Daniel had been seeking understanding. He says he got free when *Michael, one of the chief princes, came to help* him. Later, in 10:20, he reveals that he was fighting this 'prince of Persia'. Since the messenger and Michael are both angels (see 10:21), 'the prince of Persia' is probably an angel serving as Persia's advocate (see Collins 1993: 374–375; Montgomery 1927: 419–420; Newsom and Breed 2014: 332). Daniel 11:2–4 declares Persia's empire finished, so the other angel may have contended for a longer Persian dominance (Lucas 2002: 276).

Interpreting 10:13 is one of many times in Daniel when readers must embrace the symbolic nature of visions and the concept of mystery. The verse indicates that there are factors governing reality beyond what humans see. Ephesians 6:10–20 and Revelation 12:7 make this point, as does every Old Testament passage that features an angelic being. Without using mystery as an excuse for not trying to understand God's ways, a laziness Daniel 10:2–4 surely denounces, readers must embrace the ignorance native to humanity. As Wendell Berry puts it, life itself is a miracle beyond understanding, and thus always mysterious (2003: 3–12). Therefore, accepting the limitation of human ignorance can lead to humility and grace (2006: 53–67).

14. While one cannot know everything about celestial battles, this symbolism makes one thing crystal clear: the victorious chief angel is on Jerusalem's side. Persia's angel cannot overthrow God's angels, for they are doing God's will. The angel tells Daniel he has come *to make you understand what your people will encounter in later days, for the vision is for those days*, the days after Daniel's death. Thus, the message does not just address the end of time. The reference to *your people* underscores Jerusalem's importance in God's plans. What the returned Israelites have begun will take root, face challenges and ultimately triumph.

15–17. Hearing this, Daniel looks at the ground, unable to speak (10:15). Using different words from those in 7:13, he states that another angel, *one in the likeness of the sons of mankind*, reached out and *touched* his *lips* (10:16a). In Jeremiah 1:9 God touches the prophet's mouth so he can speak God's words. An angel purifies Isaiah's unclean lips with coals from the heavenly fire in Isaiah 6:7. Like these great prophets, Daniel can now speak, but still feels too weak to continue (10:16b–17). His comment causes tension, for if he cannot muster the remaining strength in his old body, how will the message be revealed?

18–19. Accepting Daniel's assessment, the *one having the appearance of mankind* touches Daniel, thereby strengthening him (10:18). The crisis has been averted. Next, the angel comforts Daniel by reminding him again that he is *very precious* to God, and exhorts him to *be very strong* (see Josh. 1:1–9). The old wise man feels better; he can carry on (10:19).

10:20 – 11:1. This is good, since the angel has other business to conduct elsewhere. He must *return to fight the prince of Persia*, the enigmatic one 10:13 mentioned (10:20a), so *the prince of Greece will come* (10:20b). The turnover of empires that 2:21–45; 7:1–8; 8:1–14; and 9:24–27 introduce must occur. God controls history. The coming of the *prince of Greece* has been *noted in the writing of truth* (10:21a), in words that cannot be false. Baldwin (1978: 182) thinks this scribal image 'conveys God's control and knowledge of past, present and future (Ps. 139:16; Mal. 3:16)'.

Moreover, this angel and *Michael, your prince*, the angel who contends for Israel, can withstand Persia (10:21b). They can bring to pass what God has written. To encourage Daniel further, the angel says he is the one who stood by Darius and gave him authority to rule (see 5:30–31; 6:28; 9:1). Daniel can trust this experienced messenger.

B. Centuries of triumph and trial (11:2 – 12:4)

Daniel's visions keep building on one another. Daniel 7 elucidates Daniel 2:21–45 by providing more details about the kingdoms that follow Babylon, and by depicting the kingdom that will never fall (cf. 2:44 and 7:9–27). Likewise, Daniel 9 and Daniel 10 – 12 describe further the four kingdoms 8:1–26 introduces, what comes after these kingdoms, and the relationship between the kingdom of God and resurrection. Daniel 11:2–45 tells a tale of costly triumph.

Daniel's people will endure, and the temple will rise again (see 9:25). But renewal will take centuries of trials (11:2–45) and will lead into devastating troubles that will make previous hard times seem easy (12:1–4).

To tell this story, this section presents a breathtaking overview of the Persian and Greek eras as they relate to the Jews, Jerusalem and the temple's future. It is important to keep this limited context in mind, since the power and influence of Persia and Greece extended well beyond Judah. Daniel 11:2–4 summarizes the rest of the years of the Persian Empire (*c.* 537–331 BC), the rise of Alexander the Great (*c.* 334–331 BC) and his kingdom's division after his death in 323 BC. Daniel 11:5–20 is only slightly less summative, covering 323–175 BC, the period from Alexander to Antiochus IV. Daniel 11:21–39 provides a more leisurely pace, summarizing 'only' Antiochus IV's terrible reign (*c.* 175–164 BC). Daniel 11:40–45 presents the end of Antiochus IV, and perhaps all such leaders.

2. The angel proceeds to give Daniel *the truth* found in the 'writing of truth' he introduced in 10:21b. Using the book's four-part scheme once again (see comments on 2:21–45; 7:1–8; 8:1–14; 9:24–27), the angel presents *three more kings standing in Persia*, followed by *a fourth*. This last one becomes enamoured by his great wealth (*richer than all of them*), and fights *the kingdom of Greece*.

There were actually more than four kings between Cyrus and Darius III (*c.* 336–331 BC; Lewis et al. 1994: 50–51). As before, the point of the four-part scheme is to summarize history, not count kings. Persian kings were known for their wealth, and Pierre Briant asserts that there is no evidence that Persian finances had declined by the time Darius III ruled (Briant 2002: 800–804). War with Greece then was more dangerous than when Cyrus fought some Greek armies in *c.* 547–546 BC (see comments on Daniel 8). Philip of Macedon had united Greece in 338 BC, and his son inherited a strong army.

3–4. As the comments on 8:20–22 explain, the *mighty king* in 11:3 is Alexander the Great (*c.* 336–323 BC), who defeated Darius III of Persia in a series of battles beginning in 334 BC. When he died leaving no heir, his kingdom *was broken and divided* (11:4) into various factions. Judah was pinched geographically between two of these: the kingdoms of Syria in the north and east, and Egypt in the south.

5. The angel mentions a *strong* man becoming *king of the south*. This phrase probably refers to the fact that when Alexander died, Ptolemy I served as satrap of Egypt until *c.* 306 BC. Thereafter he became king, leading the region until his death in *c.* 283–282 BC (Hölbl 2001: 9–34). Though this person will have great power, the angel notes, *one of his princes will become stronger*. This description can fit more than one person (Collins 1993: 378), but most scholars (e.g. Collins 1993: 378; Lucas 2002: 280; and Newsom and Breed 2014: 340) deem Seleucus I the most likely candidate. He fought alongside Ptolemy I in *c.* 316–313 BC (Hölbl 2001: 17–18). Afterwards, he ruled an area stretching from Syria across the Mediterranean. Thus, he exceeded Ptolemy in power and influence. Hereafter in Daniel, the *king of the south* may refer to Ptolemy I or any of his heirs, and 'the king of the north' to Seleucus I or one of his successors. Their dynasties were intertwined for over a century.

6. The angel uses a vague phrase (*after some years*) to skip ahead chronologically (11:6a). He says the kings *will make a* marriage *alliance*. This was a normal means of gaining power and trying to end conflict between nations. For example, during his tenure Ptolemy I used intermarriages to gain power (Hölbl 2001: 24–25). The angel states that this alliance *will not endure*. After Ptolemy I's death, the Ptolemies and Seleucids battled one another periodically for the next thirty years (Hölbl 2001: 38–46). In *c.* 249 BC, Antiochus II, a grandson of Seleucus, and Berenice, daughter of Ptolemy II, married (Collins 1993: 378). Berenice bore a child, but she and the child were murdered (Lucas 2002: 280).

7–9. In time, the angel continues, *a branch from her roots* will *enter the fortress of the king of the north . . . and prevail* (11:7). This prediction most likely refers to the activities of Ptolemy III, Berenice's brother, who sought to avenge his sister's murder by waging war during 246–241 BC (Hölbl 2001: 48–51). The angel then adds that the south will rest from attacking the north for a while (11:8), and the north will take its turn invading the south (11:9). The rivalry will continue.

10–13. Back and forth they will go. The Seleucids will gain much ground (*overflow and pass through*) against the Ptolemies (11:10). Then the Ptolemies will *raise a great* army and fight successfully against the Seleucids, which may refer to the battle of 'Raphia, an Egyptian outpost on the frontier of Palestine, in 217' (Lucas 2002: 281). When the southerners prevail, their leader will swell with pride (11:12a), *but he will not prevail*, his supremacy will not last (11:12b). The *king of the north will invade with a great army* (11:13). This statement probably refers to Antiochus III (220–187 BC), who proved very capable after early setbacks at the hands of Ptolemy IV. Under his leadership the Seleucids recovered quickly, and by 200 BC had the Ptolemies under control (Hölbl 2001: 132–138).

14–16. The angel tells Daniel that *the violent among* his *people* will support the Seleucids (11:14). High priests of Jerusalem ruled civic and religious affairs by 200 BC. Charles (1929: 288) notes that the Ptolemies bolstered a corrupt, greedy high priest in Jerusalem, which led some Jews to support the Seleucid side. If so, the angel reveals that some Jews will invite the help of a dynasty that will eventually defile the temple and city. These Seleucid allies will believe they are helping to *fulfil the vision* of bringing the temple and city's desolations to an end (see 9:24–27), *but they will be overthrown* (11:14). The king of the north will prevail (11:15), doing as he wishes to the Ptolemies (11:16a), and ruling Jerusalem as a result (11:16b). The *violent* ones back the wrong ally.

17–20. According to the angel, the king of the north will then seek peace with the Ptolemies so he can concentrate on bigger gains (11:17). He will wage war in new places (*turn his face to the coastlands*), have some success, encounter an opponent who will *put an end to his insolence* (11:18) and *will be overthrown* (see 11:14), thus having to retreat (11:19). After forcing the Ptolemies to accept his terms, Antiochus III sought to expand his territory. He ran afoul of the Roman army, which defeated him in 191 and 189 BC (Newsom and Breed 2014: 345; Astin et al. 1989: 283–289). He still retained power in his old territories. Battlefield losses are always financially costly. So it is not surprising that the angel says an *exactor of tribute*, a king seeking revenue from Jerusalem and other places, will replace the dead king (11:20). This tribute gatherer *will be shattered, but not by wrath and not by battle*. Seleucus IV replaced his father, Antiochus III, but was probably assassinated for political reasons in 175 BC, paving the way for his brother, Antiochus IV.

Baldwin rightly cautions that the predictions in 11:2–20, though indeed predictions, are more general in nature than commentators usually admit (1978: 183–185). Put another way, they are more general than one might think when reading a commentator who suggests specific historical settings for individual phrases, as I have done. The text has summarized 350 years. There are gaps in information, for the ancient records possessed today are incomplete. Still, God's revelation of events that bear on the future of Jerusalem and the temple is extraordinary.

21. The angel summarizes the next king's character and rise to power in very negative terms. He will be *a contemptible person*, possessing no *royal majesty*, the 'consistency and dignity of character' one expects of kings. A crafty one, he will arise suddenly (*without warning*) through *flatteries*. As the comments on 8:23–24 have noted, this prediction probably refers to Antiochus IV, a conniving individual. Though only fourth in line to become king, he claimed the throne by grabbing power, and then probably murdering the heir apparent (Lucas 2002: 283). Everything that follows supports the angel's assessment of this king's low behaviour.

22. Horrible people often succeed. This king will *utterly sweep away* many opponents, even *a prince of the covenant*. Baldwin (1978: 192) writes that the indefinite nature of this latter phrase means it 'could refer to a secular king with whom Antiochus is in alliance, or to a high priest appointed within the terms of God's covenant'. Like most scholars, she suggests that this *prince* may be Onias III, the high priest Antiochus IV dislodged in 175 BC 'and assassinated as the result of intrigues against him in 171 BC' (1978: 192). This king prevails for a time against God's chosen ones. Suffering and death remain part of Daniel's people's future.

23. This king will not keep agreements. When others make *an alliance* with him, *he will act deceitfully*. He will never intend to keep treaties that impede his plans. This strategy will enable him to *become strong with a small people*. He will seek power, not broad consensus. For instance, in Jerusalem, Antiochus IV sold the role of high priest to the highest bidder (2 Macc. 4:7–8), and gave power to Jews who followed his instructions (Lucas 2002: 284).

24–28. This king will grab power 'without warning' (11:21), and will likewise break treaties *without warning* (11:24). His strategy will be to target *the richest parts of the province*, most likely to gain revenue (see 11:20) and most certainly to gain influence. He will distribute *plunder, spoils, and goods* among powerful people. In short, he will bribe select persons. This is his approach for overthrowing *strongholds* in various lands.

He will particularly scheme to defeat his lineage's old foe, *the king of the south* (11:25). This strategy had practical implications, for Egypt was a lush, wealthy land. Though he will raise large armies, the king of the south will *not stand* against his northern foe. He will suffer from internal *plots . . . devised against him.* Perhaps some of the wealth the king of the north distributes to key persons (see 11:24) will buy him a few traitors down south (11:26). Neither one of these warring kings has any integrity (11:27). They *will speak lies at the same table* to gain an edge over the other, *but to no avail*, for God rules their times. He determines *the time appointed* for *the end* of their squabbles.

As 11:21, 22, 23 and 26 have stated, the conniving, lying northern king will succeed for a while (11:28). Despite gaining *great wealth*, however, he will not be satisfied. Specifically, his heart *will be set against the holy covenant.* This *holy covenant* is God's people serving him as he commands. It is the fact that by faith the Israelites were to be a kingdom of priests ministering to all peoples (see Exod. 19:5–6). This ministry grew out of love for God (Deut. 6:4–9), which then extended to love for neighbour (Lev. 19:18). Most of all, it required sole allegiance to God and his prescribed way of life, as Daniel and his friends have exemplified. The king will oppose this covenant successfully for a time, then *return to his own land.*

Verses 24–27 may predict Antiochus IV's victories over Egypt in 169 and 168 BC. In 169 BC he was successful enough that he established a puppet king in Egypt. Of course, some Egyptians had to collaborate for this plan to succeed. Very quickly, however, the divided Egyptian royal household reunited (Lucas 2002: 285), and his plans for ruling through this intermediary fell apart. In 168 BC Antiochus IV defeated Egypt, only to have Rome force him to go home (see comments on 8:22–25).

Verse 28 may reflect Antiochus's entry into Jerusalem after his 169 BC foray into Egypt. According to 1 Maccabees 1:21–23, he took treasures from the temple to fund his political and military enterprises. He could do this because he had sold the position of high priest to Jason during 175–172 BC, thereby replacing Onias, and then he had sold it to Menelaus afterwards. His heart was indeed opposed to the holy covenant.

29. The king of the north will return at God's *appointed time*, but the situation *will not be . . . as it was before*. Always in need of income, Antiochus IV invaded Egypt again in 168 BC (see comments on 8:22–26). What seemed to be simple military strategy was in fact God's sovereign design to begin to bring down the king of the north (Young 1949: 244).

30a. Things will change drastically and suddenly for the king of the north. He will invade as before, but *ships of Kittim will come against him*. As C. L. Seow states, in 168 BC 'Antiochus scored initial victories, but as he was preparing to attack Alexandria again, a Roman fleet . . . suddenly showed up' (2003: 179). Given an ultimatum by the Romans, Antiochus IV had to withdraw (see 8:22–25). This setback led him to secure his interests in Jerusalem.

30b–31. Circumstances will lead the king to *pay attention to those who forsake the holy covenant*. He will bolster his Jewish allies, and then send troops to Jerusalem. They will conquer, *profane the temple*, stop the daily *burnt offering* and set up *the abomination that makes* the temple *desolate*.

During 168–167 BC the former high priest, Jason, fought his successor, Menelaus, in Jerusalem. Hearing of this armed struggle, Antiochus IV sent troops to Jerusalem. They took the city, tore down walls and built a citadel. In 167 BC Antiochus IV decreed an end to worship of Israel's God, erected an idol (*the abomination*) and promoted Greek religions in the temple. God's house was *desolate* in the sense that it was not used for its proper purposes by the proper people (see comments on 9:26), not that it was torn down.

32. Two groups will emerge in Jerusalem during this time: those who are *seduced with flattery* and follow the king of the north, and those *who know their God* and thus *stand firm and take action*. The latter group's actions are not specified. They could include accepting martyrdom, or engaging in armed conflict, as the Maccabeans did during the rest of Antiochus IV's reign (167–164 BC) and afterwards (Seow 2003: 180). The author of Daniel does not endorse or denounce armed rebellion.

33. But the book of Daniel most certainly endorses skilfulness in knowledge and wisdom as a precious character trait (see 1:4; 5:12,

14), perhaps the most precious one. Skilfulness in wisdom sustained Daniel through decades of exile and service of foreign powers, and kept him from compromising his faith. The angel states that a group of *the skilful* will do *among the people* what he is doing for Daniel. They will make them *understand* God's will and ways (11:33). This will be a rather ragged process. The people will learn slowly, *for they will be overthrown by sword and flame, by captivity and plunder.* Warfare will not bring them the freedom they seek. The wise, 'in contrast, pursue a nonviolent course' (Collins 1993: 385). They will follow Daniel's example.

34. When the people fall to the invader, they will *receive a little help.* For centuries commentators have identified this *little help* with the Maccabees (see the surveys in Montgomery 1927: 458–459; Collins 1993: 386), though this is by no means a certain interpretation. These writers consider the Maccabees as *little help* because they revolted against Antiochus IV, and were able to restore proper temple worship by 167 BC. However, they could not secure purity and safety for long. By 161 BC they sought help from Rome, and battles with external and internal foes continued for decades (for a summary of the Maccabees, their tactics and their instability, see Schürer 2014: 199–271). Though they recovered the temple, the Maccabeans hardly solved all the problems that Antiochus IV had caused.

Many will join the members of the *little help* insincerely (*with flattery*; see 11:32). Young writes, 'Many hypocrites will associate themselves with the faithful who oppose Antiochus. This hypocritical association was doubtless due in part to the severity with which apostates were treated' (1949: 245).

35. Not even God's faithful ones will be exempt from defeat: *some of the skilful* (see 11:33) *will be overthrown* (see 11:14, 19). These losses are not evidence of God's displeasure. Rather, they happen so *the skilful* can be *refined, purified and made white.* In short, their losses will remove their flaws and bring them closer to God. In context, these words reflect the paramount need to trust God, as Daniel, Hananiah, Mishael and Azariah have. A mere change in government will not solve the people's problems.

36. Verses 36–39 'do not continue in chronological order but recapitulate the king's behavior during the persecution' (Collins

1993: 386). They provide a seven-part summary that fits Antiochus's career. First, the king will do as he wishes (11:36; see 8:4; 11:16). Second, what he wishes is to *exalt himself, and make himself great above all gods.* Thus, *he will speak astonishing things against the God of gods.* Third, he *will succeed until the indignation is completed.* Fourth, God has decreed that these things *will be done.*

37. Fifth, the king will treat his traditional gods (*the gods of his fathers*) as poorly as he treats Israel's God. He will not worship them for the same reason that he will not bow to God: *for above all he will make himself great.* This character will make Belshazzar look humble.

38–39. Sixth, he will worship what gives him power and prestige: *the god of fortresses* (11:38), represented by Zeus (Gowan 2001: 150; Collins 1993: 387) or some other militant deity (for options, see Montgomery 1927: 461). Regardless, this king loves himself most. Seventh, he will reward those who support his agenda, for he will divide *the land as payment* (11:39). Jewish collaborators will receive money or land for turning against their God.

40–45. Like 9:24–27, this passage has generated several interpretations (see Montgomery 1927: 464–66; Young 1949: 250–253; Collins 1993: 388–389; and Newsom and Breed 2014: 273–302). Four views have been prominent: (1) it proceeds chronologically, and includes events beyond 168 BC; (2) it provides a general description of what happens to Antiochus IV from 171 BC to the end of his life in 164 BC; (3) it conveys what an author writing in the mid-second century BC thought would happen, but did not; and (4) it describes an eschatological figure that the New Testament mentions, the anti-Christ.

The analysis below incorporates portions of views one and two. Daniel 11:36–39 has summarized Antiochus IV's years of triumph, 175–169 BC. Now, 11:40–45 repeats some of his victories, reviews his losses in 168–164 BC and reports his death. This reading fits the book's narrative flow, the historical records currently available and the way in which historical summary passages often move backwards and forwards in history (see e.g. Pss 77 – 78).

These verses deal with *the time of the end* (11:40), which 11:45 specifies as *his end,* the king of the north's end (Montgomery 1927: 466). The angel begins with Antiochus IV's invasion of Egypt in 168 BC. As the comments on 11:21–35 indicated, before Rome told him to leave Egypt he swept through several lands, including *the glorious land* (11:40–41a). He left Moab, Ammon and Edom alone (11:41b), most likely due to an alliance (Seow 2003: 185; Newsom and Breed 2014: 357). Antiochus IV mounted the invasion to gather revenue, and various portions of Egypt indeed had to pay (11:43). When Rome delivered their ultimatum (the *news that will alarm him*), Antiochus IV turned his wrath on lands he still ruled (11:44a), including Jerusalem, displaying *great fury to destroy* (11:44b; see 11:30–35). During 167–164 BC Antiochus IV sustained some losses, but also succeeded elsewhere (Gowan 2001: 151). In Jerusalem the Jews re-established temple worship during Antiochus IV's lifetime, but could not capture the citadel his troops had built (Schürer 2014: 217–218). Battles continued for decades.

Therefore, the angel makes the accurate assessment that the king *will establish tents of his pavilion*, an image that represents the place from which he exercises authority (Montgomery 1927: 467; BDB 66, 462; Collins 1993: 389), *between* [the] *seas*, the Mediterranean providing a northern border, *to* [as far as] *the glorious holy mountain* (11:45a), Mt Zion. With Egypt no longer his, Judea became a southern landmark in Antiochus IV's realm. Though he had great power, and never ceased trying to extend it, *he will come to his end, and there will be no-one helping him* (11:45b). He will die without allies, and without mourners.

Details of Antiochus IV's death are sketchy, but the existing materials indicate that he died in Persia, either while raiding a temple to raise money, or by a sudden disease (Hartman and Di Lella 1978: 305; Lucas 2002: 291). Daniel 11:45 does not predict how he will die. It does not specify that he will die in *the glorious land*, and indeed 11:44 places him outside it (contra Seow 2003: 186; Gowan 2001: 151; and Hartman and Di Lella 1978: 305). Therefore, Norman Porteous far overstates the case when he calls Daniel 11:40–45 a 'pseudo prophecy' and efforts to coordinate the passage with history 'a waste of time' (1979: 171–172).

Since 11:40–45 most likely refers to Antiochus IV, it does not predict a world ruler at the end of time commonly known as the anti-Christ, as some scholars argue (see Young 1949: 250–253; Archer 1985: 146–149; and Miller 1994: 309–313). A person like Antiochus IV may arise, but Daniel does not say so. The book clearly expects subsequent wicked, blasphemous rulers to arise. There is always another 'fourth kingdom' coming until God gives the final kingdom to the Son of Man and his followers (see 2:44; 7:9–27; 9:24–27).

12:1. The messenger angel does not conclude with Antiochus IV's demise. He tells Daniel more that he needs to know, without telling the much-loved one (9:23; 10:19) all he may want to know. Daniel 7:15–27; 8:15–26; and 9:24–27 have warned that all will not be well just because the king of the north dies. *At that time* the people's guardian angel (*prince*), *Michael* (see 10:21), will have to *stand over* them during *a time of trouble, such as has not been since there was a nation until that time.* The phrase *stand over* means he will rise 'as judicial advocate or executor of the judgement or both' (Collins 1993: 390). It does mean both, for to protect the faithful he must condemn the unfaithful. The messenger uses common metaphors when he promises *a time of trouble* (Judg. 10:14; Ps. 37:39; Isa. 33:2; Jer. 14:8; 15:11; and 30:7) unprecedented (*such as has not been*) in its effects (Exod. 9:24; Jer. 30:7; Collins 1993: 391). These times will be worse than earlier times, just as the little horn (7:7–8) will be worse than prior kings (Towner 1984: 165).

Thus, it is good that Michael is used to long, hard warfare. He and the angel speaking to Daniel stood between Persia and Greece, who fought one another for over a century (see comments on 10:20). The angels will need endurance again. Clashes with the Seleucids and internal disputes continued for decades (see comments on 11:31). Rome took control in 63 BC, and did little to end the people's woes. Jesus uses similar imagery to describe the persecution of God's people during the fall of Jerusalem in AD 70 (see Matt. 24:15–21; Mark 13:14–19; Luke 21:10–24). Thus, this verse does not depict the end of the world, though the end of the world will, by definition, provide the most severe troubles ever experienced.

In every time of terrible trouble, whether the era of bondage in Egypt, the exodus, the many exiles in Israelite history or the return to the land, believers cried out for God's help. The end of time will be no different. Anticipating this outcry, the angel promises Daniel, *your people will be rescued.* Then he clarifies the scope of this rescue. Only those whose *name is found written in the scroll will be rescued.* Daniel is a man of scrolls (see 1:3–20; 9:1–2), and it must resonate with him to hear again (see Exod. 32:32–33; Ps. 69:28; Isa. 4:3) that God has a scroll with every believer's name in it. Not one will be forgotten. But in what sense will they be rescued if many of them will be overthrown by wicked ones, as 11:35 asserts?

2. Echoing Isaiah 26:19, the angel moves past the long days of trouble. He states that those who are dead (*sleeping in the dust of the earth*) *will awake, some to everlasting life, and some to everlasting abhorrence.* Regardless of their other disagreements, virtually all scholars conclude that 12:2–3 describes the resurrection of individuals, 'something that each individual' will experience 'on the basis of his or her response to God' (Hartman and Di Lella 1978: 308).

The word translated *many* leads some commentators to conclude that the passage limits the number of people who rise, perhaps to the saints of Antiochus IV's era (Montgomery 1927: 471; Hartman and Di Lella 1978: 307; Gowan 2001: 153; and Seow 2003: 187–188). However, Baldwin (1978: 204) notes that Isaiah 2:2–3 uses 'all' and 'many' as synonymous terms, that Deuteronomy 7:1–2 uses 'many' as the summation of a large group of nations individually named, and that Isaiah 52:13 – 53:12 uses 'many' as an all-inclusive term. Here, *many* operates as it does in Deuteronomy 7:1–2 and Isaiah 2:2–3. It marks a specific group of people within a larger group. The whole group will rise. Within that group there are two sub-groups: those who rise to never-ending life and those who rise to *abhorrence*, which occurs only here and in Isaiah 66:24. It describes bodies burning in Isaiah, and probably deformed or rotting bodies here. The wicked will have bodies that make one turn away in horror. They are like the misshapen rulers in 7:1–8.

3. In the midst of the centuries of seemingly endless troubles, one group stands out: *the wise* (see 11:33). They are people who, like Daniel, combine knowledge, skill, prayer, Scripture reading, loyalty to God and friends and love for enemies. They *turn many to righteousness*, to the right way of living before God and with others. In life and after death they *shine . . . like the brightness of the sky . . . like the stars for ever and ever.* Their life and witness endure. They are examples to follow.

4. There is more Daniel wants to hear, but the angel stops. It is time to *seal the scroll*, to preserve its authenticity (see comments on

8:26) until *the end*, the time when it will be opened, read and shared. The author has now unsealed the scroll, told readers about Daniel and passed on his words. He has helped readers who live after Daniel's time, when many will *move about, and knowledge will increase*. This difficult phrase may mean: (1) people will seek knowledge without finding it, as in Amos 8:12 (Young 1949: 257–258); (2) people who seek God's will like Daniel has will find the truth in his scroll and elsewhere (Baldwin 1978: 207); or (3) people will go on searching for truth as they always have – in short, things will go on as before. At the very least, God has revealed precious knowledge to Daniel. Those who read this scroll do not need to roam endlessly to discover God's will.

C. Resting and rising (12:5–13)

Daniel has done all God has asked. Now it is time for the old visionary wise man to rest. One last time he sees the extraordinary. Two more angels appear (12:5), asking how long the things disclosed in 10:1 – 12:4 will last (12:6). The messenger angel gives what sounds like an evasive reply (12:7), and Daniel does not understand (12:8). No matter. Daniel must go on his way to the grave (12:9), knowing that many will follow God and many will not (12:10). Those enduring to the end will receive God's blessings (12:11–12), as Daniel has. Furthermore, Daniel can rest confident that he will stand before God, the greatest King, just as he once stood before lesser kings (12:13).

5–6. The book's longest vision draws to a close, but not before more characters make cameo appearances. Two *others* like the angel dressed in gold (see 10:4) stand on either side of the river (12:5). One asks the messenger angel (10:5–6) the age-old question: *How long?* In this case, they ask how long *the wonders*, which in 8:24 and 11:36 refer to the little horn's deeds, will last. Once again, the vision takes readers back to this loathsome character, not to the final judgment and resurrection of the dead 12:2–3 mentions (Collins 1993: 399).

7. In the Old Testament, people swearing an oath usually raise one hand (see Gen. 14:22; Exod. 6:8; Deut. 32:40; and Ezek. 20:5). Thus, it is unusual for the messenger angel to raise *both* hands.

Perhaps he raises one hand to indicate that he will tell the truth, and one hand to show that he speaks for the living God (Dan. 6:26) who rules times and seasons (2:20–23). It is impossible to be certain. He states that these negative wonders will last *a time, two times and half a time*, the same amount of time that 7:25 divulges. Most commentators take the phrase to mean approximately three and a half years. Antiochus IV desecrated the temple for a little over three years during 167–164 BC, and it was about three years between when he had Onias murdered in 171 BC and when he desecrated the temple. However, the text does not specify particular events. Rather, it emphasizes the time's brevity, and that Antiochus IV's death will not mark the end of time.

8. Daniel does *not understand* what the angel means. He desires to know *what will happen after these*, after the three and a half periods of time.

9–13. He will receive no further information. As in 9:24–27, there are more days to come, days the visions do not account for. Therefore, Daniel must accept five key truths and include them in his scroll. These truths summarize the whole book.

First, Daniel's faithful work is finished. His scroll must end, and he must go to his grave (12:9; see 12:4). Second, as 11:33–35 and 12:2–3 have stated, as time rolls on some people will act wickedly, but *the wise ones will understand* how to serve God (12:10). Daniel will have successors to take up his work with the believing community. Sadly, people like Belshazzar will also have successors. Things will proceed too much like they have in the past.

Third, the temple's desecration will last *1,290 days*, as 7:25; 9:24–27; and 12:7 have stated, using different symbolic numbers that amount to the same thing (12:11). Fourth, the numbers indicate that time remains after the temple's desecration ends, for some people will wait for *1,335 days*, and will be blessed for their endurance (12:12). Experts have long sought a suitable interpretation for this number, and for the numbers in 7:25 and 9:24–27, but with no success. A simple answer may be best: there is leftover time in each passage because these terrible events do not signal history's end. Therefore, these texts discourage speculation. Current readers know that the Greek and Roman persecutions of God's followers did not end history. Furthermore, persecution persists all over the world to this day. Therefore, these passages stress perseverance. They do not give clues about some final terrible time. Fifth, Daniel must take ultimate comfort in God's promise of resurrection (12:13).

Meaning

This long section confirms many previous emphases. It highlights God's sovereignty over and within history (see 1:1–2; 2:1–47; 7:1–27; 8:1–27; 9:24–27; 11:2 – 12:4). It states again that God's angels help his faithful ones (3:25; 7:9–27; 8:15–26; 9:20–27; 10:1–21). It stresses patient endurance by wise believers over long periods of time (1:8–21; 2:1–19; 3:8–25; 6:1–28; 8:1; 9:1–19; 10:1; 11:33–35; 12:3–13), and the inevitable slow rise of God's kingdom on earth (2:21–47; 4:34–37; 7:1–27; 9:24–27; 11:40 – 12:13). The book's unity becomes increasingly clearer.

This long section should also fuel continuing discussions about the book's view on resistance against oppression. As was noted in the comments on 11:33–35, experts have considered the mention of 'little help' (11:34) as a slap at the Maccabees. In his time Daniel's resistance consists of commitment to God's ways, to witness and to obedient suffering. In short, his resistance is wise living in uncertain times, a resistance all believers can emulate.

Finally, this passage provides a building block in the Bible's teaching about resurrection. Ezekiel 37:1–14, Hosea 6:2 and Hosea 13:14 stress national resurrection. Of course, a nation cannot rise unless individuals do, so it is not surprising that 12:2–3 stresses individual resurrection. Jesus and the Pharisees disagreed about many things, but not over the fact that the Bible teaches resurrection from the dead.[2] Awaiting resurrection becomes Daniel's hope and comfort in 12:1–13.

The author closes by reminding readers that everlasting life lies beyond days, weeks, months and years of suffering. Perseverance will be rewarded. Sufficient and appropriate knowledge of the future resides in all who believe God raises the dead. They know resurrection resolves all hopes, dreams, visions and disappointments.

---

2. For a careful treatment of resurrection in the Old Testament and the ancient world, see Johnston 2002: 218–239.

When God raises his people, his kingdom will finish rising from the ground to destroy all wicked kingdoms (see 2:44). It will rise to its full glory, and all idols will be toppled. God's will will then be done on earth as it is in heaven. Daniel can *rest*, then, knowing that he *will stand* before the greatest king, and the book commends this promise to every subsequent faithful, persevering reader.

Finding the Textbook You Need

The IVP Academic Textbook Selector
is an online tool for instantly finding the IVP books
suitable for over 250 courses across 24 disciplines.

---

ivpacademic.com